THE OUTLAW'S BIBLE

HOW TO EVADE THE SYSTEM USING CONSTITUTIONAL STRATEGY

by
E.X. Boozhie

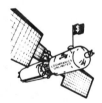

Loompanics Unlimited
Port Townsend, Washington

Neither the author nor the publisher assumes any responsibility for the use or misuse of information contained in this book. It is sold for entertainment purposes only. Be Warned!

The Outlaw's Bible

Published by:

Loompanics Unlimited
PO Box 1197
Port Townsend, WA 98368

Loompanics Unlimited is a division of Loompanics Enterprises, Inc.

ISBN 0-915179-80-6
Library of Congress Catalog Card Number 88-045203

DEDICATION

This book is dedicated to The Cops, who shall not be referred to herein as "pigs" out of respect for the species of animals.

FORWARD

Every now and then the forces of time, circumstance, and fate come together and certain lives and happenings enjoin. I met E.X. Boozhie on the yard of a maximum security prison. He was diligently studying law books, taking notes, and typing voluminous pages of material. Being a "jailhouse lawyer" myself, I instantly thought, "Wow, this guy must have *some* case!"

I was eventually introduced to our author, and as we spoke of politics, religion, and philosophy, we came to find that our experiences had brought us to a perception of the American justice system which we shared in common — that it exists only for the benefit of the ultra-rich. What E.X. had been laboring on was his own reaction to this unhappy insight; it was the book you are now holding.

The Outlaw's Bible is not just a book for lawbreakers. It is for all people who undertake to seriously learn about the "legal rights" supposedly available under the U.S. Constitution. The average man or woman never thinks about rights or legalities. I find it strange that there are absolutely no basic studies of law in any public school, yet the Law Library of Congress contains an amazing 7,000,000 books on law alone! You simply can't get through a day without breaking some law or other.

As you read this rare treatise, remember that some-day, somehow, you may need to hide from the police and avoid prosecution. This book contains the only non-violent weapon you can arm yourself with. Use it; take it very seriously.

Avi Naftel
Arizona State Prison
1985

Table of Contents

Part 1

ORIENTATION

Chapter 1

INTRODUCTION

You're likely to get into trouble.

Perhaps it's because of your weakness for some good "smoke" now and then, or because out-of-season game tends to find its way into your freezer. Maybe you keep a handgun in your car, or can't resist exaggerating a bit when you fill out loan applications, income tax forms, and the like. In one way or another, most of us do occasionally break the law. It might even be that you're into something a bit more "substantial," such that you'd be considered a professional outlaw. Maybe you deal drugs, smuggle, hustle, steal, or engage in some other illegal operation for profit. Perhaps you're already a fugitive with your name on the hot list and the law on your tail.

Whether you're a lawbreaker, or you just like the company of those who are, your ignorance about the law makes you a danger to yourself and to your friends. It could easily cost you your life. It is primarily for *your* benefit that this book was written, so read on and be the wiser.

If, on the other hand, you're as innocent as a newborn lamb, and merely harbor a little academic curiosity about how your own rights measure up against those of the police, then this book is for you, also. You probably don't like the idea of being dominated and manipulated by the police, and may have had occasion to wonder just how far the law really does entitle them to push. Such a curiosity is very healthy, because no matter how saintly a person may be, he never knows when he might find himself facing a criminal charge — a circumstance where some practical knowledge of constitutional rights can be lifesaving.

Law books are too dry and technical for most people to read, and this is why the average citizen never really learns what his rights are. It fits right into the plans of those captains of the System, the cops and the lawyers, because with the citizens in the dark, they can do pretty much what they please without recriminations. This book aims to put a stop to that situation by laying out in plain English an up-to-date overview of the citizen's legal rights against police activity. It gives an explanation from the *common man's* perspective of how the criminal justice system works in *real* life. It tells precisely *where* and to what *extent* a person has a *legally reliable* right to privacy. It tells precisely what *limits* are imposed by law upon the police. In short, it tells you how the cops operate, how far they can go, and what you can and cannot expect to get away with.

While the presentation of this material is non-technical and geared to the ordinary person, precision and completeness have not been abandoned. The idea here is to present an accurate picture of the *overall* law that governs us, regardless of which state we happen to be in at the time. Most of this information has therefore come from the federal law books. State laws are sometimes either stricter or more lenient than the corresponding federal ones, and for some types of crimes there don't even exist comparable laws in both state and federal jurisdictions. To the extent that every state is ultimately under the authority of the United States Constitution, however, state laws are controlled by federal law, and a person can pretty much rely on that during his confrontation with state and local police. You don't have to know *all* the ramifications of the law in order to get along. State law is occasionally mentioned in this book in order to give you some idea of the variations that can exist in the law from one place to another, but no attempt is being made here to provide an exhaustive summary. This book is strictly for getting the "big picture." If you want to know *exactly* where you stand, you'll have to go to a local law library and look up the state and federal statutes that apply to you where you are — either that, or ask a lawyer.[1]

Every person knows that he doesn't want to go to jail; you don't need a book to tell you that. Unless you've had personal experiences with the criminal justice system, however, it isn't likely that you really know what you're up against. Those of you who've already taken a fall know what the System is all about. You've met the players on the field and seen them in action; you may skip on ahead to Chapter 5. But if you haven't yet been in trouble with the law, the next three chapters will give you a valuable opportunity to make the acquaintance of your enemies before they meet you. They aren't anything at all like those mythological creatures which our middle-class orientation has taught us to believe in. You've seen them on the street... you've had drinks with them at the Club... perhaps you're even related to one of them. No matter how well you think you've known them, however, you really don't know them at all until you've seen them from behind bars. The insight that comes from that perspective is very important, for it teaches you to beware of them and to avoid underestimating them; underestimation is the deadliest sin of all.

The criminal justice system, which we'll henceforth refer to simply as "the System," can be likened to a predatory beast. From the point of view of its prey, there are three significant parts to the beast: the claw, which it uses to reach out and snatch up prey; the jaws, into which the prey is stuffed and processed for digestion; and the belly, where the chewed-up prey is digested and sapped of all its nutrients. The prey in this simile is the citizen — you. The claw represents the police, the jaws the court system, and the belly the prison system. All three organs work together toward the ultimate benefit of each other, and all three live off the destruction of the prey. Meet each one of them now — the Cops, the Courts, and the Keepers.

REFERENCES

1. You can learn to look up the law for yourself by reading *Legal Research in a Nutshell,* by Morris L. Cohen, West Publishing Co., St. Paul (1978). Then go to any county courthouse to use the law library, because they'll have all the local law books there, and citizens are entitled to use them.

Chapter 2

THE COPS

"Thou hast seen a farmer's dog bark at a beg-
gar?... And the creature run from the cur? There
thou might'st behold the great image of
authority: a dog's obeyed in office.

William Shakespeare, *King Lear,* Act iv, Scene 6,
line 159 (1608)

The most visible member of the System, and the first
one you'll come in contact with, is the cop. He isn't
always recognizable as such, because it's his state of
mind, rather than his clothes, which makes him what he
is. His ambition is to control the behavior of other
people. He lacks imagination and tends to think in a linear
fashion, so he usually relies upon rules to solve everything. In this respect, he has much the same mentality as
the religious zealot; indeed, many cops are religious in
addition to being legalistic. They believe that the world
is in conflict between absolutes of right and wrong, and
that rules exist for the purpose of sustaining the
triumph of the "right" over the "wrong." Whether these
rules are God's or the government's, the cop sees it as his
duty to enforce them.

Organized government holds the championship title
for rule-making, so it's not surprising that this kind of
person would be attracted to it for a livelihood. He's
deeply impressed by the government's status as domi-
nant authority in our society, and he's likely to attribute
the quality of justness to its rules simply on that basis
alone. When asked why he puts his support behind the
establishment, he's likely to reply, "because it's the law."
What he's actually doing is aligning himself with what he

perceives to be the "winning side." He chooses established government to join up with so that he can share in
the security that comes from the legitimacy and prevailing balance of power that it holds.

Cops tend to have fragile egos, and it's very important
to them that their pride be continually bolstered. Police
work meets this need by clothing them with the government's authority. Instantly the cop becomes far more
powerful than he could ever hope to be on his own
merits. The fact that the authority he wields is actually
the government's, and not his own, is unimportant to
him; for all outward appearances, *he's* the boss. Sometimes he can use the government's authority to further
his own personal interests, and at other times he must
be content to exercise the authority for the sole interests of the government. Either way, however, he derives
satisfaction from being "The Man" and reaffirming his
prestigious self-image.

Cops hardly ever get rich, because they spend their
lives doing the footwork necessary to make other
people's rules work. Those other people — the "movers
and shakers" who are the brains behind the power
structure of society — are the real beneficiaries of the
cop's labors. They make the rules, and the rules serve
their interests. They set the System up so that it
provides the cop with a decent living in return for his
services, but the economic reality is that he's strictly
hired help. Unless he can get a hustle going on the side,
or somehow work his way up into politics, a cop will
never get much financial reward from his job.

Very few of them have enough originality or ambition
to turn a police job into something lucrative. The rare
entrepreneur might succeed by putting his police skills
onto the commercial marketplace, as Alan Pinkerton and
William J. Burns have done, but most ambitious cops
attempt to further their careers via the political route.
They get a law degree, go to work for the local prosecutor's office, and attempt to build up a reputation by

convicting people of crimes. The more people they send to prison, and the more newsworthy the cases are, the better the press coverage is for them. Thus, with sufficient publicity, political shrewdness, and a gullible electorate, an ambitious cop can claw his way up into public office and become one of the rule-makers himself.

As you may have already noticed, the term "cop" is being used in a very inclusive manner. Policemen are cops, to be sure, but there are many other types of cops, too. Once you realize this and learn to recognize them as the threats that they are, you'll have neutralized one of their most potent weapons — the element of surprise.

Think of cops as being of two basic types — the professionals and the amateurs. Professional cops are in police and security work as a full-time vocation, and may be either governmentally- or privately-employed.

At the lowest rung of government are the municipal cops, notably the police and fire departments. City police — the "boys in blue" — are the most visible of all cops, since they patrol the streets in uniform. Their brothers in the fire department, however, shouldn't be underestimated just because firemen aren't primarily concerned with crime. They work closely with the police; in fact, fire inspectors are the ones who are in charge of arson investigations. Moreover, firemen are often likely to come across contraband or other evidence while putting out a fire. Their mentality and sympathies are basically the same as the police.

At the next tier of government, the county and state level, there's a massive profusion of cops doing the government's work. The most important ones are the state police and county sheriff's departments and their respective state and county attorney's offices. These are the cops that handle most of the felony prosecutions. The prosecutors are sometimes referred to as "district attorneys" (D.A.s), and their big boss is the state attorney general (although the governor is technically the top executive officer of the state). Other cops at this level of government include those of the coroner's office, tax office, health department, and forest service, to name a few.

On the federal level we find a further plethora of cops — what we'll henceforth refer to in this book as "the feds." Some of the better-known agencies include the Federal Bureau of Investigation (F.B.I.), Bureau of Alcohol, Tobacco and Firearms (A.T.F.), Drug Enforcement Administration (D.E.A.), Secret Service, Marshals Service, Postal Inspectors, Internal Revenue Service (I.R.S.), Federal Aviation Administration (F.A.A.), Securities and Exchange Commission (S.E.C.), Federal Communications Commission (F.C.C.), and National Park Service. Looking out for our national frontiers are the Coast Guard, Border Patrol, Bureau of Customs, and Immigration and Naturalization Service. We mustn't forget the military, either; the armed forces are the country's police force on the international level. Of particular significance are the spy outfits, such as the Central Intelligence Agency (C.I.A.) and National Security Agency (N.S.A.), as well as the various internal police agencies within the Department of Defense (military police, O.S.I., etc.).

Other countries, of course, have their own equivalents of all these officers. There's also a non-governmental organization called Interpol which helps the government cops of different countries to coordinate their efforts on a world-wide scale.

Privately-employed cops should generally be recognized within two basic categories — those of the "private sector" and those who conduct certain business services. The "private sector" refers to all manner of police and security-type jobs which are hired commercially. Private investigators, detective and guard agencies, insurance investigators, and private industrial watchmen make up this category. These jobs usually require government licensing, and they're often filled by ex-government cops. Skip tracers, bounty hunters, and repossessors occupy the lower echelon of the private sector. They provide the muscle for tracking down welchers, bail jumpers, and unpaid-for vehicles for the benefit of the private concerns which have a financial interest in them. Various business services, notably credit bureaus, computer services, and informational services, also represent a category of private cops. Their low visibility and the subtlety of their "police" functions make it inapparent to most people that these are indeed cops. They compile vast files of information on you and make it available to insurance companies, private concerns, and the government... any of which can use it against you.

Amateur cops are ordinary people who get involved in police work without making their living off it. They're often simply public-spirited citizens who are gulled into aiding the police by virtue of their good-natured desire to help people. Some of them are members of organizations such as the Boy Scouts, Civil Air Patrol, Jaycees, and Radio Hams, which incidentally happen to support the police. Others are police "groupies" who hang around law enforcement agencies in order to satisfy a psychological need. In many places the police have actually solicited senior citizens, youths, and other folks with spare time on their hands for their participation in police auxiliary groups. They put the volunteers to work doing repetitive or unskilled tasks so that the paid police can be freed up for other duties. In some localities the amateur cops are organized into "block watch" patrols which drive around with walky-talkies, reporting on anything suspicious that they happen to see. Moralistic and often prejudiced, the police groupy tends to suffer from an exaggeration of all the worst qualities of the cop mentality.

The sleaziest species of amateur cop, and the only one who might occasionally turn a profit from his activities, is the informer. He's known colloquially by a variety of names — snitch, rat, stoolie, squealer — and the police refer to him these days as a "C.I.," or "cooperative individual." He runs to the authorities with incriminating information that he learns from his friends and associates. He's usually prompted to such betrayal by one of five motives: (1) moralistic indignation (i.e., "Why should *he* get away with that?"); (2) revenge; (3) desire to eliminate competition; (4) hope of reward; and (5) fear (of either the persons he's snitching on, or of police extortion).

The snitch is the single most powerful tool that the police have. Through his assistance, there have been more undetectable crimes disclosed, more unbreakable cases broken, and more invulnerable suspects convicted than by all the combined technology of the law enforcement arsenal. Professional cops exploit this valuable resource by appealing to the five snitch-motives wherever and whenever they can, always hoping to develop a new "source." The government cops create many of their snitches by extorting cooperation from people they've caught but have refrained from filing charges against. Junkies are particularly vulnerable to this ploy because the prospect of even a minor bust is a nightmare for someone who's physically dependent on narcotics.

A chilling illustration of the significance of a snitch is the trial of Irish Republican Army (I.R.A.) suspects which began May 8, 1984 at the Belfast Crown Court in Northern Ireland. A single informer named Raymond Gilmour was responsible for bringing 39 people up on 190 charges ranging from "helping an illegal organization" to murder.[1] In our country, it's more common for the police to refrain from even identifying their informers, much less bring them into court to testify. They prefer to keep them out there working in the community until they're either discovered and killed, or no longer useful. Nobody really likes or respects the snitch, not even the police; he's merely an effective tool for them to use up and discard.

Bearing in mind their different perspectives, we can now briefly discuss what the various cops intend to accomplish by their activities.

Amateurs are ostensibly involved in police work to provide a "service to mankind." If motives are honestly appraised, however, it's usually the satisfaction of a personal psychological need which they're really out to achieve. In the case of an informant, the purpose is to satisfy his indignation, revenge, jealousy, greed, or fear. Amateur cops can snoop around and perform a variety of auxiliary tasks, but invariably they must get their objectives accomplished through the police, since they have no real authority of their own.

Private cops are out to protect the interests of their paying clients (or employers). They're the only ones who actually *are* out to accomplish their stated purpose. There may be secondary benefits, such as ego satisfaction, but the profit motive is their principal driving force. They snoop, develop data files on people, and collect evidence for their clients' use. They track down missing persons and things. They stand guard over property and transport valuable cargoes. Unlike the amateur cops, they're usually authorized to carry guns and use them, and they can get down to business on the physical level if it's necessary.

Government cops are purportedly out to take care of citizens — "to serve and protect," as the police motto claims. Their real purpose, however, is something which few of them ever consciously think about. It has nothing to do with making "right" triumph over "wrong." Their true mission is to protect the status quo for the benefit of the ruling class.

A few outrageously powerful concerns own most of the wealth of this country, and indirectly control most of what they don't own. The legal machinery, which consists of the courts and lawmaking bodies, is part of that controlled realm. Laws are created by the legislatures and interpreted by the courts so that the interests of the controlling powers are best served. Naturally, they consistently process the laws in their own best interests as well. A complex system of prerogative has thus been created, whereby the lion's share of the wealth and power is retained by the elite, and generous portions are allowed to filter down within privileged circles. The bulk of the population, those middle-class working folks whose labor has generated all this wealth, are lucky if they get enough to make ends meet. The poor get a few bones to chew on.

Many of the middle-class folks, including the cops, occupy government jobs. These jobs don't generate any wealth at all; government regulates, it does not create or produce anything. Ultimately, then, all the government parasites and elitist fat cats are supported by the overburdened working stiff, who consequently finds himself staring blankly at his empty hand and wondering where all the money has gone. Some plausible explanation is in order to assuage his discontentment.

Enter the poor man. Crude and scantily-educated, he fails to communicate well with middle-class people. He's culturally and socially a world apart from them, and he lives in places where they wouldn't go in broad daylight. They cannot understand or empathize with him, and it's only a one-step journey to go from ignorance to hatred. They're prepared to believe the worst about him; and the worst is what they hear.

Reports come pouring out of government agencies raising the hue and cry that crime is on the rise in America. Newspaper headlines and the Six O'Clock News broadcast graphic stories of murder and mayhem on the streets. Politicians pontificate about cleaning up crime and bringing back the "good old days." Movies and television programs dramatically portray innocent citizens being brutally assaulted by grotesque-looking thugs. And who are the thugs that receive all this bad press? You guessed it — it's the ghetto people.

Like the Jews, who provided Hitler with a convenient scapegoat for rallying the support of the German people, the urban poor in America supply our government with the alibi it needs to rationalize its excesses to the middle class. Police, courts, lawyers, and prisons generate vast expenses which must be paid for in order to control the "ghetto menace." Under the pervasive effects of establishment-inspired propaganda, the working folks are convinced that their tax money is being wisely used in the worthwhile cause of protecting them from their lower-class "enemies." With their resentment and blame diverted against the poor, they offer no resistance to the real crooks, who continue to fleece them openly and legitimately under the guise of governmental need.

To make good their function of protecting the status quo, the police work toward two principal objectives — getting the lawbreakers out of circulation and deterring the populace from violating the law. They usually succeed in the first objective by getting the citizen into court, where he's convicted and sentenced to prison. In the case of a foreigner, an alternative approach is to have him deported out of the country. Sometimes the police get to exercise a third option by killing the suspect while apprehending him.

By the use of deterrence, the police can exert their control over the entire population, rather than just the few individuals who actually get caught breaking the law. Most of the citizenry can easily be intimidated into cooperating with the government because they don't want to risk upsetting their own little status quo; jobs, reputations, possessions, and freedoms can readily be compromised by the government. When the unusual citizen decides that he's not going to be intimidated, and openly defies the government, he's likely to be vigorously pursued until he's either reformed or eliminated. An old farmer named Gordon Kahl was such a fellow; he refused to pay his income tax, and when the usual police harassment failed to "rehabilitate" him, he was goaded into armed resistance, hunted down, and executed John Dillinger-style.[2/3]

Like the private ones, government cops spend much of their time snooping, developing data files, and collecting evidence. Sometimes they'll work in secrecy for years before they're ready to bring charges against a suspect. Police bugging and wiretapping of American citizens reached its peak in 1971, then saw a temporary decrease in the wake of the Watergate scandal. With 208 authorized taps in 1983, however — a 60% increase over the previous year — the feds have returned to their record levels of activity, and promise to go much higher. Most of this surveillance relates to narcotics investigations and is directed against single-family homes. Although each phone tap eavesdropped on an average of 147 people, the feds admit that only about 16% of the conversations were "incriminating." All this surveillance is quite expensive; each one of the warranted taps done in 1983 cost the taxpayers an average of $65,300. One wiretapping operation alone — that of Katherine Boudin, who was being investigated for a 1981 Brinks truck robbery — involved 50 cops, and cost two million dollars![4] All these figures represent *authorized* wiretaps, of course; the extent of *un*authorized electronic surveillance in America is many times greater.

Police spend a sizeable portion of their time these days setting up crimes of their own so they can bust whoever is willing to participate with them. They impersonate buyers and sellers of drugs, stolen goods, prostitution, murder contracts, bribes, or anything else that's illegal. The Abscam and DeLorean investigations are well-known examples of this type of scam. The F.B.I. alone conducted 316 such probes during 1983, and they've earmarked 12.5 million dollars for undercover work in 1984.[5] Legislators have been worried about this sort of police activity, since it's often directed at their own lily-white necks instead of at a lowly bunch of ghetto tramps. Following the lead of the Senate Select Committee which deliberated on the subject in 1982,[6] the Democratic majority of a House Subcommittee recently recommended that the cops be required to get a warrant before launching a secret probe.[5] It's unlikely that there'll be any such legislation in the near future, however, and for the time being everyone is fair game for an undercover "sting."

Aside from their spying and entrapment activities, the police are capable of a variety of other dishonorable things that the ordinary citizen doesn't realize. The author can testify from personal experience that they will falsify physical evidence and coach witnesses to tell lies in order to assure that their criminal prosecutions will result in conviction. They occasionally carry around small quantities of dope to plant on people in order to create the pretext for an excuse to hold them. Some of them even keep an untraceable handgun in their squad car in case they shoot someone who turns out to be unarmed. The "throw-down" gun is simply tossed near the body so that the officer can easily vindicate himself by claiming that he had shot in self defense.[7]

Once the police have enough evidence to justify bringing charges against somebody, they go through a litany of legal procedures which culminates in the suspect's trial. First, they file a "complaint" with the grand jury, and it in turn issues an "indictment" (the formal charge). Based on the indictment, a judge then issues a "warrant" authorizing them to arrest the person. They can skip the grand jury if they want to, and the judge will still give them their warrant, but then they have to issue their own version of the indictment, which is called an "information." With an "information" the cops are generally required to give their suspect the benefit of a "preliminary hearing" or "prelim," wherein the judge must determine whether there's probable cause to believe that he's guilty. The cops generally prefer to avoid this, since it gives the suspect a chance to block their prosecution; the grand jury indictment, on the other hand, is practically a sure thing.

With their warrant in hand, the cops are ready to arrest their man. If they have probable cause to believe that he's guilty of a crime, they can arrest him without a warrant, and do the paperwork later. Either way, the arrest that follows is standard operating procedure which is familiar to all TV viewers: they inform the suspect that he's under arrest, read him his "rights," frisk him for weapons, put on the handcuffs, and cart him off to jail. This is the ultimate "high" for a cop, especially if he has an audience; in one dramatic and glorious spectacle it gives expression to everything that holds purpose for him in life.

REFERENCES

1. *The Christian Science Monitor,* May 9, 1984, p. 2
2. "Shootout in a Sleepy Hamlet," *Time,* June 13, 1983
3. Manu, D., "Update on Kahl — What the News Didn't Tell," *The Justice Times,* September 1983, (Box 562, Clinton, AR 72031)
4. Grier, Peter, "Federal Use of Wiretaps," *The Christian Science Monitor,* May 10, 1984, p. 5
5. "When Government Tempts," *The Christian Science Monitor,* May 3, 1984, p. 19
6. *The Criminal Law Reporter,* 32 CrL 2297, 1/12/83
7. *Webster v City of Houston,* 689 F2d 1220 (5th Cir. 1982)

Chapter 3

THE COURTS

"The hungry judges soon the sentence sign,
And wretches hang that jurymen may dine."

Alexander Pope, *Rape of the Lock*, Canto iii, line
21 (1714)

The engine of the mighty C., C., & K. Railroad, which first
began to crank over its massive wheels at the time of indictment, will be steadily chugging down the track by
the time its new passenger gets his first view of the
courtroom. This will occur within about 48 hours of arrest, because that's when they're supposed to bring
every arrested person in front of a judge for his "initial
appearance." The purpose of this hearing is to establish
who the arrestee is, what the charges are, and whether
or not he can get out of jail on a pre-trial release agreement. If it's a penny-ante beef they might let him out on
his "own recognizance" (O.R.), which means that he gives
his word that he'll show up for trial later. If the charges
are substantial enough to threaten a penalty of prison,
they'll require the suspect to post a bail bond as an incentive to assure that he'll be back at trial time. Depending on the amount of bail that the judge sets, it might
be necessary for a guy to sign over his house, his company stock, the beach front property, and his wife — all
of which is forfeited if he skips out. When the charges are
very serious, or when the suspect can't afford bail, the
hoosegow will become home until his trial's over; and
that can often be more than a year.
    The next step of the prosecution process is "arraign-
ment," which takes place within a week or so. This is

when the suspect is brought in front of the judge to plead either "guilty" or "not guilty" to the charges. A trial date is set, and if the person is still locked up it's another opportunity for him to ask the judge for pre-trial release.

By this point in time one usually knows whether the cops have an airtight case or one that could go either way at trial. In most instances of the former, it's customary for the prosecutor to approach the defendant with an offer of a "plea bargain," which is a contract between the accused and the court. The plea agreement specifies a conviction and penalty, and takes the place of the trial; it's like an out-of-court divorce settlement. The government likes to make plea agreements because it saves the expense and time of a trial, which can easily cost the state a five-figure sum and weeks of court time. The fact of the matter is that if they had to give a trial to every person they brought charges against there wouldn't be enough judges, jurors, or courtrooms to go around.

The prosecutor creates the incentive to accept his terms in several ways, all of which boil down to plain, old-fashioned extortion. First of all he'll file as many "counts" of as many different charges as he can dream up. It's a little bit like going through the line at the cafeteria. You take three pads of butter, some sour cream, and a few chives for your baked potato. You stack some mushrooms on top of your steak, and — oh, better make it two beverages, since they're small. When you get to the cashier she charges you three times for butter, twice for the drink, and again separately for each helping of sour cream, chives, and mushrooms — all in addition to the steak and potato. That's the way they pile on the criminal charges. With a dozen people in the bank, a simple five-minute stickup can be described by the cops as "twelve counts of kidnapping, twelve counts of displaying a deadly weapon not in self-defense, and one count each of armed robbery, carrying a concealed weapon, possession of an unregistered firearm, possession of a firearm by an ex-felon, and commission of a felony while on parole."

As if the multiplicity of charges isn't bad enough, the prosecutor will threaten to try for consecutive, rather than concurrent, sentences (a proviso that's colloquially referred to as "running the sentences wild"). If he's successful it would mean that the convicted person would have to serve out each sentence before starting on the next; four 5-year sentences could take twenty years to kill, instead of just five years with all sentences running concurrently.

Since the punishment for a given crime is generally greater for a person who's had prior convictions than it is for the first-time offender, a prosecutor will also use this as a selling point; having "priors" can effectively triple the penalty that a person receives.

Other factors known as "aggravating circumstances," which the judge can use to "enhance," or worsen, the sentence that he hands down, include "dangerousness" (i.e. whether a weapon was used), "heinousness" (i.e. whether cruelty was notable), and "repetitive nature" (i.e. whether the guy keeps getting into trouble for the same crime).

All these options give the prosecutor bargaining power. Even if the defendant mentioned above were actually innocent of all charges, he might be inclined to plead guilty to one count of armed robbery, with a sentence of ten years, rather than risk going to trial and facing 29 counts carrying about 300 years with the allegations of dangerousness, repetitiveness, and priors all hanging over his head. Having been through the System before, he'd be all the more likely to sign because he's already seen how easily the courts can railroad a person when they want to.

If the prosecutor can't scare his defendant into signing a plea agreement, or if he wants to take the case to trial so he can write a book about it and get more publicity for himself, the next event will be the "pre-trial hearing." This is when the defendant's lawyer tries to get the judge to throw out the prosecutor's evidence. To do this, he accuses the cops of acquiring their evidence by violating his client's rights. When they can't refute this charge the judge is supposed to "suppress" the evidence, which means that they can't use it. No evidence, no case.

This is the juncture at which most of the information in this book will prove its value, because the wise reader will pay close attention to the constitutional limits that are drawn and conduct himself and his affairs in such a way that the cops won't be *able* to get any evidence against him legitimately. Anything they get on him will have to be acquired through a constitutional violation, and will be properly quashed at the pre-trial hearing.

One word of forewarning here, however — frequently the judge doesn't do his job, and allows evidence into the trial which should have been suppressed. When that happens, and the defendant gets convicted because of it, he has to go to prison and work his way back into court on appeal so that the evidence can be suppressed as it should have been in the first place. This is all very unfair because it usually takes a couple of years to get a case overturned on appeal. It's all part of the game; the cops and the courts are partners in the System, and they see this as an opportunity to burn a guy who's obviously guilty but technically beyond the reach of the law. Cops don't like the idea of a suspect going free on a technicality, and the courts are often willing to play along with them by bending the rules in order to illegitimately punish such a person. They realize that he'll probably win his case on appeal, but they figure to get at least a couple of years out of him before he does. This little aside is made merely to clear up the misconception that most folks harbor about legal "loopholes;" they're genuine lifesavers, and the professional outlaw uses them to limit his losses and prevent a real disaster, but they aren't talismans. Metaphorically speaking, they'll protect you from the knockout punch but they can't always guarantee that you won't get skinned up a little.

Everything comes to a climax with the trial, which is the System's mechanism for branding the defendant as "government property." Theoretically it's a formal arena where a wise and impartial judge and a disinterested panel of civilians hear both sides of the story (the defendant's and the cops'). The prosecutor strives to convince them that the defendant is the Devil himself and should be shown no mercy, while the defendant's lawyer tries to show that the whole affair is a terrible mistake and that his client hasn't done anything to deserve punishment. The jurors have to decide what the facts are, while the judge tells them what the law is. After doing some more deciding the jury eventually either (1) "acquits" the defendant (which means that he's free to go home), (2) "convicts" him (which means that he must be sentenced to some kind of punishment), or (3) fails to come to a unanimous decision — a "hung jury" (which means that he has to go through a whole new trial with a whole new jury).

The reality is that most of the time the defendant gets convicted. That "impartial" judge is just as anxious to get him into prison as the prosecutor is, since he too is a cop and was once a prosecutor himself. That "disinterested" jury might better be described as an "un-interested" jury because the half that wasn't either knitting or snoozing during the trial is likely to consist of members of the local lunatic fringe who share the prejudices of the police groupy. And contrary to the popular government-inspired myth that people are held to be innocent until proven guilty, it's likely that most of the jurors made up their minds the moment they first saw the defendant and heard the charges. The average citizen's faith in government, coupled with his lack of personal experience to the contrary, leads him to *assume* that a man standing trial must be guilty, "or otherwise he wouldn't be there." The Irish-American social satirist Finley Peter Dunne parodied jury deliberation in the following manner: "When the case is all over, the jury'll pitch th' tistimony out iv the window, an' consider three questions: 'Did Lootgert look as though he'd kill his wife? Did his wife look as though she ought to be kilt? Isn't it time we wint to supper?'"[1]

After the bad news comes in from the jury there's one more stop that the legal locomotive makes on its way through the courthouse — the defendant, now a "convicted felon," must be sentenced. The jurors have all gone home to their housework or park benches, and it's up to the judge to do the honors. Though not required, it's often customary to delay sentencing until a couple of weeks after conviction so that a social worker from the probation department can write up a "presentence report" for the judge. This is a brief summary of the convict's life story as seen through the eyes of the cops — untried accusations from the police files, prior appearances in criminal courts, bail-jumping or escape attempts, conflicts with probation or parole officers, negative prison reports, other pending charges — it's all there. The social history bears a closer resemblance to a pedigree than to a profile of a man's life; it lists his vital statistics, his family members, places of residence, and occupation, but gives no indication that he might be a devoted family man, a worthwhile citizen, or a valuable employee. The real kicker in this report comes under the section entitled "Statement of Offense," where the writer gets his big chance to stack the deck. There'll be vivid accounts of the dastardly deeds, heart-rending statements from the "victims," and enough opinionating by the writer to justify the posting of a caption reading "Why I Believe the Defendant should Be Drawn and Quartered."

Logically enough, the purpose of the presentence report is to give the judge a factual background on the person so he can tailor his sentence with wisdom and foresight. Unfortunately, the cop mentality that judges have extinguishes both of these qualities; if the report has any effect, it will be to justify in the judge's mind the imposition of a harsher sentence. The damaging effect of a presentencing report can be particularly bad in the case of a plea bargain, where the heavily-biased version of events in the report may be the judge's only source of information about the case. Hitherto undisclosed allegations which the reporting officer has dug up are catapulted to prominence as sentencing criteria, and the defendant doesn't even have the opportunity to deny or explain them. Since plea agreements often allow the judge to choose from a range of penalties for the stipulated charge, this often results in the imposition of the maximum penalty — all on the word of a minor functionary.

In case you still nurse the illusion that justice will surely be preserved in the end through the mature wisdom and human sensibility of the judge, pause and consider what the judge's background is and where his interest. ... He's a lawyer who earned his credentials by distinguishing himself in the public eye as a government cop, usually a prosecutor. He got his position through public recognition, and if he's going to lose it, it will be for offending public sentiment. Any question in his mind about the severity of his sentences will therefore be resolved in favor of his own safety from possible adverse reaction; and the safest way to go is to "throw the book at 'em." This is why it's so pathetic to hear about people who place themselves at the mercy of the court in the naive belief that it knows the quality of human kindness. That fatherly old gentleman who tells you that he has "a great deal of respect for people who are willing to step forward and admit their responsibility" is liable to show you just how much respect he has by awarding you three death sentences.[2]

"The first thing we do, let's kill all the lawyers."

William Shakespeare, *II Henry VI*, Act iv, Scene 2, line 85 (1592)

Having briefly described what goes on in the trial court, it's worthwhile now to devote a few lines to the lawyers; after all, they're the ones who run the place. The judge, whom you've already met, is the head honcho. All the other lawyers and clerks in the courtroom kowtow and fawn before him like vassals of a medieval king. They call him "Your Honor," and refer to "The Honorable Judge So-and-So" and his "Honorable Court," always being careful to capitalize the written words. Everybody rises when His Honor enters the courtroom.

The most active players in the courtroom farce are the trial lawyers — the prosecutor and the defense counsel. The prosecutor is a cop who specializes in the legal aspects of police work. The defense counsel is a private lawyer who's paid to represent the accused, although he might draw his paycheck from the government if the defendant can't afford to pay. The government keeps a stable of lawyers on contract for just such occasions — the "public defenders." They're usually youngsters or people who are new to the area and haven't yet built up a busy office practice of their own.

As you might imagine, it's in the best interests of a defendant to get a highly-skilled lawyer who has the time and motivation to give him the most vigorous defense possible. This is where money makes the difference. The public defender is paid a very small fee for each case, so he's motivated to take on as many of them as possible and handle them in assembly line fashion. The heavy caseload of most courts makes it a virtual certainty that he'll be overworked, and the only way he can keep up is by resolving a large percentage of his cases through plea bargains. The privately-paid attorney, on the other hand, can afford to apportion his time so as to allow him to develop an effective defense for his client and pursue it to the bitter end in court. Moreover, he's often socially in a position to pay off the judge, which the public defender and his indigent client have neither the cash nor the connections to accomplish. A seventeenth-century commentator once observed that "a man may as well open an oyster without a knife, as a lawyer's mouth without a fee,"[3] and it remains equally true today that a criminal defendant's hope for a favorable outcome will be directly proportional to the size of his bankroll.

Some folks would say that this is unfair — that every defendant should be entitled to the same high level of competency, attention, and care with his legal defense regardless of his ability to pay. For public relations purposes, certainly, the government and the legal profession like to entertain that impression. But the truth is that people are *not* guaranteed an equal level of representation. The U.S. Supreme Court has declared that "a criminal trial is not a game in which the participants are expected to enter the ring with a near match in skills;"[4] every lawyer has to try his first case sometime, and the government doesn't care if it is your life that he ends up practicing with.[5]

We could attempt to do a detailed characterization of lawyers the same way we did of cops, but it really wouldn't serve a useful purpose here. It's sufficient, and probably a lot more interesting, to simply take a look at what other folks have thought of lawyers down through history:

Socrates (c. 400 B.C.) —

> "(He has) practiced deception and retaliation, and has become stunted and warped. And so he has passed out of youth into manhood, having no soundness in him; and is now, as he thinks, a master in wisdom. Such is the lawyer, Theodorus."[6]

Jesus Christ (c. 31 A.D.) —

"Woe to you lawyers also! for you load men with burdens hard to bear, and you yourselves do not touch the burdens with one of your fingers."[7]

Jonathan Swift (1727) —

"You have clearly proved that ignorance, idleness, and vice, are the proper ingredients for qualifying a legislator; that laws are best explained, interpreted and applied, by those whose interest and abilities lie in perverting, confounding and eluding them."[8]

Oliver Goldsmith (1768) —

"Lawyers are always more ready to get a man into troubles than out of them."[9]

Samuel Taylor Coleridge (c. 1820) —

"He saw a lawyer killing a viper
on a dunghill hard by his own stable;
and the Devil smiled, for it put him in mind
Of Cain and his brother Abel."[10]

Henry Peter, Lord Brougham (c. 1840) —

"A learned gentleman who rescues your estate
from your enemies and keeps it to himself"[6]

Oscar Wilde (c. 1890) —

"Lawyers have been known to wrest from
reluctant juries triumphant verdicts of acquit-
tal for their clients, even when those clients, as
often happens, were clearly and unmistakably
innocent."[11]

Carl Sandburg (c. 1930) —

"Why is there always a secret singing
When a lawyer cashes in?
Why does a hearse horse snicker
Hauling a lawyer away?"[12]

Grace Hibbard —

"An Honest Lawyer" — book just out —
What can the author have to say?
Reprint perhaps of ancient tome —
A work of fiction any way."[13]

The job of the court is to air both sides of a controversy and let the judge resolve it according to what the
written law says (of which he professes to be the
expert). There are big laws (such as the "Constitution"),

medium-sized laws (such as the "statutes"), and small laws (such as the "case law" that the courts themselves create). When there's a conflict between them, the bigger law is supposed to take precedence over the smaller one, and the party backed by the bigger law wins over his adversary. That's the way it's supposed to be, anyway.

In practice the courts generally do their utmost to rule in favor of the government, even when the individual has the bigger law in his corner. They do this by twisting their reading of the law (a process known as "construction") so that they can make it seem to say what they want it to say. They see nothing wrong with straining the words and stretching the meaning of the law when it suits their purpose.[14]

They're all for playing by the rules as long as the government wins, but when those rules sustain the individual citizen the courts claim that it's not a game anymore, so they don't have to recognize them.[15] That dualistic, black-and-white mentality that's so characteristic of the cop is at the bottom of this attitude. As one Supreme Court cop revealed, they see themselves as being charged with the twin purposes of "the conviction of the guilty and the vindication of the innocent,"[16] and to judge from recent rulings the functional corollary to this iron-heel principle is that "the end justifies the means."[17]/[18]/[19]

New laws that are likely to benefit the citizen are held to be non-retroactive so that prisoners can't use them to overturn their unfair convictions,[20] yet new laws which support police endeavors are cheerfully given retroactivity.[21]/[22] In matters where the courts have discretion, they invariably back the cops and rebuff the defendant; they'll go out of their way to slap him down if he's winning,[23] but when the defendant comes begging for a smidgen of justice they'll tell him that it's not their job to do what's "prudent or appropriate, but only what is constitutionally compelled."[24]

When a citizen is confronted by the law in all its technical perplexity, it's common for him to exercise poor judgment out of ignorance or mental instability. Instead of observing common notions of fair play and an understanding of human frailties, the court grasps this as an opportunity to pin the defendant down to the letter of the law. Unwise blunders, such as the making of incriminating statements and admissions of guilt, are welcomed and encouraged by the courts,[25]/[26]/[27] and if a defendant further entangles himself in the government's web by foolishly giving away all his constitutional rights, that pleases them even more.[28]

There are several different types of courts, but for the purposes of this book we shall consider only the three types involved with criminal cases — trial courts, appeals courts, and grand juries.[29]

Trial courts are where all the prosecutions and lawsuits take place, and they consist of two levels — the "limited jurisdiction courts" and the "general jurisdiction courts."

A limited jurisdiction court is portrayed on the popular television program "People's Court." Various petty affairs are handled in these courts, and criminal matters are generally limited to misdemeanors that carry no more than a year in jail and a $1,000 fine. They're called by a number of names: Justice of the Peace Court, City Court, Municipal Court, Police Court, Mayor's Court, Magistrate's Court, and Claims Court. The judge runs a one-man show, so things tend to move along pretty quickly there.

Although the ostensible mission of such courts is to "impartially apply the law," most of the city and county governments that run them are in fact dependent upon their ability to generate public revenues through fines. They also serve to intimidate local citizens into desired patterns of behavior, and persuade drifters to keep on traveling.

General jurisdiction courts are where the felony prosecutions and big lawsuits take place, and most of them handle a few misdemeanor cases and appeals from limited jurisdiction courts as well. Federal ones are called "District Courts," whereas those which are run by the various states are known by names such as Superior Court, Criminal Court, Circuit Court, Chancery Court, Common Pleas Court, County Court, Recorder's Court, and District Court. This is the kind of court portrayed in "Perry Mason" episodes, with the jury, the battling lawyers, and all the other rigamarole that comes to mind when one thinks of a "trial."

General jurisdiction courts don't actually sit to "impartially apply the law" in any more real sense than the limited ones do; as we've discussed previously, they exist in order to assert the will of the government. By imposing penalties on behalf of the cops, they protect the status quo for the ruling class. They dispatch as many folks as possible from the hands of the cops into the hands of the keepers, thus fueling the System with the bodies it needs to continue functioning. They intimidate citizens into snitching on others, thus expanding the range of police investigations. They also exert an intimidating effect on the behavior of the general populace by deterring people from doing things that the government doesn't want them to do (which it labels as "crime").

If the parties aren't satisfied after a case has gone through trial, it might proceed on to the second major type of court — the appeals court. There's no jury in an appeals court; everything's done by lawyers and judges, and few real people ever witness what goes on there. Two levels of appeal exist — the "intermediate appeals court" and the "court of last resort."

Intermediate appeals courts in the federal system are called the "Circuit Courts of Appeals," and there are thirteen of them around the country. Each one governs the federal law in a different region, most of which cover several states. The corresponding state courts are generally called "Courts of Appeals," although New

Yorkers had to be different by calling theirs the "Appell-ate Division Supreme Court."

When state appeals aren't settled at the intermediate level, they might go on to the state's court of last resort, which is generally called the "State Supreme Court" (except by those contrary New Yorkers, who persist in calling theirs the "Court of Appeals"). The federal version of the court of last resort is the "United States Supreme Court" in Washington, D.C. Through the decree of its nine judges, who are called "Justices," it has the final word over all the other courts, both federal and state.

The third type of court we're going to discuss is the grand jury. Actually it isn't a separate type at all, but is rather an arm of the trial court. Since it functions al-together differently, however, we need to draw the distinction. Theoretically it's a panel of citizens with a power which is independent of both the cops and the courts; its power comes directly from the people.[30] It was originally instituted in the American colonies so that no backbiting neighbor could get a person brought up on criminal charges without substantial grounds. The grand jury would review a criminal complaint in order to determine whether there was really anything to it. If there wasn't, the matter would go no further; if it seemed to have merit they would issue an "indictment," which gave the cops the green light for their pro-secution.

Lawyers being as they are, it didn't take them long to learn how to manipulate the grand jury to their own purposes. It's responsive to the prosecutor to the extent that he determines what witnesses to call and who examines them.[31] It's responsive to the court to the extent that it depends upon the court to compel the production of the witnesses and evidence.[32] Since he's the central figure in the grand jury investigative process, the prosecutor can thus orchestrate the proceedings so that *he,* and not "the people," will make the prosecutive determinations.[33] As Justice William O. Douglas has said,

"It is, indeed, common knowledge that the grand jury, having been conceived as a bulwark between the citizen and the Government, is now a tool of the Executive"[34] (which means the cops). Similarly, another commentator has observed that "this great institution of the past has long ceased to be the guardian of the people for which purpose it was created at Runnymede. Today it is but a convenient tool for the prosecutor — too often used solely for publicity. Any experienced prosecutor will admit that he can indict anybody at any time for almost anything before any grand jury."[35]

Not only is it a good "rubber stamp" for getting prosecutions started, but it's also better than thumbscrews for getting information out of people. This angle will be discussed more thoroughly in Chapter 14, but as a quick illustration consider the approach taken by the Nixon administration when it took over. Attorney General John Mitchell instructed all the federal prosecutors around the country to cooperate with the F.B.I. by directing their federal grand juries to subpoena people who refused to talk to investigators. These people had a *right* to refuse to talk to the F.B.I., but once they were brought into court before a grand jury, they could be forced to choose between talking and going to jail.[36]

REFERENCES

1. Dunne, Finley Peter, "On Expert Testimony," *Mr. Dooley in Peace and in War,* 1898

2. *Strickland v Washington,*＿US＿, 104 SCt 2052, 2057-2058 (1984)

3. Holyday, Barten, *Technogamia,* ii, 5 (c. 1640)

4. *U.S. v Cronic,* ＿ US＿, 104 SCt 2039, 2045-2046 (1984)

5. *Id.,* 104 SCt at 2050

6. Quoted by Bob Boze Bell in *New Times,* March 16-22, 1983, pp. 14-15 111 W. Monroe, Phoenix, AZ 85003

7. *Luke* 11:46

8. *Gulliver's Travels:* Voyage to Brobdingnag

9. *The Good Natured Man,* Act iii

10. *The Devil's Thoughts,* St. 4

11. *The Decoy of Lying*

12. *The Lawyers Know Too Much*

13. *Books Received,* quoted by Burton Stevenson in *The Home Book of Quotations,* Dodd, Mead & Co., NY, 1947, p. 1091

14. *Ullmann v U.S.,* 350 US 422, 433, 76 SCt 497, 504 (1956)

15. *McGuire v U.S.,* 273 US 95, 99, 47 SCt 259, 260 (1927)

16. *Florida v Royer,* 460 US _, 103 SCt 1319 (1983), J. Rehnquist dissenting

17. *Segura v U.S.,* _US _, _SCt (1984)

18. *U.S. v Leon,* _ US _,_SCt_ (1984)

19. *New York v Quarles,*_US_, 104 SCt 2626 (1984)

20. *State ex rel Collins v Superior Court, Etc.,* 132 AZ 180, 189-190, 644 P2d 1266, 1275-1276 (1982)

21. *State v Espinoza,* AZ Sup. Ct., 2/22/84

22. *Ramia v State,* Md. Ct. Spec. Appls., 3/1/84

23. *Florida v Meyers,* _US_, 104 SCt 1852, 1855-1856 (1984), J. Stevens dissenting

24. *U.S. v Cronic,* 104 SCt at 2050, n. 38

25. *Michigan v Mosley,* 423 US 96, 108-109, 96 SCt 321, 329 (1975), J. White concurring

26. *Dunaway v New York,* 442 US 200, 222, 99 SCt 2248, 2261-2262 (1979), J. Rehnquist dissenting

27. *U.S. v Washington,* 431 US 181, 187, 97 SCt 1814, 1818 (1977)

28. *Edwards v Arizona,* 451 US 477, 489, 101 SCt 1880, 1887 (1981), J. Powell concurring

29. *National Survey of Court Organization,* U.S. Department of Justice, Law Enforcement Assistance Administration, U.S. Government Printing Office, Washington, DC (1973)

30. *In re April 1956 Term Grand Jury,* 239 F2d 263, 268-269 (7th Cir. 1956)

31. *The Grand Jury as an Investigatory Body,* 74 Harv. L. Rev., 590, 596 (1961)

32. *U.S. v Calandra,* 414 US 338, 346 n. 4, 94 SCt 613, 619 n. 4 (1974)

33. *Proceedings of the 36th Annual Judicial Conference of the District of Columbia Circuit,* 67 FRD 513, 538 (1975), Seymour Glanzer

34. *U.S. v Dionisio,* 410 US 1, 24, 93 SCt 764, 777 (1973), J. Douglas dissenting

35. *Delays in Criminal Cases,* 55 FRD 225, 253 (1973), J. Campbell

36. Harris, Richard, *Freedom Spent,* Little, Brown & Co., Boston, 1976, p. 392

Chapter 4

THE KEEPERS

"'All hope abandon, ye who enter here.'
Such characters, in color dim, I mark'd
Over a portal's lofty arch inscribed."

Dante Alighieri, *The Divine Comedy,* Inferno,
Canto III (1321)

After the court is through with him, the person is no longer the same human being that he was when he went in. He's been transformed through the legal process from a "decent," esteemed citizen to a loathsome convicted felon. He may not look or feel different at first, but the effect of this process on his life will ultimately prove to be as drastic as any "altered state" that Paddy Chayefsky ever dreamed up.

Those supposedly "inalienable" rights to life, liberty, and the pursuit of happiness have been dispatched with an ease that betrays the hollowness of their promise. A new standard of civil rights is applied in their stead, giving the unfortunate person a status somewhere between that of a farm animal and a human being — just about the same as that which was enjoyed by the slaves prior to the Civil War. The convict, in fact, is the twentieth-century version of the plantation slave; he's owned by the government rather than a private individual, and he often has a fixed release date to look forward to, but otherwise the comparison is a fair one. He's little more than government livestock. The Thirteenth Amendment to the Constitution, which supposedly abolished slavery, admits as much: "Neither slavery nor involuntary servitude, *except as a punishment for crime whereof the party shall have been duly convicted,* shall exist within the United States, or any place subject to their jurisdiction."[1]

Regardless of his prior accomplishments and expertise, the convict is considered unworthy of credibility or respect. It's as though the court's ritual has effectuated some magical spell with the power to eradicate everything in his life except the fact that he's been convicted of a crime. It's that same old dualistic cop mentality at work; you're either a "good guy" or a "bad guy," and once they've labeled you as the latter your credibility is shot.

What they do with the convict will depend upon many factors, such as the nature of the crime, the amount of publicity it generated, the particular state having jurisdiction, and whether or not the judge has been "fixed." Basically it will fall into one of two categories — probation or incarceration. In some cases fines and forfeitures might be imposed in addition to either of these categories.

Probation is the most lenient sentence a judge can hand out. It means the convict can go home, just as though he'd been acquitted; there are strings attached, however. Any number of terms and conditions can be applied, and if the person screws up and violates one of them he can be sent directly to prison. Probation is a form of supervision, and a special type of cop called a "probation officer" is assigned to ride herd over the person. These cops wear plain clothes and pretend to be social psychologists, but they're phonies; their real job is solely to keep tabs on the probationer, and the sum of what they know about psychology comes from watching "The Bob Newhart Show." One could search the corridors of government for a long time before finding a more useless bureaucrat than the probation officer.

Probation is uncommon; the usual destiny of the convict is incarceration, and for this there are two distinct types of facilities — jail and prison.

As you'll recall, misdemeanors that are tried in courts of limited jurisdiction are only subject to sentences of a year or less, and the local jail is used to consummate these penalties. Jails are typically filthy and inadequate for housing people (or animals either, for that matter). They're often poorly heated, overcrowded, and devoid of luxuries like mattresses, pillows, and blankets. The city and county police departments which operate them are always anxious to lock folks up, but are too cheap to spend the money that it takes to care for them properly. They couldn't care less if you have to sleep on the floor and go without bathing for a few days. They're not interested in the worries and frustrations that you're likely to be suffering after having just been locked up —like what's happening to your family and your business, and why your lawyer hasn't been in to see you. Once they have you filed away in a cell, they can more or less ignore you until somebody on the outside summons you for a visit or a court appearance.

Those local citizens who have enough clout to force the cops to run a humane jail rarely do so; they're more likely to draw heat down on a kennel or stable which mistreats animals than to focus attention on a jail where people are abused. The politicians and other "good" citizens of the community have little empathy for folks who wind up in jail; they assume that such people probably deserve a little discomfort, and dismiss the problem as being one of only temporary abuses anyway. Most folks are only housed for a few days, and those who do stay for longer periods of time tend to be derelicts and poor people whose opinions count for little with the politicians. The whole subject of the caretaking of jail detainees is too sordid for most "decent" citizens to want any part of anyway.

The principal type of institution used by the keepers is the prison. This is a large warehouse type facility which is run by state or federal cops for the purpose of holding convicted felons for long periods of time. Colloquially it's referred to as "the joint," "the slammer," or "the big house;" and some of them have been affectionately nicknamed according to their peculiar geographical features ("The Rock;" "up the river").

What the physical features of a prison consist of will depend upon which level of security one wants to consider — most prison systems have four of them.

For people who are under the death sentence, and others who are considered to be especially desperate or dangerous, there's "Supermax." The security there is the tightest of anywhere in a prison system. Each prisoner is kept in a separate cell, and he generally only leaves it for a few minutes of exercise or to shower a couple times per week. If somebody comes to visit him, they have to talk to each other from either side of a partition, because there's no physical contact allowed. Prisoners might be allowed to do certain hobbies in their cells, such as painting, but there's really very little for them to do or look forward to in Supermax. Aside from providing a "death row" for those who are awaiting execution, facilities such as this are used to house people whom the prison administration has singled out for special punishment. The isolated environment occasioned by the heavy security measures provides the guards with an excellent opportunity to work prisoners over without witnesses, and the lower quality of life there compared to other parts of the prison system is itself a continual form of punishment.

The next lower category is "Maximum Security," which is the stereotyped facility shown in prison movies such as *Stir-Crazy* and *On-The-Yard*. Prisoners live in huge buildings called "cellblocks" containing a hundred or more cages, and they work at various jobs within the compound, such as doing laundry, preparing meals, or making license plates. Unlike Supermax, they get to socialize, walk around outside, and take part in various activities such as athletic events, educational classes, church, etc. When people come to visit, they're allowed to sit at tables in the same room with the prisoners. Encircling the maximum security unit there's always a high wall or fence fortified with razor wire and interspaced with towers where rifle-toting guards are stationed.

Many prisons have a third level of custody called "Medium Security," where the prisoners live in dormitories instead of barred cells. The freedom to walk around and participate in recreational activities is generally greater than in Max, and there might not be any gun towers, but the fence and razor wire are still there.

The least oppressive custody level in a prison is "Minimum Security," where there are neither fences nor gun towers (an improvement which does wonders for a prisoner's morale). Those who are housed in such facilities are called "trustys," and they often work in nearby communities with little or no supervision by prison staff. When outside visitors come to see them, they can spend several hours together having a picnic on the lawn, and some prisoners even get to go home on short furloughs every so often.

Regardless of whether a person is housed in a super-max, maximum, medium, or minimum security unit, he's subject to certain standard deprivations because he's a prisoner. It's a level of repression that insidiously damages the psyche and warps the personality, ultimately with unfortunate consequences for society. Restrictions on freedom can take various forms.

There are many things you simply can't do when you're in prison — things which may be important to your mental, spiritual, or physical well-being. You can't travel or get around to the businesses and institutions you need to see in order to handle your personal affairs. You're deprived of an opportunity to do your own line of work, and instead are forced to do some meaningless scut work for little or no pay. You're separated from your family, and the loss of your personal and financial impact on their lives usually results in the decay of the relationship. You're denied a normal sex life. Some medical and dental services are not furnished to prisoners, and you can't choose your own doctor or seek a second opinion. There's no stability in your life because you can be moved away at any time, regardless of any plans or friendships you may have made. You can't have certain worldly pleasures that you may be accustomed to, such as booze, fine foods, custom tobaccos, and clothing of your choosing. Recreational diversions which are usually disallowed in prison include shooting, flying, motoring, swimming, photography, martial arts, computers, and animals.

Regimentation is the order of the day; you're locked up, let out, fed, showered, counted, and turned out for exercise according to schedule, just like dairy cattle.

There's no such thing as privacy. They censor your mail and reading material, listen in on your phone conversations, and search your property when they feel like it, confiscating whatever they please. They force you to strip naked so they can search your body and clothes, and they constantly watch you, whether you're working, lying in bed, taking a shower, or on the toilet.

You're forced to live constantly with unpleasantness. You sleep in cramped quarters on an uncomfortable bed, breathing stinky, smoky air, and trying to ignore the noise of loudmouths and morons who think that the whole world wants to hear what they're playing on their radios. You have to put up with all kinds of ignorance and irritation, including frustration and discouragement from prison administrators, and stupidity and disrespect from churlish guards.

Prison systems are big business; it requires the investment of huge sums to build the facilities, and even bigger sums to operate them. There are 6,661 of them now, and they hold nearly 724,000 people.[2] At the cost of between $25,000 and $125,000 to build each cell, and between $7,000 and $30,000 per year to keep each prisoner in it, this mounts up to one hell of a lot of bucks.[3]

Between 1970 and 1980 the yearly expenditures on prison construction in America rose from $74 million to

$450 million, and by 1982 they had doubled to $946 million. There are currently 717 *new* prisons and jails under construction in this country, and at that cost of over $5.6 billion, that should be sufficient to allow them to lock up another 132,829 people more than they have room for now. California alone plans to spend $1.2 billion on prisons during the next five years; it has its heart set on doubling the size of its prisoner herd within that period.[4]

Building the prisons is only the beginning of the scam; it provides a healthy boost to the private economies of certain individuals, to be sure, but the real dividends come from their operation after they're built. It takes numerous guards, maintenance, medical, and food personnel, industrial managers, secretaries, and administrators to adequately featherbed a prison operation. There are 40,000 of them that belong to one union alone.[5] All these salaries come out of tax revenues, so they don't have to be justified by the demonstration of profits, as would be the case with a legitimate business enterprise. At various junctures along the line many of the operational funds are diverted into private pockets. All told, it can be a pretty sweet deal for a lot of people. The state of Arizona has evidently found it to be so; its annual prison budget of $27 million in 1979 has leaped to five times that amount over the past five years[6] (Arizona has added a fifth "C" to its list of major industries: Cattle, Climate, Copper, Cotton, and *Convicts*). It's estimated that the operating costs for those 100,000 new prison beds which are currently under construction will end up costing the taxpayer some $70 billion over the next 30 years.[4]

Realizing how lucrative this racket is, even private companies have started to get on the bandwagon. A firm out of Nashville called the Corrections Corporation of America has opened up a 350-bed prison in Houston, while another one, Buckingham Security, Ltd., is building a 722-bed facility near Pittsburgh. These companies provide the whole "prison package" for federal or state governments that wish to contract prisoners out to them. The feds alone are currently spending $21 million per year for the use of privately-run prison facilities.[5]

After a person has done his time and gets out of prison, the System still isn't through with him — not by a long shot. Most prison systems have early release programs called "work furlough," whereby the prisoner goes to live in a "halfway house" and works during the day at a regular job. Halfway houses are dormitories operated by the prison administration, and the residents have to follow most of the same rules as when they were in prison. The government makes a double-barreled killing off this scam: it gets operational funds from tax sources, since it's part of the prison system, and it gets a big chunk of the prisoner's earnings as well. Actually the prisoner is still technically "in custody," and he can be jerked right back to the joint for the slightest infraction. Parole is a less tightly-controlled program whereby the prisoner signs an agreement to abide by a number of conditions in return for being allowed to live and work in the community. These conditions include frequent visits to a "parole officer," who can be described in much the same language as the probation officer. More government payrolls are added at this point by supplying the ex-con with a variety of "counseling services" which he's forced to accept "for his rehabilitation." A person who's on parole doesn't have the rights of an ordinary citizen, and if he violates one of the conditions of release prior to the expiration of his term he loses credit for all the parole time he did on the street. A person with a ten-year parole term could do nine years of it without a hitch, and then be jerked back into prison to do the whole ten years all over again just for drinking a beer!

All these people who fulfill the role of the keepers — probation officers, jail and prison personnel, administrators, parole officers — are basically cops. They're motivated by the same love of government, the same crusade against "evil," and the same play of egos that characterize the street cops.

In the case of the keepers, their fondness for government work is even more likely to be a result of laziness than with street cops. Prison jobs are much easier to get than police commissions, and as often as not, the prospective prison guard is simply looking for steady work that's close to home. Prison work is easy job security that requires no real skills. People who become prison guards are generally a calibre of individual that would have washed out of a real police academy. Most of them are fat, misshapen, or impaired by various other physical handicaps, and invariably lack the capacity for original thought.

The keepers see themselves as members of a team fighting the battle against evil. Their job is to isolate, punish, and rehabilitate the bad guys, while simultaneously satisfying society's thirst for retribution and deterring similar conduct in the future. In a word, they think they're *correcting* society's problems, so they prefer to call themselves "correctional officers."

Their ego problems are as bad as those of the police, but they're a much more cowardly breed of cop; they know that their captives have been stripped of all weapons and are incapable of effective resistance, and those are the kinds of odds that appeal to them.

The upper-eschelon keepers who run the prison systems have attempted to legitimize what they're doing by rhetorically elevating it to the status of a science, which they call "corrections." Some of them have even acquired a title of Ph.D. in the endeavor to pass themselves off to the public as professionals; presumably they have to justify their exorbitant salaries somehow. Once you've cleared away all the blarney, however, the plain fact is that a slaver by any other name is still nothing but a slaver. These guys aren't practicing a "science" any more than Adolph Eichmann or Klaus Barbie were. One of the so-called "doctors of corrections" recently revealed his level of sensitivity and understanding of prisoners when he quipped that a person who's housed in Supermax is "making $20,000 a year" (which is the amount of money it costs the state to keep a man caged up in that particular hellhole).[6] With such a lack of insight into the human mind by those who are supposed to be in the know, one can hardly be optimistic about the attitude and philosophy that their subordinate goons are likely to exhibit.

The people of the legislature play their part in the prison system scam as well. Crime is always a hot issue, and some lawmakers rally much of their constituency from the ranks of the meek and the terrified. Such legislators can be counted on to back the steady expansion of an oppressive prison system. One such lawmaker from Arizona recently showed her level of concern for state prisoners by suggesting "if some of those swamp coolers would break down, that might get rid of some of our prison population." When asked to clarify herself, the good woman replied, "What I meant was that if some of the coolers were to break down or come unplugged, it would make them rather uncomfortable. Or maybe it would just smother them to death."[7]

After probation, incarceration, fines, forfeitures, and post-release supervision are all behind him, the convicted person will continue to suffer a form of punishment through the loss of various rights. Some of them are cancelled through official decree, while others simply disappear by social prerogative.

There are federal laws foreclosing such things as the right to be a juror,[8] deal in firearms,[9] (indeed, even to *possess* one),[10] or hold office at a bank.[11] If the person's conviction pertained to an abuse of trust or an act of treason, they have statutes making him ineligible to work for the government,[12] and there are various agency regulations which declare that any conviction eliminates him from consideration. Certain government freebies may also be withheld from an ex-con: depending on the type of crime he was convicted of, he might lose his Veterans' or federal retirement benefits,[13] his entitlement to educational assistance,[14] or his bed at the Old Soldiers' Home.[15]

State laws exact a toll in lost civil rights as well. They can deprive the ex-con of his right to vote,[16] hold public office,[17] or practice his profession.[18]

Unofficial suppression of an ex-con's rights and privileges in society can be extremely hurtful. Once the credit bureaus lock the conviction into their memory banks, that information becomes forevermore accessible to creditors, banks, employers, unions, and other organizations. The effects of this on a person's candidacy for loans, job applications, etc. should be obvious. Social organizations are frequently loathe to admit an ex-con into their membership, and general popular prejudice can wind up stinging him in countless unforeseeable ways. Police will jump on with all fours whenever an ex-con becomes suspected in connection with a crime, and there's a standing presumption of guilt that he must struggle against in his efforts to get bail and defend himself. Truly, the Curse of the Keepers haunts a person long after he has left the prison walls.

REFERENCES

1. The United States Constitution, Amendment XIII, Section 1 (1865)

2. *Jericho,* Newsletter of the Unitarian Universalist Service Committee National Moratorium on Prison Construction, No. 34, 1984, p. 12 (309 Pennsylvania Ave. S.E., Washington, DC 20003)

3. Corey, Bruce & Gettinger, Stephen, *Time to Build? The Realities of Prison Construction,* The Edna McConnell Clark Foundation, 1984, p. 15

4. *Id.* at p. 7

5. Gest, Ted, "Prisons For Profit: A Growing Business," *U.S. News & World Report,* July 2, 1984, pp. 45-46

6. *La Roca,* Magazine of the Arizona State Prison, Vol. 10 No. 3, May-June 1984, pp. 9-10, quoting James G. Ricketts, Ph.D., Director (PO Box 629, Florence, AZ 85232)

7. *New Times,* Vol. 14 No. 74, January 5-11, 1983, p. 2, quoting Arizona state legislator Jane D. Hull (111 W. Monroe, Phoenix, AZ 85003)

8. Title 28 U.S.C. Section 1861 (1)

9. Title 18 U.S.C. Section 922 (g)

10. Title 18 U.S.C. Appendix, Section 1201 et seq.

11. Title 12 U.S.C. 1730 (h) (1)

12. Title 18 U.S.C. Sections 593, 1901, 2071, 2381, 2383, 2385, and 2387

13. Title 5 U.S.C. Section 8312; Title 38 U.S.C. Section 3505

14. Title 42 U.S.C. Sections 1862 & 2459, notes re campus disrupters

15. Title 24 U.S.C. Section 50

16. *Richardson v Ramirez,* 418 US 24, 56, 83 n. 27, 28, 94 SCt 2655, 2672, 2685-2686 n. 27, 28 (1974), J. Marshall dissenting

17. E.g. Arizona Revised Statute (A.R.S.) 13-904

18. E.g. A.R.S. 32-1422 (A) (4)

Chapter 5

THE
CONSTITUTION

So, what's the point in worrying about all this? If a person can be abducted by the cops, railroaded through the courts, and cast into bondage for exploitation by the keepers, isn't it all rather hopeless? What possible chance could one mortal have of resisting the imperious will of the State with all its well-greased organizational machinery, limitless funds, armies of specialists, and the support of the people to back it up? Isn't the government holding *all* the cards? The answer is no... not here and now, anyway. In this country there's a trump card left to the individual that makes the critical difference between life under our system and that under the Commissars; we have the United States Constitution. It pre-empts all the other laws that the bureaucrats and power-players keep devising to impose control over our lives. It is, as the courts acknowledge, "the fundamental law of the land."[1]

Every American child learns about the Constitution at school; and what a royal bore it is at the time! They tell the kiddies a stirring tale about how some old men wearing wigs and knickerbockers and three-cornered hats wrote this famous document so that we could all live happily ever after. The kids don't relate to any of this, of course. They fail to realize its relevance to modern-day life, and as the years go by they grow into adults who know that they have "constitutional rights," but don't know exactly what that means. "I know my rights" and "You can't do this to me" are boasts that quickly leap to the lips of the average citizen when he's confronted by the discretionary power of the police. The unfortunate truth is that people *don't* know their rights... and the ones they do know they either give away or fail to assert. Trusting as they do in the fairness of the System, they soon discover that they've misplaced their faith, and that it's too late to avoid disaster. Such is the tragedy that this book seeks to prevent; its purpose is to spell out for the average person (1) precisely what rights he has against the police, (2) how to use them to avoid trouble, and (3) how to use them to get out of trouble if the unthinkable does occur.

HOW THE CONSTITUTION WORKS

Without launching into a tiresome discussion of civics, on which too many books have already been written, a few words must be devoted to placing the Constitution into perspective with the other laws. As the "fundamental law of the land," the Constitution is the highest order of authority that we have. It is, in effect, the charter that lays down the ground rules for all the other laws, and in that way it determines how our society is organized. If a theological metaphor may be forgiven, it's our Ten Commandments. Nobody questions it — not the F.B.I... not the Supreme Court... not the President... not even the phone company.

Unfortunately, it's one thing to acknowledge the Constitution and quite another to obey it. This is so because the Constitution is a law without penalties. The laws that do have penalties attached to them are called "statutes," and someone who gets caught violating one of those can be charged a fine or sent to the pokey (or both). Besides the Constitution and the statutes, there's a third kind of law called "case law." Every time someone is dragged into court, whether for violating one of the statutes or to settle a dispute, the court has to make a decision; who's right, and who's wrong? To punish or not to punish — that is the question. Once it makes its mind up, that's called a "holding" or "decision," and it becomes "case law." The next time a case just like that one comes in, they don't have to go through all the same reasoning again; they're supposed to use the same decision the earlier court made.

When the First Congress wrote the Constitution, the idea was to let the legislators and the judges be the ones to set any penalties for violating it.[2] Since it was the public officials that the Constitution was designed to restrain, it's no surprise that they've done very little in the way of establishing punishment for violators. Occupants of one branch of the government tend to characterize their colleagues in other branches as honorable, just, and possessed of praiseworthy intentions (like themselves). It must seem unthinkable to them that their official brethren would ever be guilty of wrongdoing.

Nevertheless, there are a few measures by which our constitutional protections can be enforced. An example of a statute that's been created for this purpose is Title 18 U.S.C. Section 2511; it provides for a fine of up to $10,000 and/or a prison term of up to 5 years for violating a person's privacy with unauthorized electronic surveillance. An example of case law that's been developed to enforce the Constitution is the famous "exclusionary rule." It threatens the violator with none of the standard kinds of punishment, yet its unique penalty has become one of our most important means of protection from the System. It's the key to the strategy laid out in this book, so it needs to be thoroughly understood.

THE EXCLUSIONARY RULE

This subject is a current "hot potato" in the law enforcement field. The Reagan Administration hates it, the Supreme Court's trying to erode it, and the criminal defendant needs it. It's been a subject of controversy ever since its birth in 1914, but the Draconian mentality of the Moral Majority has recently focused a rising level of censure against it. Law-and-order buffs complain that it offends their notion of justice. Police lament because it diminishes their conviction rates and forces them to think before they act.

A series of landmark Supreme Court cases[3]/[1]/[4] has formalized a rule that, when police acquire evidence against a person by violating his constitutional protections, they shouldn't be allowed to use it to convict him. The protections we're talking about here are our rights of privacy and security under the Fourth, Fifth, Sixth, and Fourteenth Amendments to the Constitution. The Fourth forbids unreasonable searches and seizures (of a person, his home, or his belongings); the Fifth prohibits the forcing of a person to give testimony against himself; the sixth protects a person's communications with his lawyer; and the Fourteenth guarantees that the state government will give the defendant a fair shake when it prosecutes him. If the cops step out of line in any of these areas in order to "get the goods" on somebody, the exclusionary rule says that the evidence they acquire from it can't be used. Even if it proves conclusively that he's guilty, and there's no way of getting another shot at him, the tainted evidence must be barred, or "suppressed" from the courts.

Such evidence might consist of tangible articles,[5] such as drugs or weapons; an incriminating statement or confession made by the suspect;[6]/[7] testimony of the officers concerning things that they have seen[8] or heard[9] as a result of their unlawful intrusion; or testimony of eye-witnesses concerning their identification of a suspect.[10] None of these types of evidence may be used in any way to convict a person who's been harmfully victimized by unconstitutional police conduct;[11] not as direct evidence in his trial... not as grounds for arrest... not even as grounds for a search warrant. Moreover, if the police exploit an unlawful intrusion by gathering leads that direct them to further evidence, that too is subject to suppression; it's known as the "fruit of the poisonous tree" because it grew directly out of an initially illegal act.[12]

The purpose behind the exclusionary rule is to deter the police from violating the average citizen's constitutional rights,[13] although there don't seem to be adequate studies to substantiate its effectiveness in doing so.[14] When the court refuses to admit tainted evidence it weakens the prosecutor's case, and in losing the conviction he's losing out on press mileage that he needs for furthering his political career. He vents his spleen onto his police subordinates, and the blundering patrolman ends up with a tongue-lashing from the Captain and the removal of his name from the Officer-of-the-Month competition. In cases where their disregard of the citizen's rights failed to turn up any incriminating evidence, the police might even find themselves on the wrong end of a civil lawsuit.

Although it's been said many times that this exclusionary rule exists for the benefit of the guilty and the innocent alike,[1/15] the basic intent behind it doesn't focus on the suspect at all. Its real purpose is to maintain the people's trust in government.[16] Nobody really cares whether the criminal gets a fair shake or not; indeed, there are many who believe that he deserves a raw deal. The concern lies in dispelling the idea that the courts are in an unholy partnership with police lawlessness. Government can continue to hold the status quo only as long as it maintains its credibility with the general public. The "imperative of judicial integrity"[1] that the courts established by refusing to become a party to constitutional violations served to assure the common folk not only that they wouldn't be rousted about in Gestapo fashion, but also that the courts were above the inconstancy of men's discretion. In recent years, this noble concept of an imperative of judicial integrity has been discarded by the Supreme Court behind the claim that only the deterrent effect justifies excluding evidence.[17]/[18] Perhaps this is just an admission that the Court itself no longer has the judicial integrity that it used to have. At any rate, it's the indirect protective effect on the millions of innocent citizens that makes the courts willing to allow an occasional outlaw to walk away free.

The exclusionary rule is not a fundamental constitutional right that automatically goes into effect whenever anyone's constitutional protections are violated.[19]/[20] The only person who can claim the right, or "standing," to invoke it is the very one whose constitutional rights have been transgressed.[21] Moreover, he can only block the use of the evidence against himself, not its use against other parties. For example, a man can't use it to suppress evidence against him that was illegally obtained from his crime partner; true, it's dirty evidence, but the only one who has a legal gripe against it is the crime partner. It was his crime partner's constitutional rights that were disrespected, not his own, and except in narrow circumstances where their privacy rights are co-extensive (such as a private conversation at one of their homes),[22] such a man cannot invoke the exclusionary rule. In order to keep objectionable evidence from being used, a "motion to suppress" should be raised sometime before the trial. This requirement of a "timely objection" was set down to prevent duplication of effort and wasted time in court,[23] but exceptions to it can sometimes be made.[24]

Courts, consisting as they do of confirmed advocates of the System who generally feel compelled to join in the fight against Evil, have developed many ingenious excuses for denying the use of the exclusionary rule. It does not apply, for instance, to any proceeding other than a criminal trial; grand jury hearings[16] and civil tax proceedings[14] are acceptable arenas for unlawfully acquired evidence. Neither does it apply in a variety of criminal trial contexts where the High Court's specious logic has managed to finesse a way around it. If the act of police misconduct is followed by enough intervening events, independent circumstances,[25] or lapse of time[26] before leading to the actual evidence, it might be determined that the causal connection has been either broken or so attenuated as to "dissipate the taint."[27] Such a rationalization gives small consolation to the defendant, who knows only that, if it weren't for the violation of his rights, the cops never would have gotten the evidence against him.

Another subterfuge that neutralizes the exclusionary rule is the demonstration of an independent source of access to evidence that was unlawfully obtained.[11] According to this proposition, the evidence that the police illegally acquired might have been gotten lawfully by another means if they had thought of it, which they didn't, so it's okay to use it. Now, doesn't that make perfect sense? Similar in logic is the "inevitable discovery" exception, which reasons that if the government hadn't trampled over a person's rights to get its evidence, it probably would have found it sooner or later anyway.[28]

For some unfathomable reason, a live witness is considered an exception to the rule of excludable evidence;[25] even though such testimony would never have existed but for the illegitimate police conduct, the courts nevertheless permit it. The lack of deterrence value is also cited as grounds for passing over the exclusionary rule. For this reason, the Supreme Court refused to overturn the convictions of prisoners with Fourth Amendment grievances who had already received the full course of appeals in the state courts and sought federal relief under petitions of habeas corpus. The High Court didn't think that at such a late stage of the appeals process the exclusionary rule would have any deterrent effect on the behavior of the cops involved six years earlier.[18]

Police often rely in "good faith" on a law that's later held to be unconstitutional,[29] or on a belief concerning the law that's later proven to be erroneous.[30] When such a reliance results in the breach of a defendant's constitutional rights, the courts generally refuse to apply the exclusionary rule. What behavior, they ask, could they hope to modify by punishing the police for doing what they thought was their duty? Following up on this "good faith" nonsense, the Supreme Court delivered the coup de grace to the warrant requirement with its recent ruling that, even when the cops and the judge screw up and issue a bum warrant, they can still use the evidence they've acquired with it as long as nobody can prove that they deliberately cheated.[31] Cops and judges, who are presumed to be acting in "good faith" rather than from self-serving expediency, have but to assert that they placed their "objectively reasonable" reliance on the sufficiency of their probable cause. Maybe the "probable cause" will turn out to be zilch once somebody looks at it closely, but no matter — the warrant and its resultant evidence still stand.

Even when evidence must be suppressed from use in the prosecutor's case-in-chief, it can still be slipped into the trial if the defendant approaches the subject from the witness stand, because the exclusionary rule doesn't apply to evidence used for impeachment purposes.[32]

Criticism of the exclusionary rule has been voiced by the more truculent and punitory members of the legal community. Their main complaint charges that it subverts the ends of justice by preventing the whole truth from being told. The "whole truth" that they're talking about doesn't demand an accounting of all the factors which kindled a crime and made it necessary. Such considerations are deemed irrelevant, and in their minds there's no excuse for breaking the law anyway. It's that precious evidence that might be used to convict somebody that their "whole truth" contemplates. It must be remembered that punishment is the lifeblood of the System; without it the whole framework would break down. It shouldn't be any surprise that sanctimonious egotists who have seized the role of running other people's lives would object to the loss of a good piece of incriminating evidence.

The consequence of vital evidence suppression is that the guilty escape punishment; as Justice Cardozo has cynically commented, "the criminal is to go free because the constable has blundered."[33] In addition to the trauma that this works on authoritarian egos, there's the allegation that it endangers society. The decent, law-abiding citizens are placed in peril by exposure to criminals (viz. people who might have been locked up but for the exclusionary rule). Folks who break drug laws are especially likely to benefit from this rule, according to a recent study. Between the years 1976 and 1979, police search-and-seizure violations in California caused the prosecutors to drop 4.8% of their more than 4,000 felony cases; they had to drop 30% of their felony drug busts.[34]

In summary, it can be seen that the courts have drawn a balance between the individual's rights and government's interests, and the prevailing state of this balance at the time of trial determines whether or not they will allow the use of the exclusionary rule. On the one pan of the scales we have the so-called "societal interests," which claim that "everything rationally related to ascertaining the truth is presumptively admissible."[35] The police and other partners in the System endeavor to expand the stacking of this side of the scales, with the discretionary standard of the Gestapo envisioned as the ideal. Even they, however, admit to limitation from such strong constitutional rights as privileged communications and the refusal to testify against oneself.[35] Balanced against "societal interests" is the constitutional right of the individual to be left alone. He's entitled to be free from police "invasion of his indefeasible right of personal security, personal liberty and private property," as well as "any forcible and compulsory extortion of a man's own testimony or of his private papers to be used as evidence to convict him of crime or to forfeit his goods."[36]

In a larger sense, however, the individual's interests are identical to those of society, rather than being at war with them. Admittedly, it's in a criminal's best interests if he can exploit the exclusionary rule to beat his case, but that's only a side effect of the personal rights issue. The heart of the issue is the citizens' trust in government, as Justice Brandeis has warned: "If the government becomes a lawbreaker, it breeds contempt for the law; it invites every man to become a law unto himself; it invites anarchy."[37] This is why the idea of an "imperative of judicial integrity" was felt to be so important at one time; "Nothing can destroy a government more quickly than its failure to observe its own laws, or worse, its disregard of the charter of its own existence."[38] Citizens perceive their government as being fair, honorable, and worthy of support only when it treats them respectfully and acts in behalf of their interests as individuals. Society is nothing more than the sum of those individuals, so the genuine societal interest is far more deeply concerned with personal rights than with governmental services such as law enforcement. Government telling us what's best for our society is like the spider giving navigational directions to the fly.

REFERENCES

1. *Elkins v U.S.,* 364 US 206, 222, 80 SCt 1437, 1447 (1960)
2. Madison, James, I Annals of Congress 439 (1789)
3. *U.S. v Weeks,* 232 US 383, 34 SCt 341 (1914)
4. *Mapp v Ohio,* 367 US 643, 81 SCt 1684 (1961)
5. *Wong Sun v U.S.,* 371 US 471, 485, 83 SCt 407, 416 (1963)

6. *Brown v Illinois*, 422 US 590, 95 SCt 2254 (1975)

7. *Miranda v Arizona*, 384 US 436, 86 SCt 1602 (1966)

8. *McGinnis v U.S.*, 227 F2d 598 (1st Cir. 1955)

9. *Silverman v U.S.*, 365 US 505, 81 SCt 679 (1961)

10. *U.S. v Wade*, 388 US 218, 87 SCt 1926 (1967)

11. *Silverthorne Lumber Co. v U.S.*, 251 US 385, 392, 40 SCt 182, 183 (1920)

12. *Wong Sun v U.S.*, 371 US at 488, 83 SCt at 417

13. *Rea v U.S.*, 350 US 214, 217, 76 SCt 292, 294 (1956)

14. *U.S. v Janis*, 428 US 433, 449-453, 96 SCt 3021, 3029-3032 (1976)

15. *McDonald v U.S.*, 335 US 451, 453, 69 SCt 191, 192 (1948)

16. *U.S. v Calandra*, 414 US 338, 357, 94 SCt 613, 624 (1974)

17. *Michigan v Tucker*, 417 US 433, 450 n. 25, 94 SCt 2357, 2367 n. 25 (1974)

18. *Stone v Powell*, 428 US 467, 485, 96 SCt 3037, 3048 (1976)

19. *Id.*, 428 US at 486, 96 SCt at 3048

20. *Mapp v Ohio*, 367 US at 661-662, 81 SCt at 1695

21. *Alderman v U.S.*, 394 US 165, 89 SCt 961 (1969)

22. *Id.*, 394 US at 179 n. 11, 89 SCt at 969-970 n. 11

23. *U.S. v Barletta*, 500 FSupp 739 (D. Mass. 1980)

24. *Smith v Estelle*, 451 US 454, 468 n. 12, 101 SCt 1866, 1876 n. 12 (1981)

25. *U.S. v Ceccolini*, 435 US 268, 98 SCt 1054 (1978)

26. *Wong Sun v U.S.*, 371 US at 491, 83 SCt at 419

27. *Nardone v U.S.*, 308 US 338, 341,60 SCt 266, 268 (1939)

28. *Nix v Williams*, _ US _ , 104 SCt 2501, 2511 (1984)

29. *U.S. v Peltier*, 422 US 531, 95 SCt 2313 (1975)

30. *U.S. v Williams*, 622 F2d 830 (5th Cir. 1980)

31. *U.S. v Leon*, _ US _, 104 SCt 3405, 3423 (1984)

32. *U.S. v Havens,* 446 US 620, 100 SCt 1912 (1980)

33. *People v Defore,* 242 N.Y. 13, 21, 150 NE 585, 587 (1926)

34. National Institute of Justice, *The Effects of the Exclusionary Rule: A Study in California 2* (1982)

35. *Rios v U.S. & Elkins v U.S., Dissenting Opinions,* 364 US 233, 80 SCt 1453, 1454 (1960)

36. *Boyd v U.S.,* 116 US 616, 630, 6 SCt 524, 532 (1886)

37. *Olmstead v U.S.,* 277 US 438, 485, 48 SCt 564, 575 (1928)

38. *Mapp v Ohio,* 367 US at 659, 81 SCt at 1694

Part II

THE FOURTH

Chapter 6

THE
FOURTH
AMENDMENT

"The right of the people to be secure in their persons, houses, papers and effects, against unreasonable searches and seizures, shall not be violated, and no Warrants shall issue, but upon probable cause, supported by Oath or affirmation, and particularly describing the place to be searched, and the persons or things to be seized."

The United States Constitution, Amendment IV (1787)

It's a principle as old as mankind that a small, well-armed gang can freely push its way around among less-organized masses of people by using the threat of violence. The writers of the Constitution were fed up with the English version of police harassment, so they wrote the Fourth Amendment to make sure that the same kind of cancer wouldn't creep into their own newly-formed government. Its guarantees "are not mere second-class rights but belong in the catalog of indispensible freedoms. Among deprivations of rights, none is so effective in cowing a population, crushing the spirit of the individual and putting terror in every heart. Uncontrolled search and seizure is one of the first and most effective weapons in the arsenal of every arbitrary government."[1] It's an issue that was "so deeply felt by the Colonies as to be one of the potent causes of the Revolution."[2]

The gist of the Fourth is that people have a right to expect privacy from governmental intrusion. It's implicit in the amendment that this privacy is not absolute; it's subject to be overcome whenever the common good demands it. Yet, who's entitled to make that decision? A warrant is a judge's authorization for the police to interrupt a citizen's privacy and take something (or someone), so the mention of warrants suggests that such a decision should be made by a judge. The wording doesn't say that the police *always* have to have a warrant, however. This point has left the door open to a wide variety of circumstances under which a cop may use his own discretion to violate a citizen's privacy. Indeed, there seems to be a movement within the Supreme Court to drop the requirement for a warrant altogether.[3] It's also a significant point that enforcement of the Fourth Amendment through the exclusionary rule doesn't apply if the intrusion is made by a private citizen[4] or foreign police.[5] Such people are not entitled under our law to violate a person's privacy, but what they expose to the police by doing so can be used as evidence against him just as surely as if they had wielded a warrant. The guarantees of the Fourth Amendment in this country apply not only to American citizens, but to aliens,[6] corporations,[7] and non-incorporated groups[8] as well.

CONSENT

"Consent searches are permitted... because we permit our citizens to choose whether or not they wish to exercise their constitutional rights."
Justice William J. Brennan dissenting in *Schneckloth v Bustamonte*, 412 US 218, 283, 93 SCt 2041, 2076 (1973)

The easiest way for the police to break through a citizen's expectation of privacy is to get his consent. Once he invites them into his home, his car, or his pockets, he has given them carte blanche to use whatever they may find against him. Once he willingly goes along with them, he has voluntarily placed himself under arrest and relieved them of the burden of justifying it. He may not even realize the illegality of items in his possession, or things that he does in the privacy of his home. He might well overlook the insignificant traces left from previous activities that he does know are illegal. In either case, however, the police won't be inhibited from seizing upon such evidence to convict him of a crime;[9] a pistol that he innocently keeps in his glove compartment, or some marijuana seeds in the pile of the carpet, might thus become the unexpected means for a rather harsh lesson in how the System works.

Society implants into its young minds the notion that they have nothing to fear from the exposure of their affairs to inquiring officials; "If you have nothing to hide, you have nothing to fear." Children grow up naively believing that the details of their lives are harmless, insignificant trivia that the police would never be interested in. Why not expose them to inspection, as long as there's nothing flagrantly illegal? This philosophy is buttressed by the myth that the government is good, that its agents are our friends, and that they're fair and just. The result of such conditioning is that average Joe Citizen is quick and generous in giving his consent to inquisitive officials. He's even likely to feel guilty at the thought of refusal. He assumes that the police would never actually hold his harmless peccadillos against him. He's willing to believe that they'd probably overlook insignificant little incriminating details. He even believes that they might be dissuaded from a prosecution by appealing to reason. Furthest from his mind is the thought that the police would ever stoop to planting or faking evidence in order to set him up. After all, "they're just good ol' boys like ourselves... and besides, they're representatives of our government!"

In order for consent to be valid it must be given willingly; mere submission to police authority is not the same as consent.[10] There are numerous pressures that the police might bring to bear upon a person in order to coerce him into playing ball with them, and the circumstances surrounding his grant of consent will show whether or not it was truly voluntary. Some of the factors that have been important in past cases include the subject's youth,[11] low intelligence,[12] lack of education,[13] lack of advice of his constitutional rights,[14] exploitation of his religious beliefs,[15] the use of "third degree" interrogation tactics,[16] a lengthy period of detention,[17] repeated and prolonged questioning,[18] the use of physical punishment, such as depriving him of food or sleep,[19] and overbearing police demands.[20] The subject's own behavior can provide an indication of the voluntariness of his consent; what he says[21] or doesn't say,[22] his attitude, and his actions[23] are all inferential to what his true state of mind is. When somebody consents to a police intrusion, and later complains to the court that his consent was involuntary, it's the court's job to evaluate all these circumstances and decide the issue on an individual basis.[24] Voluntariness of consent doesn't require a showing of the person's positive desire for the intrusion;[25] it's enough that he simply agrees to it. Nor is it relevant that he may have consented to something that's against his own interests.[26] The Supreme Court looks upon that situtation as a sort of constitutional right to commit suicide: "Unless an individual is incompetent, we have in the past rejected any paternalistic rule protecting a defendent from his intelligent and voluntary decisions about his own criminal case."[27] The Court hasn't committed itself to insuring that those decisions are always intelligent, either. A person might conceivably be unaware of his right to refuse, yet still be considered to have made a "voluntary" consent.[28] Even if a person does realize that he has a right to withhold consent, there's a tremendous potential for him to make a foolish decision (as most grants of consent are). People have no way of knowing from where and in what form harm to them might arise as a result of giving their consent to a search. The courts realize this, and seem to take a perverse satisfaction in seeing people fall prey to their own poor judgement.[25] A good many convictions are scored by duping gullible folks into giving their consent to searches that the police otherwise couldn't have made.[26/29/30/31]

It would come as a great surprise to many people to learn that their consent might be acquired automatically in some circumstances, and be bypassed altogether in others. The first condition occurs when a person agrees to work under a government contract; he has automatically given his implied consent to warrantless audit and seizure under statutory authority.[32] The second condition can happen when a person shares his property and privacy rights with someone else. Whether it's his duffel bag,[33] his bedroom,[34] or a conversation[35] that he shares, he's giving up a measure of his expectation of privacy. The other person, having an equal right to consent to police intrusion, can thus open the doors to them for their searches, electronic bugging, or whatever.

PROBABLE CAUSE

"Why, sho' I got probable cause to lock you up, Boy! Y'alls PROBABLE guilty CAUSE I sez you is."

Sheriff Buford T. Justis, Bullhead County, Texazona

If they can't get his consent, the police may legitimately override a person's expectation of privacy by establishing "probable cause" to believe that he's in some stage of committing a crime. This "probable cause" is simply a fact or two that the cop knows — something he's seen, or something he's heard from a reliable source — combined with what he knows from his training and experience.[36]/[37] If his facts would be sufficient in themselves to warrant a reasonable person to believe that a crime has been committed, then he has probable cause.[38] He doesn't have to be certain about the crime;[36] his reasonable inference, based on a substantial fact, is sufficient. "Fact" is the keyword here. Just believing that a person is guilty of a crime, without any facts to back it up, is not probable cause — it's prejudice.[39] The Anglo patrolman who defines "grand theft auto" as "six Chicanos in a new Cadillac" has failed to meet the criterion of probable cause.

WARRANTS

"The warrant requirement... is not an inconvenience to be somehow 'weighed' against the claims of police efficiency. It is, or should be, an important working part of our machinery of government, operating as a matter of course to check the 'well-intentioned but mistakenly overzealous, executive officers' who are a part of any system of law enforcement."

Justice Potter Stewart, *Coolidge V New Hampshire,* 403 us 450, 481, 91 SCt 2022, 2046 (1971)

Police officers who have plans to arrest somebody or search his property are supposed to get the go-ahead in the form of a warrant from a magistrate. They have to convince him that probable cause exists, and they do this by stating their facts on paper. This is called a "complaint" in the case of an arrest warrant and an "affidavit" in the case of a search warrant, and the officer must swear an oath to its truthfulness. Basically, the same standard for probable cause is used with either type of warrant.[40] If the judge is convinced that there's justification to overcome the citizen's expectation of privacy, he issues the warrant. The facts that he relies on might consist of third-party "hearsay" evidence, such as the testimony of a victim or witness to a crime,[41] the word of a fellow policeman,[42] or a tip from an informant with inside information.[43] This kind of evidence must have a substantial basis to be acceptable, and the High Court says that when details supplied by a snitch can be corroborated by the police through their own independent observation, the evidence is substantial.[44] Just making the claim that their snitch is "reliable" isn't good enough[45] unless the police can support that claim by showing that he has been unusually dependable on previous occasions.[46] In any case, the judge reserves the right to use his own common-sense discretion in determining under the "totality of circumstances" whether the facts are sufficient.[47] The probable cause that supports a warrant must still exist at the time the police serve it.[48] If they wait too long before making their search or arrest, there might not be any reason to believe that the same facts that justified the warrant are still true; in that case, the warrant's no good.

Great respect and adherence has been accorded the warrant concept all the way down through American history.[49] "Absent some grave emergency, the Fourth Amendment has interposed a magistrate between the citizen and police. This was done not to shield criminals nor to make the home a safe haven for illegal activities. It was done so that an objective mind might weigh the need to invade that privacy in order to enforce the law. The right of privacy was deemed too precious to entrust to the discretion of those whose job is the detection of crime... And so the Constitution requires a magistrate to pass on the desires of the police before they violate the privacy of the home."[50] Evaluation of the facts by a neutral and detached magistrate provides an objective element of protection to our privacy that the cops wouldn't bother with.[51] It's no rubber stamp for the police, like the grand jury;[52] papers have to be filled out, and they become formal records that an arrestee can challenge in court. As we pointed out in the last chapter, however, the success of such a challenge will depend upon whether or not the defendant can show that the cops acted *deliberately* or *with reckless disregard of the truth* in preparing their warrant.[53]

The factual basis for the complaint or affidavit can be attacked,[54] although the courts tend to allow a generous leeway for technical imperfections, typographical errors, and such.[55]/[56]/[57] Bare-faced lies, of course, are not tolerated.[58] Attacking the complaint might be effective in making the police release a man from jail (because the arrest warrant is therefore void), and at the same time ineffective as grounds for the suppression of incriminating evidence acquired during his arrest.[59] The warrant itself can be challenged on several fronts. The person who issued the warrant might not have been entitled to do so, as in the case of a Justice of the Peace who happened to also be the prosecutor;[60] the guarantee of an impartial evaluation of probable cause would seem to be threatened under such an arrangement. The exact place or extent of the search might not be adequately described on the warrant, as in the case of a barn that is undistinguished from any other barn in the county,[61] or a whole building where the apartment to be searched isn't specified.[62] The person or things that were supposed to be seized might not be adequately described on the warrant;[63]/[64] the wording might be imprecise, have descriptive errors, or neglect to mention items altogether. If its terms are too inclusive it's said to be "overbroad," and that smacks of the infamous "general warrant" that the Redcoats used to employ when they wanted to rummage through the early colonists' homes. A warrant is supposed to be specific enough in describing, or "particularizing," the things to be seized that it doesn't leave any discretion to the cops at all.[65] Flaws such as these can be a defendant's ticket out of jail, and they only become available if the warrant process is forced into operation. Depending upon which aspects of a warrant are faulty, a person might get part[66] or all[40] of it quashed in court, and everything that came into police custody because of it might have to be thrown out as "fruits of the poisonous tree" — a real windfall for somebody who was caught with the goods.

REFERENCES

1. *Brinegar v U.S.*, 338 US 160, 180, 69 SCt 1302, 1313 (1949), J. Jackson dissenting

2. *U.S. v Rabinowitz*, 339 US 56, 69, 70 SCt 430, 436 (1950), J. Frankfurter dissenting

3. *U.S. v Ross*, 456 US 798, 102 SCt 1290 (1982)

4. *U.S. v Jacobsen*, 466 US __, 104 SCt 1652, 1656-1657 (1984)

5. *Govt. of Canal Zone v Sierra*, 594 F2d 60, 72 (5th Cir. 1979)

6. *Abel v U.S.*, 362 US 217, 80 SCt 683 (1960)

7. *G.M. Leasing Corp. v U.S.*, 429 US 338, 353, 97 SCt 619, 629 (1977)

8. *Mancusi v DeForte*, 392 US 364, 369, 88 SCt 2120, 2124 (1968)

9. *U.S. v Dornblut*, 261 F2d 949 (2d Cir. 1958)

10. *Florida v Royer*, 460 US __, 103 SCt 1319, 1324 (1983)

11. *Haley v Ohio*, 332 US 596, 68 SCt 302 (1948)

12. *Fikes v Alabama*, 352 US 191, 77 SCt 231 (1957)

13. *Payne v Arkansas*, 356 US 560, 78 SCt 844 (1958)

14. *Davis v North Carolina*, 384 US 737, 86 SCt 1761 (1966)

15. *Brewer v Williams*, 430 US 387, 97 SCt 1232 (1977)

16. *Miranda v Arizona*, 384 US 436, 86 SCt 1602 (1966)

17. *Chambers v Florida*, 309 US 227, 60 SCt 472 (1940)

18. *Ashcraft v Tennessee*, 322 US 143, 64 SCt 921 (1944)

19. *Reck v Pate*, 367 US 433, 81 SCt 1541 (1961)

20. *U.S. v Berryman*, 706 F2d 1241, 1243 (1st Cir. 1983)

21. *U.S. v Canales*, 572 F2d 1182, 1184 (6th Cir. 1978)

22. *Florida v Royer*, 103 SCt at 1322

23. *Schneckloth v Bustamonte,* 412 US 218, 220, 93 SCt 2041, 2044 (1973)

24. *Id.,* 412 US at 248-249, 93 SCt at 2059

25. *U.S. v Vickers,* 387 F2d 703, 707 (4th Cir. 1967)

26. *U.S. v Mendenhall,* 446 US 544, 559, 100 SCt 1870, 1880 (1980)

27. *Michigan v Mosley,* 423 US 106, 108-109, 96 SCt 321, 329 (1975), J. White concurring

28. *Schneckloth v Bustamonte,* 412 US at 234, 93 SCt at 2051

29. *U.S. v Gooding,* 695 F2d 78 (4th Cir. 1982)

30. *U.S. v Forero-Rincon,* 626 F2d 218 (2d Cir. 1980)

31. *U.S. v Henry,* 615 F2d 1223 (9th Cir. 1980)

32. *Zap v U.S.,* 32B US 624, 66 SCt 1277 (1946)

33. *Frazier v Cupp,* 394 US 731, 740, 89 SCt 1420, 1425 (1969)

34. *U.S. v Matlock,* 415 US 164, 169-170, 94 SCt 988, 992-993 (1974)

35. *U.S. v White,* 401 US 745, 751-752, 91 SCt 1122, 1125-1126 (1971)

36. *Texas v Brown,* 460 US __, 103 SCt 1535, 1543(1983)

37. *Cortez v U.S.,* 449 US 411, 418, 101 SCt 690, 695 (1981)

38. *Carroll v U.S.,* 267 US 132, 162, 45 SCt 280, 288 (1925)

39. *Aquilar v Texas,* 378 US 108, 112-113, 84 SCt 1509, 1512-1513 (1964)

40. *Giordenello v U.S.,* 357 US 480, 485-486, 78 SCt 1245, 1250 (1958)

41. *U.S. v Swihart,* 554 F2d 264, 269 (6th Cir. 1977)

42. *U.S. v Ventresca,* 380 US 102, 111, 85 SCt 741, 747 (1965)

43. *Illinois v Gates,* 462 US __, 103 SCt 2317, 2335-2336 (1983)

44. *Id.,* 103 SCt at 2334

45. *Spinelli v U.S.,* 393 US 410, 416, 89 SCt 584, 589 (1969)

46. *Illinois v Gates,* 103 SCt at 2329

47. *Id.*, 103 SCt at 2332

48. *Sgro v U.S.*, 287 US 206, 210, 53 SCt 138, 140 (1932)

49. Wright, Federal Practice and Procedure, Criminal 2d, Section 666

50. *McDonald v U.S.*, 335 US 451, 455-456, 69 SCt 191, 193 (1948)

51. *Johnson v U.S.*, 333 US 10, 13-14, 68 SCt 367, 369 (1948)

52. *U.S. v Dionisio,* 410 US 1, 24, 93 SCt 764, 777 (1973), J. Douglas dissenting

53. *U.S. v Leon,* __US__, 104 SCt 3405, 3423 (1984)

54. *Franks v Delaware,* 438 US 154, 155-156, 98 SCt 2674, 2676 (1978)

55. *U.S. v Ventresca,* 380 US at 108, 85 SCt at 746

56. *Jaben v U.S.*, 381 US 214, 224-225, 85 SCt 1365, 1371 (1965)

57. *Massachusetts v Sheppard,* __US__, 104 SCt 3424 (1984)

58. *People v Garcia,* Ill. App. Ct., 1st Dist., 9/8/82

59. *U.S. v Fernandez-Guzman,* 577 F2d 1093, 1097 (7th Cir. 1978)

60. *Coolidge v New Hampshire,* 403 US 443, 450, 91 SCt 2022, 2029 (1971)

61. *McGinnis v U.S.*, 227 F2d 598, 601-602 (Ist Cir. 1955)

62. *U.S. v Parmenter,* 531 FSupp 975, 976-977 (D. Mass. 1982)

63. *West v Cabell,* 153 US 78, 14 SCt 752 (1894)

64. *Coolidge v New Hampshire,* 403 US at 471, 91 SCt at 2040-2041

65. *Marron v U.S.*, 275 US 192, 196, 48 SCt 74, 76 (1927)

66. *U.S. v Riggs,* 690 F2d 298, 300-301 (Ist Cir. 1982)

Chapter 7

EXCEPTIONS TO THE WARRANT REQUIREMENT

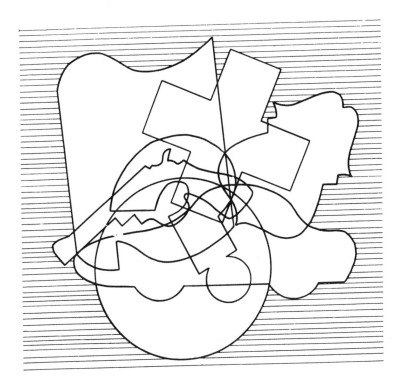

EXIGENCIES WITH CAUSE TO SUSPECT CRIME

"The creation or recognition of an exception to the 'warrant-based-on-probable-cause' requirement is generally premised on a tripartite weighing of public necessity, efficacy of the search and degree of the intrusion."

Judge Carl Bue, *Collier v Miller*, 414 FSupp 1357 (S. D. Texas 1976)

Many situations furnish the police with probable cause to make a search or arrest, but not enough time to get a warrant beforehand. Since most outlaws are unwilling to wait around for them to go after their warrant, the cops have acquired the authority to act upon their own judgment of probable cause in cases of emergency. The need to catch a fleeing suspect is one such emergency; it's well-recognized that the police do not need a warrant to search when they're in hot pursuit of a criminal suspect.[1] Another emergency is the need to prevent evidence from disappearing. With their inherent capability to travel out of a court's jurisdiction and thus escape a warrant, vehicles pose a risk in this regard. A combination of probable cause and the likelihood of their being moved is therefore recognized as justification for the police to search cars, boats, and aircraft without a warrant.[2]/[3] Situations where evidence might be destroyed, either by nature[4] or by a quick-thinking outlaw,[5] are also contemplated by this exception.

Such exigencies justify warrantless search and seizure when supported by probable cause, but what do the cops do when they think "something's going down" but have no probable cause to act upon? The element of exigency is still there, they suspect that somebody's about to get away with something, but they don't have the legal justification to breach his Fourth Amendment protections. Under the ground rules discussed thus far, they'd be limited to the options of (1) a search and seizure that's unsupported by probable cause (which would be thrown out of court), (2) asking the suspect for his consent to be searched (which might be refused), and (3) just letting the matter pass (which they aren't about to do). The Supreme Court created an answer to this dilemma in 1968 by defining another level of justification to intrude, together with its own limited level of intrusion.[6]

This new justification might be thought of as the bastard stepchild of probable cause; instead of being "probable" it's merely "reasonable," and instead of being "cause to believe" it's merely "reason to suspect." It's just a less substantial form of probable cause which gives a cop the right to pry. Like probable cause, it must be based on facts that can be put into words — it must be articulable. Unlike probable cause, the facts needn't be sufficient to warrant a reasonable person to believe that a crime has been committed. They can be observations of circumstances that would only arouse the suspicion of one who is specially trained in crime detection. This less-substantial level of justification to intrude will be henceforth referred to as "reasonable articulable suspicion."

The level of intrusion that goes along with it is a similarly limited form of search and seizure; after all, if the standard of excuse to intrude is to be relaxed, the level of intrusion ought to be lessened proportionately. Instead of an arrest (based on probable cause) the officer conducts a brief "stop" or "detention" (based on reasonable articulable suspicion). Instead of a "full field search" of the person, as would be done upon arrest, he merely conducts a "frisk" or patting down of the clothing to feel for weapons. The subject is not supposed to be moved from the place of the encounter, is not under any obligation to answer the questions, and must be free to leave after a brief time if there's no probable cause to arrest him. It's an "intermediate intrusion." Originally, the whole purpose of this limited form of intrusion was to give the policeman a mechanism for protecting himself from someone carrying a concealed weapon. He could stop the person and inquire about the suspicious circumstances, and if he should become fearful he could frisk the person and remove any weapons as a self-protective measure — the "stop and frisk" policy. Law enforcement, however, has predictably exploited this type of intrusion as a means of threshing out other evidence of crime, such as contraband,[8] illegal aliens,[9] and administrative motor vehicle violations.[10] Police who proceed to search somebody under the auspices of a weapons frisk are not supposed to use the situation as a pretext to look for other things, such as dope;[11] if they should happen to accidentally turn up something interesting, however... well, those are the breaks.[7] The usefulness to the police of a limited intrusion is that it gives them an opportunity to start investigating something at the earliest indication of an irregularity. Once a cop gets his foot in the door, the facts that he digs up might become grounds to turn a brief detention based on reasonable articulable suspicion into an arrest based upon probable cause.

EXIGENCIES TO PROTECT LIFE AND RENDER AID

Exclusive of any considerations regarding whether or not a crime may have been committed, the police have a duty to protect the public safety and come to the aid of anyone who might be in physical danger. Their presence at the scene of a life-and-death crisis, such as a fire,[12] a shooting,[13] a potential explosion,[14] or a medical emergency,[15] may lead them to cross somebody's Fourth Amendment privacy barrier. Such an exigency is a well-recognized exception to the warrant requirement.

SEARCH INCIDENT
TO LAWFUL ARREST

In case all this talk about reasonable suspicion and probable cause has created the impression that cops are reasonable people, this is a good time to correct that misconception. These are legal concepts which are used by the courts to decide the propriety of a search and seizure long after it's been done. The only interest the police have in such concepts is their use as guidelines for making the decision to arrest or not to arrest; to search immediately or wait for a warrant. They can memorize rigid policy, where there's a "bright line" to show them the limits of permissibility, but they're not thinkers. Their adequacy is in the realm of following orders, not in that of intelligent reasoning. One such bright line is the fact of a suspect's arrest. Police procedure dictates that certain things will happen upon a person's arrest, regardless of the circumstances; he'll be handcuffed, "read his rights," booked in at the station house, etc. It's irrelevant whether or not he poses a threat sufficient to justify the handcuffs. It doesn't matter if he's an attorney and already knows his rights. The constable's only concern is that a lawful arrest be made and the proper procedure observed. The courts have recognized this talisman-like quality of lawful arrest as being one more exception to the requirement for a search warrant.[16]

There are three basic issues surrounding the "search incident to lawful arrest:" (1) the scope of the search (how far they can go), (2) its extent (how deep they can dig), and (3) the timing (when they can do it). The scope has been defined by the Supreme Court to include the person of the arrestee and the area under his immediate physical control (the "grabbable area").[17] This logically includes any parts of a room or vehicle that a defendant might be physically capable of reaching at the instant of arrest. The rationale is that a person might go for a gun or destroy evidence, and the courts recognize that a lawful arrest is in itself justification to take measures to see that neither of those things will happen. Unfortunately, the question of exactly what "grabbable area" consists of remains open to courtroom interpretation. The Supreme Court attempted to clarify it in the case of a car by saying that the passenger compartment, but not the trunk, is grabbable area;[18] this clears up any doubts about the trunk being off-limits to search incident to arrest, but at the same time it raises the new possibility that the cops may be entitled to search the passenger compartment of a person's nearby car simply because of his arrest, regardless of his separation from it in time or space.[19] Moreover, since this mechanistic approach defines grabbable area on a spatial rather than a functional basis, it allows area searches even when the arrestee is hog-tied and physically incapable of actually doing any grabbing.[19]/[20]

The extent to which such searches may be conducted includes full field search of the individual's person[21] and the opening of any closed containers within the grabbable area (i.e. briefcases, packages, desk drawers, a glove compartment, etc.).[18] The High Court hasn't specifically stated that locked containers may be forced open, but at least two of its Justices understand the holding to mean as much.[19]/[22] The search incident to lawful arrest is completely unlimited as to its objective; any type of evidence that they can turn up is fair game.[13]

The issue regarding the timing of these searches is embodied in the phrase "incident to," which suggests that the search should occur at approximately the same time as the arrest. If there's probable cause to arrest someone, and the police go ahead and do a search incident to lawful arrest just before making the formal arrest, the search is valid.[24] If they don't have cause to arrest, however, any search they do cannot be considered "incident to lawful arrest;" the evidence that turns up can't be used to justify the arrest, and both search and arrest are invalidated.[25] Because the justification for a search incident to lawful arrest ceases after the arrestee is safely in custody, these searches are generally invalid when done at a later time or place,[26]/[27] unless intentionally deferred for some overriding reason.[28] One thing there isn't any disagreement about is that the arrest must be valid — that's why the word "lawful" is always included in the phrase. If the arrest is without sufficient cause,[29] or if the warrant's either invalid[30] or invalidly executed,[31] the arrest and its incident search both fail. Police detention that's less than a formal arrest (such as the protective confinement of drunks in some states) might fail to justify such a search, also.[32]

ADMINISTRATIVE SEARCHES

A further class of exceptions to the warrant requirement is that of administrative searches. Any type of blanket search that's conducted in the interests of an institution or society in general can be thought of in this category. The government has its fingers into everyone's business, but those industries which affect the public safety are especially vulnerable to its regulation. Congress has specifically authorized warrantless searches in some types of business as part of a regulatory scheme — gun dealerships and mining operations are two of them.[33] The average man on the street, however, is more likely to be familiar with the warrantless personal searches that we have to submit to in order to get past various security checkpoints. Some, such as those at the entrances of federal buildings and airport boarding gates, merely require the subjects to pass through a metal detector and show the contents of their briefcases, etc.[34]/[35] The feds have conducted plant quarantine programs whereby travelers' effects were submitted to the same type of search that Customs officials do.[36] People seeking entrance to military restricted areas may have to submit to warrantless vehicle searches,[37] and acceptance of a prison staff position might entail a standing consent to undergo surprise "strip searches."[38] He who receives the hospitality of the local jail is likely to be treated to the works: a complete strip search (which includes a peek into whatever orifices the jailer may fancy) and a routine "inventory search" (which produces a written accounting of every item brought in, from his dentures to the contents of his automobile).[39] The widest range of discretion to search is held by the feds who control the frontier. Their authority to perform warrantless searches is backed up by statute,[40] and extends from 12 miles offshores[41] to 100 miles inside the border, plus "functional border equivalents" such as airports.[42] The intensity of their searches can range from brief questioning to the limits of the imagination.

All these exceptions to the warrant requirement are the offspring of that capricious slut, Lady Luck. There seems to be no end to the number of possible hands that she's capable of dealing. Under practically identical circumstances, two people committing the same crime might fall victim to warrantless search and seizure under totally different justifications, and a third might not be searchable at all. Nobody can foresee every little detail in life; an outlaw can't anticipate every hitch, and the cops can't always pick up on his mistakes. Police know that there's more than one way to skin a cat, however, and they look for every excuse they can find to justify an intrusion. These warrant exceptions often overlap in a given situation, allowing more than one basis of justification to violate a person's Fourth Amendment rights.

Consider a hypothetical situation. A police patrol car receives an all points bulletin to be on the lookout for a distinctive automobile carrying two men who have just committed an armed robbery. Being in the vicinity of the crime, the cops decide to cruise around in search of the car. As they round a corner they see a vehicle of the correct description pull up along the curb, and two men carrying shotguns get out and enter a house. There are no license plates on the car. First of all, the cops have probable cause to conduct an immediate warrantless search of the entire car under the automobile exception,[43] since the car and its occupants answer the description and locality reported in the A.P.B. Additionally, they have probable cause to arrest the driver for operating a vehicle without license plates, and thereby conduct a warrantless search of the passenger compartment incident to lawful arrest.[18] Since they were actively searching for the getaway car, and have probable cause to believe that the men they saw were the robbers, they're justified in entering the house without a search warrant under the hot pursuit exception.[1] Moreover, the circumstance of two armed desperadoes running loose among the taxpayers justifies the warrantless entry as an exigency to protect life and render aid.[13] In the event that they make an arrest and take the suspects and their car into custody, they would be justified in making a complete inventory search of the car and the men's personal effects.[39] At the very least, they have reasonable articulable suspicion enough to warrant inquiry and brief detention of the men while they try to arrive at an explanation.[6]

Exceptions to the warrant requirement provide police with an excuse to invade a person's privacy, and the circumstances of an occasion often allow it for more than one reason. Let the area within the boundaries of the diagram (see page 95) represent all possible incriminating seizures, and let each of the figures represent a portion of them that can be had under a different exception to the warrant requirement. Notice how the exceptions overlap one another, with a very small proportion of the total area being covered by several exceptions simultaneously. The dashed area represents those seizures which cannot be made except by warrant. The figures represent the automobile exception (car), the hot pursuit exception (gun), the exigency to protect life (first aid cross), incidence to lawful arrest (badge), administrative searches (sheet of paper), reasonable articulable suspicion (question mark), and consent (circle).

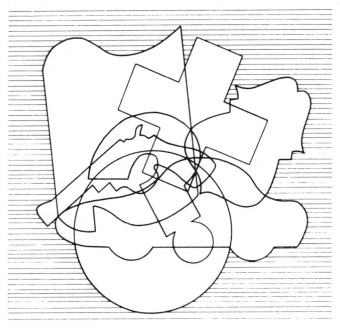

Figure 1

A supplement to these warrant exceptions is the "plain view doctrine:" Any time a cop has a legitimate reason for being where he is, and inadvertently happens to see something that he has cause to believe is evidence of a crime, he may seize it immediately without a warrant.[44]/ [45] Out in public, where there is no privacy, a policeman doesn't need any special justification to seize a suspicious object. Anyone stupid enough to flaunt his business in the Man's face deserves to be busted. Once that cop enters private turf, where an individual has a recognized expectation of privacy, it's a different story.[45] The Fourth Amendment demands reasonableness in any seizure, and unless there's a legitimate reason for a cop to be trespassing, no seizure will be considered reasonable. Seeing something and having probable cause to seize it isn't by itself sufficient excuse for him to make the seizure.[44] He must also have a prior justification for being there — either consent, a warrant, or one of the recognized exceptions to the warrant requirement, such as an emergency,[12] an arrest,[46] or an administrative search.[47] Assuming that the officer is legitimately on the scene, a second condition of the plain view doctrine dictates that he discovered the evidence inadvertently.[48] It would be a simple matter for a cop to arrange an "exigency" to occur so that he can gain access to something he wants to seize — deliberate cheating of the warrant requirement — so the law holds that evidence which isn't discovered inadvertently isn't valid under this doctrine. A third condition for plain view seizure is that it should be immediately apparent that whatever is found is indeed associated with some crime.[44] In the case of a brick of marijuana, there'd be little question that it constitutes evidence of crime. When personal papers, firearms, and other possibly innocent items are concerned, however, the spectre of a pretext looms in the background. It's therefore considered reasonable to require police to demonstrate at least a common-sense degree of probable cause to believe that what they saw and seized in plain view was in fact evidence of a crime.[49] Although there are limits on the scope of these warrantless searches, it's been allowed that when an officer sees evidence in plain view beyond the area he's authorized to be in, he may still validly seize it as long as his search has been properly limited. The idea is to keep the police from turning a valid warrantless search into a general exploratory rummaging from one item to another until something incriminating turns up.[44]

What constitutes "plain view" is an interesting point to consider. Nobody would argue with the contention that marijuana seeds which are on a table and visible from the doorway are in plain view.[46] In their semi-religious zeal, however, law enforcement officials have taken the concept of plain view to ludicrous heights. Texas cops recently did so quite literally as they employed helicopters and a 600 mm telescope in desperate attempts to get a peek through the 5-inch gap of a greenhouse vent. They felt confident that there had to be a cannabis crop inside, and spent a month of such shenanigans before finally concluding that they could indeed see the weed growing right there "in plain view." That one was laughed out of court,[50] but it's well accepted that anything an inquisitive passerby might conceivably be able to see is in plain view for police seizure purposes.[49] The concept isn't restricted to the sense of sight, either; it can be applied to "plain smell," such as the odor of marijuana,[51] "plain feel," such as a weapon that's palpable through the side of a cloth knapsack,[52] and "plain hearing," such as things told in misplaced confidence to a police informant.[53] In short, anything that a chump is careless enough to put out "on front street" is fair material for the police to use as evidence against him.

REFERENCES

1. *Warden v Hayden,* 387 US 294, 298-299, 87 SCt 1642, 1645-1645 (1967)

2. *Carroll v U.S.,* 267 US 132, 153-154, 45 SCt 280, 285 (1925)

3. *U.S. v Montgomery,* 554 F2d 754, 758 (5th Cir. 1977)

4. *Schmerber v California,* 384 US 759, 770-771, 86 SCt 1826, 1835-1836 (1966)

5. *Ker v California,* 374 US 23, 40-41, 83 SCt 1623, 1633-1634 (1963)

6. *Terry v Ohio,* 392 US 1, 88 SCt 1868 (1968)

7. *People v Lewis,* Colo. Sup. Ct., 2/28/83

8. *U.S. v Mendenhall*, 446 US 544, 559, 100 SCt 1870, 1880 (1980)

9. *U.S. v Brignoni-Ponce*, 422 US 873, 95 SCt 2574 (1975)

10. *Delaware v Prouse*, 440 US 648, 663, 99 SCt 1391, 1401 (1979)

11. *Sibron v New York*, 392 US 40, 64, 88 SCt 1942, 1950 (1978)

12. *Michigan v Tyler*, 436 US 499, 509, 98 SCt 1942, 1950 (1978)

13. *Mincey v Arizona*, 437 US 385, 392, 98 SCt 2408, 2413 (1978)

14. *People v Clements*, Colo. Sup. Ct., 3/28/83

15. *U.S. v Dunavan*, 485 F2d 201, 204-205 (6th Cir. 1973)

16. *Michigan v DeFillippo*, 443 US 31, 35, 99 SCt 2627, 2631 (1979)

17. *Chimel v California*, 395 US 752, 763-764, 89 SCt 2034, 2040-2041 (1969)

18. *New York v Belton*, 453 us 455, 460, 101 sct 2860, 2864 (1981)

19. *Id.*, 453 US at 468-470, 101 SCt at 2868-2869, J. Brennan dissenting

20. *People v Levan*, N.Y. Sup. Ct., App. Div., lst Dept., 2/10/83

21. *U.S. v Robinson*, 414 US 218, 235, 94 SCt 467, 477 (1973)

22. *New York v Belton*, 453 US at 471-472, 101 SCt at 2870, J. White dissenting

23. *U.S. v Robinson*, 414 US at 234, 94 SCt at 476

24. *Rawlings v Kentucky*, 488 US 98, 111, 100 SCt 2556, 2564 (1980)

25. *U.S. v Di Re*, 332 US 58l, 595, 68 SCt 222, 229 (1948)

26. *Preston v U.S.*, 376 US 364, 367-368, 84 SCt 881, 883 (1964)

27. *Michigan v Tyler*, 436 US at 511, 98 SCt at 1951

28. *U.S. v Edwards*, 415 US 800, 803-805, 94 SCt 1234, 1237-1238 (1974)

29. *Jones v U.S.*, 357 US 493, 78 SCt 1253 (1958)

30. *Giordenello v U.S.*, 357 US 480, 485-486, 78 SCt 1245, 1250 (1958)

31. *U.S. v Macri*, 185 FSupp 144, 150 (D. Conn. 1960)

32. *U.S. v Gallop*, 606 F2d 836 (9th Cir. 1979)

33. *Donovan v Dewey*, 452 US 594, 600-606, 101 SCt 2534, 2538-2539, 2542 (1981)

34. *U.S. v Henry*, 615 F2d 1223 (9th Cir. 1980)

35. *Downing v Kunzig*, 454 F2d 1230, 1233 (6th Cir. 1972)

36. *U.S. v Schafer*, 461 F2d 856 (9th Cir. 1972)

37. *U.S. v Miles*, 480 F2d 1217 (9th Cir. 1973)

38. *Gettleman v Werner*, 377 FSupp 445, 452 (W.D. Pa. 1974)

39. *South Dakota v Opperman*, 428 US 364, 375-376, 96 SCt 3092, 3100 (1976)

40. Title 8 U.S.C. Section 1357; Title 19 U.S.C. Sections 482, 1581, 1582, 1701

41. *U.S. v Villamonte-Marquez*, 462 US _, 103 SCt 2573, 2578 (1983)

42. *U.S. v Brignoni-Ponce*, 422 US at 882-884, 95 SCt at 2581-2582

43. *U.S. v Ross*, 456 US 798, 102 SCt 1290 (1982)

44. *Coolidge v New Hampshire*, 403 US 443, 466-468, 91 SCt 2022, 2038-2039 (1971)

45. *Texas v Brown*, 460 US _, 103 SCt 1535, 1540-1541 (1983)

46. *Washington v Chrisman*, 455 US 1, 9, 102 SCt 812, 818 (1982)

47. *Harris v U.S.*, 390 US 234, 88 SCt 992 (1968)

48. *Coolidge v New Hampshire*, 403 US at 469-470, 91 SCt at 2040

49. *Texas v Brown*, 460 US __, 103 SCt at 1542

50. *Wheeler v State*, Texas Court of Criminal Appeals, 9/29/83

51. *U.S. v Norman*, 701 F2d 295, 297 (4th Cir. 1983)

52. *State v Ortiz*, Hawaii Intermediate Ct. App., 4/18/83

53. *Hoffa v U.S.*, 385 US 293, 302-303, 87 SCt 408, 413-414 (1966)

Chapter 8

SEARCH AND SEIZURE OF THE PERSON

"The overriding function of the Fourth Amendment is to protect personal privacy and dignity against unwarranted intrusion by the State."

Justice William J. Brennan, *Schmerber v California*, 384 US 757, 767, 86 SCt 1826, 1834 (1966)

Now that we have a grasp on the general meaning of the Fourth Amendment, we can discuss its specific impact on the individual. Certainly the most vital of our protected interests is that of the person; the ownership of home and property can be a fleeting thing, but the integrity of our bodies remains always with us. It's the last thing we have to lose when we've lost everything else, and it's inseparably tied to our deepest feelings of self-worth and will.

The most meaningful way of looking at search and seizure of the person is to consider it in terms of levels of intrusiveness. The emphasis of this book is on showing precisely what the police in America are authorized to do and what their legal limits are. For this reason, the present chapter will progress from the discussion of their most minimal impositions through their more oppressive ones. A "minimal" intrusion is not necessarily an inconsequential one; any encounter that a person has with the police is potentially harmful. A piece of evidence is just as damning, whether it's picked up during a minor intrusion or a major one.

It should be remembered that, while each level of police intrusion has its limits, the facts and circumstances that develop can push it beyond them into the next higher level. A little belligerence here, and a bit of incriminating evidence there, and what began as a casual chat can wind up with somebody in handcuffs.

WITH LESS THAN REASONABLE ARTICULABLE SUSPICION

Though it may disagree with some folks' preference regarding formal social conduct, there exists a "common law right of inquiry" which permits one to approach a total stranger and ask a question. This right applies no less to a policeman than to the next person, and likewise invests him with no more authority than anyone else.[1] It simply means that there's nothing wrong with one human being speaking to another. As a natural courtesy during such an encounter, it wouldn't be unusual for the inquirer to introduce himself; depending upon the circumstances, he might even identify himself as to his background or profession. It happens all the time when a person offering his help to a stranger qualifies himself with a disclosure that he's bilingual, a mechanic, a paramedic, or whatever the situation calls for.

It's no different when a policeman approaches a citizen out of idle curiosity. He's entitled to identify himself as an officer,[2] display his credentials,[3] or show off his Dick Tracy two-way wrist radio, if that's what turns him on; but none of this constitutes an imposition of authority. Cops are pathetically addicted to the outward symbols of their job, such as their credentials, uniforms, equipment, etc. They love to show them off for anybody who will look. They're fiercely proud of their status as law enforcement officers, since more often than not it constitutes the nearest facsimile to a genuine accomplishment that they've ever had. This eagerness to impress people with their title or credentials should no more suggest an exercise of authority than a self-introduction by any other citizen. A tramp's begging or a street corner hawker's solicitation demands no response at all; a cop's idle prattle carries the same force of authority, and merits the same level of respect. They may not like being ignored, but unless they can put their suspicion into words and confront you with it they have no authority to waste your time.

Except by consent, the only personal search that the police can generally do without at least reasonable suspicion is a border search. As was pointed out in the last chapter, the feds can do warrantless searches of anyone and anything coming into the country, whether by land, by air, or by sea. A person's decision to enter the United States carries the implicit understanding that he may be subjected to as thorough a personal search as the authorities may wish, and he's committed to it as soon as he attempts entry. A special situation exists in the case of people who are under conviction for a crime; their constitutional rights have been diminished by the court as a part of conviction, and even if they're released on probation they can expect personal searches at the whim of the officials.[4]

Security searches, such as one encounters at airports, federal buildings, etc., often involve no more of an intrusion than passing through a metal detector. They are best regarded as consensual searches, since the person has the option to turn around and leave if he doesn't want to submit to it.

One form of personal intrusion that the courts haven't universally agreed about yet is the dog sniff. Canines which are specially trained to detect drugs can easily point out someone who's "carrying" by sniffing him over. This sort of "search," when applied indiscriminately as a screening tactic, has been upheld by courts in some places[5] and forbidden in others.[6] Those cases where it has been upheld were justified within the narrow context of drug screening in public schools. There have been attempts to sanction it by claiming that it isn't really a search at all, so it doesn't violate the Fourth Amendment search and seizure protections.[5] It nevertheless remains a significant intrusion, and as one court stated, "Intentional close proximity sniffing of the person is offensive whether the sniffer be canine or human."[6]

A person doesn't become subject to a search just because he happens to be in the right place at the right time, or just because he happens to keep company with people who are under suspicion. The police would love to be able to shake everyone down whenever they raid a place, but unless they have an articulable reason to suspect each person in particular, they don't have authority to search him in any way.[7] This holds true whether the encounter occurs in a private residence,[8] a public establishment,[7] or an automobile.[9] If the cops can't point to a specific reason to fear him, such as belligerent or suspicious behavior, they aren't authorized to frisk for weapons. If they can't specify probable cause for believing that a given person has incriminating evidence on him, they aren't authorized to search him for it. They aren't even authorized to detain him on the scene if he isn't an official occupant of the premises.[8] A casual visitor who's behaving himself, and doesn't present the police with at least reasonable articulable suspicion, is therefore officially immune from any form of search or detention.

WITH REASONABLE ARTICULABLE SUSPICION

Once a policeman has more than just a hunch that something illegal is afoot — when he has some objective reason to suspect a particular person of being dangerous or committing a crime — then he becomes justified to exercise authority. This minimum standard of justification is known as "reasonable articulable suspicion."[10] On the basis of it the police may stop a person, question him, and detain him for a brief period of time while they attempt to determine whether or not he's guilty of something. If the circumstances of the encounter or the demeanor of the suspect suggest the likelihood of danger, they're also justified in frisking him for weapons. This involves a patting down of the outer garments to feel for anything that might be a weapon, then reaching in for the purpose of removing it. It doesn't give them an excuse to rummage through pockets for other things,[11] or to remove something that doesn't feel like a weapon.[8/12] This basic level of intrusion is generally known as a "*Terry* stop," referring to the name of the historic Supreme Court case which established it. It's characterized as being an "intermediate intrusion"[13] because there are limits on the extent to which the cops can go; they're to use the least intrusive means available to dispel their suspicion within a short time period.[14] The presumption is that, on such flimsy grounds as reasonable articulable suspicion, the officer must still consider his suspect to be innocent of any wrongdoing and treat him accordingly.

The brevity of this encounter has been suggested by the American Law Institute (A.L.I.) to be of less than 20 minutes,[15] but there's no firm time limit set by law. It appears that the length of time required for police to run a check for outstanding warrants is accepted as reasonable.[16]

During this limited detention, it's considered improper for the police to move a suspect away from the scene of the encounter so as to isolate him.[17] It's not an arrest, and they're not supposed to make a person feel like he's under arrest. It might be okay to ask him to step inside the building to get out of the weather,[18] but it would be improper for the police to take him to an interrogation room unless he indicated a voluntary willingness to go there.[19] If the suspect happens to be in a vehicle, the police may order him either to stay inside[20] or to get out.[21]

A wide range of circumstances can provide the reasonable articulable suspicion to warrant an intermediate intrusion, but in all cases there should be an element of particularity for the individuals concerned. Stopping people because they happen to be strangers to the area,[22] or by selection at random,[23] fails to meet the particularity requirement. General area-sweep tactics, where everybody encountered within a given area is stopped and searched, are also improper.[24] Though just being in a particular place is of itself insufficient grounds to stop somebody, additional circumstances might throw a different light on it. Thus, when a person who was already suspect from prior investigation shows up at the scene of an anticipated crime, the combination of circumstances does constitute reasonable articulable suspicion, even though he hasn't done anything suspicious or illegal yet.[25]

The officer's fear of danger from a suspect is the original and still predominant justification for a stop-and-frisk. Cops insist on always having the upper hand in any situation, and the courts agree that this is reasonable. Therefore, the slightest hint of danger from any source gives a cop the right to protect himself by frisking his suspect for weapons. An isolated or treacherous place, a late hour of night,[26] an exigent situation that's just developed,[27] or knowledge of a suspect's assaultive reputation[28] might all be reasonable grounds for the intrusion. An anonymous tip claiming that a given person is carrying a weapon is also adequate grounds,[29] although the pretextual possibilities to that sort of excuse should be obvious.

Various law enforcement agencies have attempted to add an element of science to their specialties by creating lists of abstract characteristics that describe the type of offender they're interested in. They cull these descriptions from numerous prior cases and consolidate them into "profiles" which purportedly have statistical authority. The implication is that a person in the general population who matches the characteristics of such a profile should have a statistically greater likelihood of being a criminal than those who do not. While this may have an element of truth, the important point to realize is that profiles contain many descriptions that would be just as likely to characterize an innocent person as a guilty one. Subjecting someone to a *Terry* stop on the sole basis of his conformity to an abstract profile has been held valid in some cases[2] and invalid in others.[30]/[31] Validity seems to be based on both the degree of suspiciousness of the particular profile characteristics and the presence of consent. This subject will become clearer in Chapter 16, where a detailed discussion is devoted to the significance and use of a police profile.

With a warrant the police can detain a person on reasonable articulable suspicion in order to accomplish part of an investigation, such as fingerprinting,[32] photography,[33] voice analysis,[34] or an identification lineup.[35] Detentions of this sort must be conducted in such a way as to minimize the level of intrusion on a person's privacy and freedom: the subject should be given advance notice of the detention, and allowed an opportunity to arrange for a convenient time when he can have his attorney present. Such investigations must be capable of producing reliable evidence, and be free of abuse, coercion, or intimidation to the subject.[32] Even when the focus of the investigation is on one's property rather than his person, his detention might be valid. Such is the case when someone is detained on the scene while his home is being searched pursuant to a warrant.[36] Other types of property, such as luggage, do not carry such a liability; although the police may temporarily hold onto luggage during a *Terry* investigation, they have no authority to detain its owner along with it.[37]/[38] Of course, many people would feel themselves to be effectively detained once their luggage, driver's license, and travel ticket have been held up; and the longer they're withheld, the closer it comes to constituting a personal seizure.[39]/[40]/[41]/[42] Only the ticket and ID are considered by the courts to bear upon a person's freedom to leave, since they would presumably be necessary for his departure. If a person voluntarily submits these items during a *Terry* investigation, it doesn't constitute a personal seizure until such time as they are clearly being withheld as a means of detaining the suspect.[40]

The extent of a search based on reasonable suspicion is limited to the type of weapons frisk described above. Under the circumstances of a *Terry* stop, however, it's common for the cops to finagle enough consent from people to accomplish a much more extensive search; if anything incriminating should then happen to turn up, the level of justification immediately rises to probable cause, and a full search incident to lawful arrest ensues. One type of personal search that falls into the basic *Terry* category is the dog sniff applied to a person.[6] With reasonable articulable suspicion that a person may be carrying drugs, police may subject him to a confirmatory sniff by trained dogs and thereby acquire probable cause for an arrest and a full search.[43]

Part of the *Terry* search is directed toward gaining information, and it's appropriate to point out that, while a person may be under a certain degree of physical constraint, he's under no compulsion to answer questions.[44] It's true that the whole idea behind a *Terry* stop is to give the policeman an opportunity to maintain the status quo while gathering more information;[45] however, there's no law that says a suspect must provide the information. It's been pompously suggested that citizens have a "duty" to cooperate and respond to such questioning,[46] but that can be dismissed as mere propaganda.

One piece of information that the cops are likely to insist on is the subject's identity. Some state and local governments have gone so far as to enact statutes requiring a citizen to identify and explain himself when requested to do so by the police.[47] They've even tried to legislate the compulsory showing of "credible and reliable identification" by pedestrians.[44] Such laws are unconstitutional and tend to be overturned eventually in the Supreme Court,[22]/[44] but in the meantime they provide the cops with an excuse to badger and oppress folks who stray into their jurisdictions. As was pointed out in Chapter 5, incriminating evidence is not suppressible under the exclusionary rule when it's rooted out during a "good faith" adherence to a law that's later proved unconstitutional. In other words, a person cannot rely upon constitutional protections when confronted by a bad law that hasn't yet been overruled. Supplemental to the identification laws are the ones that make it a crime to give the cops false identification;[48] they justify themselves with the claim that it's an "obstruction of justice" to deceive the police.

Special identification laws aside, the police are legitimately entitled to detain a person against his will on the basis of reasonable articulable suspicion while they try to gather more information. However, the investigation must "be temporary and last no longer than is necessary to effectuate the purpose of the stop."[14] If the subject refuses to help them, his brief detention is the only threat they can pose against him.[43] After a while he must be allowed to leave, whether they're satisfied or not."

The forcefulness of such a detention depends upon the circumstances of the moment. It's usually imposed by virtue of a simple request from a policeman, and no physical constraint is involved as long as the suspect complies with the request. Whether the citizen is walking,[10] driving,[23] or navigating,[49] the cops are authorized to stop him once they have reasonable articulable suspicion. They're not supposed to use physical force, the displaying of weapons, a show of numbers, a threatening tone of voice, or any other coercive method unless it becomes absolutely necessary.[3] Even minor intrusions must be minimized, lest several of them should result in a cumulative effect that raises the level of seizure impermissibly high.[14] Nevertheless, if a suspect refuses to stop,[50] or if the cops get scared,[51] they can escalate the degree of force as far as necessary, justified by the fear for personal or public safety. They can apply handcuffs,[27] draw down with their guns,[52] or do anything else that's necessary to maintain the status quo.

WITH PROBABLE CAUSE

The third and highest tier of police intrusiveness occurs at the point where there's probable cause to believe that a crime has been committed. This is the classical level of justification that the police need before they can really dig in and go to work. Up to this point they're pushing hard just to squeeze themselves into a person's business, and relying heavily upon both consent and their ability to coax something incriminating out into the open. Once they have probable cause, however, the question of personal search and seizure becomes one of "when" more than of "if," and it extends to whatever lengths are justified by the probable cause.

A person's arrest confers the probable cause necessary to justify a full field search — a general rummaging through everything a person has on him, including the contents of closed containers.[53] Such a search is justified without an arrest if there's probable cause to search for something in particular and the circumstances constitute an exigency.[54] The use of a warrant is a formal declaration that there exists probable cause to search. It's a matter of standard procedure that "the police must, whenever practicable, obtain advance judicial approval of searches and seizures through the warrant procedure."[55] Inserting a magistrate into the decision-making process places a greater level of certainty on the probable-cause justification for a search, and gives authorization for some types of personal intrusion that are too aggressive to be left to the discretion of a mere cop.

Arrest is the basic personal seizure that occurs upon a showing of probable cause. It marks the beginning of an individual's guided tour through the System — "guided," because from this point on he's in the custody of the government. The message is driven home when they clap the cuffs on, a standard bit of police procedure for any arrest. If arrest is made at a time when no probable cause exists, it's invalid; nothing they can do thereafter

— neither the finding of incriminating evidence, nor the giving of *Miranda* warnings, nor even the issuance of a warrant — will cure the unlawful arrest.[56]/[57]/[58] Also, arrest for a misdemeanor is supposed to be done under a warrant, unless the crime was actually committed in the cop's presence;[59] in some states, this technicality might be used to challenge an improper arrest.

As we've said earlier, probable cause is based on fact which is sufficient to warrant a reasonable person to believe that somebody has committed a crime.[54] It's pretty cut-and-dry when the facts point objectively and conclusively to an inference of guilt. Difficulty arises, however, when it becomes likely that either the facts or the inferences are wrong.

Probable cause based upon an informant's tip, for example, is notoriously risky; the type of mentality that would snitch to the cops is no stranger to lies made in the self interest. Nevertheless, an inside tip will be sufficient when it comes from a rat who's known for his reliable information.[60]/[61]

Associations may constitute probable cause if they appear to be substantial and relevant enough. Thus, if the police have probable cause to arrest one person, and there appears to be a working relationship between him and a second party, the probable cause applies to the second person as well.[60] Likewise, the probable cause against a suspect might be imputed to all the members of his family who share his company.[62] Association with a suspect parcel is equally as incriminating as that with a suspect person; by taking control of something which is under surveillance, a person brings probable cause upon himself.[60]/[63]

A further source of probable cause is the suspect's own behavior. If the cops want to make an arrest but aren't justified in doing so, they can acquire the justification by provoking the suspect into resisting arrest.[64] Citizens have no right to resist an illegal arrest, whether actively (with fists, guns, etc.)[64] or passively (as by going limp).[65]

A person who resists arrest will therefore provide the police with the probable cause they need for a valid arrest, even though the initial unlawful one would have been thrown out of court.

There's a variety of Fourth Amendment police intrusions other than full search and arrest. Any procedure to which a person is physically subjected for the purpose of gathering more information about him can be considered a search; any tangible evidence the police get from it constitutes a seizure. Viewed in this fashion, identification procedures such as visual lineups, photography, voice analysis, and fingerprinting are "searches" which result in the "seizure" of a person's image, voice recording, fingerprints, etc. These are such minimal intrusions that the police can get warrants for them on just reasonable suspicion.

At the national border, a person may be subjected to a strip search if the Customs agents have reasonable articulable suspicion that he's carrying contraband.[66] These same grounds can also serve as justification to subject him to an abdominal x-ray,[67] or alternatively, to hold him prisoner for as long as it takes to evacuate his bowels of any contraband he may have swallowed.[68] The Ninth Circuit Court of Appeals (which controls the states of Alaska, Arizona, California, Hawaii, Idaho, Montana, Nevada, Oregon and Washington) says that it takes more than just "reasonable suspicion" to justify an X-ray; it takes a "clear indication," a "plain suggestion," or "substantial suspicion" that the subject has contraband in his belly.[69]/[70] This "clear indication" level, which lies somewhere between reasonable suspicion and probable cause, is satisfied by a solid tip from a snitch, but not by mere suspicious observations.[69] The same "clear indication" is also necessary before Customs agents may conduct body cavity searches[69] or administer emetic in order to cause the suspect to throw up.[71] Any time the cops want to go poking around inside a person's body, or remove something from it, they must either have his consent or satisfy several conditions. The conditions are:

(1) there must be a "clear indication" that incriminating evidence will be found during the proposed intrusion, (2) there must be either a warrant or an emergency so urgent that it would be impractical to get one, and (3) they must use a "reasonable" method of intrusion.[72]

It's interesting to note how the lower courts have followed these Supreme Court guidelines. In reference to the first condition, one federal circuit court held it to be justifiable for the police to run in the wife and four small children of an alleged drug dealer and do rectal and vaginal searches on all of them.[62] Evidently, the Honorable Court saw a "clear indication" that the fellow must have hidden his contraband there (he didn't, of course)...

Following the second condition, one state court held that the police cannot do a vaginal search against the suspect's will unless they can justify it with either a warrant or an emergency that won't wait for a warrant. They don't automatically get to do it just because they have her in jail.[73] This particular state law represents a greater degree of protection to the individual than the Supreme Court has demanded, since body cavity searches of prisoners and pre-trial detainees is generally permissible, even without probable cause to search.[74]

The third condition was found to be satisfied in the use of the so-called "no-choke position" for extracting evidence from an uncooperative suspect's mouth; the cop jams the suspect's head down so that his jaw is forced against his chest, making it difficult to swallow. Then he pries open the guy's mouth to get the evidence out.[75] By contrast, the forcing of emetic solution down a person's throat with a stomach pump has been declared to be an unreasonable method of intrusion. Though it's an effective way to make someone throw up any evidence he may have in his stomach, it was considered by the Supreme Court to be "too close to the rack and the screw."[76]

Modern blood-drawing techniques are innocuous enough that the method is universally regarded as reasonable. While a warrant is generally necessary,[77] blood samples may also be seized incident to lawful arrest.[78] If the subject refuses to permit his blood to be drawn incident to arrest, some states allow the refusal itself to stand as evidence of guilt (e.g. in drunk driving cases).[79]

The severest level of personal intrusion is that of surgery. It occasionally happens that the police will want a piece of evidence that's out of reach to anyone but the surgeon. A federal court recently considered such a case, where the cops wanted a bullet that was lodged in a man's chest. Medically speaking, it was preferable to leave it alone, but the cops wanted it to use as evidence against him in his trial. The court held that a "minor" operation, involving a 1.5 cm incision, going just beneath the skin, and performed under local anesthesia, would be a justifiable intrusion for such a purpose; but a 5 cm incision, going deep into muscle tissue, and performed under general anesthesia (as would have been necessary in this case), would be too severe a measure. The court declared that it was "appalled at the prospect of government authorities rendering a person unconscious, cutting him open, and probing around inside his body for evidence which might, or indeed might not, aid them in convicting him of a crime.[80]

REFERENCES

1. *People v DeBour,* 40 N.Y.2d 210, 352 NE2d 562 (1976)

2. *U.S. v Mendenhall,* 446 US 544, 555, 100 SCt 1870, 1877 (1980)

3. *U.S. v Collis,* 699 F2d 832, 834-835 (6th Cir. 1983)

4. *Owens v Kelley,* 681 F2d 1362, 1367-1368 (11th Cir. 1982)

5. *Doe v Renfrow,* 631 F2d 91 (7th Cir. 1980)

6. *Horton v Goose Creek Independent School District*, 690 F2d 470, 478-479 (5th Cir. 1982)

7. *Ybarra v Illinois*, 444 US 85, 93-94, 100 SCt 338, 343 (1979)

8. *State v Broadnax*, 98 Wash.2d 289, 654 P2d 96, 100-101, 104 (1982)

9. *U.S. v Butts*, 704 F2d 701, 704 (3d Cir. 1983)

10. *Terry v Ohio*, 392 US 1, 88 SCt 1868 (1968)

11. *State v Hobart*, 94 Wash.2d 437, 617 p2d 429, 434 (1980)

12. *Sibron v New York*, 392 us 40, 65, 88 SCt 1889, 1904 (1968)

13. *People v Lewis*, 659 P2d 676, 681 (Colo. 1983)

14. *Florida v Royer*, 460 US __, 103 SCt 1319, 1325 (1983)

15. A.L.I., *A Model Code of Pre-Arraignment Procedure*, Section 110.2 (1), 1975

16. *People v Ellis*, Ill. App. Ct., 4th Dist., 3/24/83

17. *U.S. v Jefferson*, 650 F2d 854, 858 (6th Cir. 1981)

18. *U.S. v Moya*, 704 F2d 337, 342 (7th Cir. 1983)

19. *U.S. v Mendenhall*, 446 US at 557-558, 100 SCt at 1878-1879

20. *People v Harrison*, N.Y. Ct. App., 11/18/82

21. *Pennsylvania v Mimms*, 434 US 106, 111, 98 SCt 330, 333 (1977)

22. *Brown v Texas*, 443 US 47, 51-52, 99 SCt 2637, 2641 (1979)

23. *Delaware v Prouse*, 440 US 648, 659-661, 99 SCt 1391, 1399-1400 (1979)

24. *U.S. v Best*, 563 FSupp 1075, 1080 (D.D.C. 1983)

25. *U.S. v Long*, 705 F2d 1259, 1262 (10th Cir. 1983)

26. *Adams v Williams*, 407 US 143, 147-148, 92 SCt 1921, 1924 (1972)

27. *U.S. v Bautista*, 684 F2d 1286, 1289 (9th Cir. 1982)

28. *State v Miller*, Vt. Sup. Ct., 9/7/82

29. *U.S. v Mason*, D.C. Ct. App., 9/9/82

30. *Reid v Georgia*, 448 US 440, 100 SCt 2752 (1980)

31. *U.S. v Berryman*, 706 F2d 1241, 1244 (lst Cir. 1983)

32. *Davis v Mississippi*, 394 us 721, 89 SCt 1394, 1398 (1969)

33. *Baker v State*, Indiana Sup. Ct., 6/21/83

34. *People v Davis*, 669 P2d 130, 133 (Colo. 1983)

35. *State v Hall*, New Jersey Sup. Ct., 7/14/83

36. *Michigan v Summers*, 452 Us 692, 101 SCt 2587 (1981)

37. *U.S. v Moya*, 704 F2d at 339

38. *U.S. v Walraff*, 705 F2d 980, 990 (8th Cir. 1983)

39. *U.S. v Mendenhall*, 446 US at 570 n. 3, 100 SCt at 1885 no. 3, J. White dissenting

40. *U.S. v Black*, 675 F2d 129, 136 (7th Cir. 1982)

41. *U.S. v Elmore*, 595 F2d 1036, 1041-1042 (5th Cir. 1979)

42. *Florida v Royer*, 460 US at __, 103 SCt at 1326-1327

43. *Id.*, 103 SCt at 1328-1329

44. *Kolender v Lawson*, __ US __, 103 SCt 1855, 1862 (1983), J. Brennan concurring

45. *Adams v Wiliiams*, 407 US at 146, 92 SCt at 1923

46. *Coates v U.S.*, 413 F2d 371, 374 (U.S. App. D.C. 1969)

47. Louisiana H.B. 360, Act 686

48. *People v Kelly*, Calif. Ct. App., 3d Dist., 2/25/83

49. *U.S. v Gollwitzer*, 697 F2d 1357, 1362 (11th Cir. 1983)

50. *U.S. v Thompson*, 558 F2d 522, 524 (9th Cir. 1977)

51. *U.S. v Russel*, 546 F2d 839 (9th Cir. 1976)

52. *U.S. v Merritt*, 695 F2d 1263, 1273-1274 (10th Cir. 1982)

53. *U.S. v Robinson*, 414 US 218, 235-236, 94 SCt 467, 477 (1973)

54. *Carroll v U.S.*, 267 US 132, 153-156, 45 SCt 280, 285-286 (1925)

55. *Terry v Ohio*, 392 US at 20, 88 SCt at 1879

56. *Rios v U.S.*, 364 US 253, 261-262, 80 SCt 1431, 1436 (1960)

57. *Dunaway v New York*, 442 US 200, 217, 99 SCt 2248, 2259 (1979)

58. *U.S. v Hughes*, 201 FSupp 615, 616 (W.D. Pa. 1962)

59. Wright, *Federal Practice and Procedure: Criminal 2d*, Section 77 (1982)

60. *U.S. v Swayne*, 700 F2d 467, 469-471 (8th Cir. 1983)

61. *Illinois V Gates*, 462 US __, 103 SCt 2317, 2329 (1983)

62. *Salinas v Breier*, 695 F2d 1073, 1075-1076 (7th Cir. 1982)

63. *U.S. v Wilkerson*, 478 F2d 813, 815 (8th Cir. 1973)

64. *U.S. v Bailey*, 691 F2d 1009, 1015-1016 (11th Cir. 1982)

65. *U.S. v Danehy*, 680 F2d 1311, 1313-1315 (11th Cir. 1982)

66. *U.S. v Vega-Barvo*, 729 F2d 1341, 1345 (11th Cir. 1984)

67. *Id.* at 1348

68. *U.S. v Mosquera-Ramirez*, 729 F2d 1352, 1355 (11th Cir. 1984)

69. *U.S. v Ouintero-Castro*, 705 F2d 1099, 1100 (9th Cir. 1983)

70. *U.S. v Vega-Barvo*, 729 F2d at 1352, J. Hatchett dissenting

71. *U.S. v Briones*, 423 F2d 742, 744 (5th Cir. 1970)

72. *Schmerber v California*, 384 US 757, 770-771, 86 SCt 1826, 1835-1836 (1966)

73. *State v Clark*, 654 P2d 355, 362 (Hawaii 1982)

74. *Bell v Wolfish*, 441 US 520, 558; 563, J. Powell dissenting; 578, J. Marshall dissenting; 594, J. Stevens dissenting; 99 SCt 1861, 1884, 1886, 1894, 1903 (1979)

75. *People v Lara*, 166 Cal. 475 (1980)

76. *Roschin v California,* 342 US 165, 172, 72 SCt 205, 209-210 (1952)

77. *Gentry v State,* Tex. Ct. Crim. App., 10/27/82

78. *U.S. v Harvey,* 701 F2d 800, 807 (9th Cir. 1983)

79. *South Dakota v Neville,* _ US _, 103 SCt 916, 921 (1983)

80. *Lee v Winston,* 551 FSupp 247, 261 (E.D. Va. 1982)

Chapter 9

PLACES OF PRIVACY

"The poorest man may in his cottage bid defiance to all the force of the Crown. It may be frail, its roof may shake; the wind may blow through it; the storms may enter, the rain may enter, — but the King of England cannot enter; all his forces dare not cross the threshold of the ruined tenement!"

William Pitt, Earl of Chatham, Speech to Parliament on the excise bill for cider (1763)

It's been aptly said that the Fourth Amendment protects people, not places,[1] yet there are certain places that are so intimately associated with a person as to acquire constitutional protections in his behalf. We refer to this protection as a "privacy interest" or an "expectation of privacy." The principal factor which determines whether or not a privacy interest exists is the recognition by society that it's legitimate and permissible.[2] Though society doesn't recognize unlawful conduct to be deserving of a privacy interest, it does allow that there are certain times and places where a person should be free from public scrutiny.

One such privacy interest is the peace and quiet of the home.[3] Physical disruption of this peace and quiet occurs the moment an unauthorized intruder enters a person's house,[4] and reaches its zenith when he ransacks the place and assaults the occupant.[5] It can also occur without an actual entry of the home, as in the case of a police helicopter which noisily hovers 20 ft. above a man's roof looking for evidence of crime.[6] The Fourth Amendment protects this privacy interest by prohibiting these sorts of physically disrupting intrusions.

Another recognized privacy interest is the right to relax without the fear of public scrutiny.[3] It's an important psychological need of many species, including man, to be able to relax away from the stresses of society. People need to have a place where they can retire and do or say as they please; society recognizes the home as being such a place. A person should feel free to do things there that he'd be inhibited from doing in public. Closely related to this is the interest in public esteem — the right of a person to keep to himself what he thinks might bring him public censure.[3] People often have thoughts, beliefs, customs, or habits that they prefer not to advertise due to public prejudices, among other reasons. Of course, society doesn't include illegal activities among the "legitimate" sorts of things that a citizen might be entitled to do in private,[2] but it's pretty difficult for the police to make the distinction without first violating the privacy. The Fourth Amendment protects these relaxation and public esteem interests by prohibiting unauthorized spying on an individual's private life.[7]/[8]

There's no all-or-none limitation on the extent or nature of a person's expectation of privacy. He may retain it with regard to certain people — uninvited guests as opposed to invited ones, for example — or with regard to certain parts of his home, where even invited guests are not welcomed.[9] Just because he invites a large group of people into his home, that doesn't make it a "public place" where the cops are entitled to go.[10] Privacy expectations can be contracted and expanded independently for different aspects of a situation. Thus, when someone uses a public phone booth to make a private call, he resigns himself to the public view while retaining an expectation that his conversation will not be overheard. Similarly, when a person uses a hotel room, he doesn't expect the same level of privacy from the walls of adjoining rooms or the hallway outside his door that he enjoys in his own house; he realizes that he shares these aspects of hotel life with other people.

Nevertheless, he maintains the same privacy interest in the security of the room as for the bedroom of his own house.[9]

A time-honored maxim, sometimes attributed to the Roman statesman Pliny, claims that "home is where the heart is." Although this does reflect the general philosophy of the law, there are criteria which define the home more specifically for the purposes of the Fourth Amendment. It's a person's use and control of a place that makes it his home and gives him a corresponding expectation of privacy in it. If he owns it, so much the better; but a person has the same privacy interest in a rented home as he does in one he owns. Likewise, a short-term rented home, such as a hotel room, is no less a sanctuary than a long-term home.[11] The fact that he lives in it justifies his expectation of privacy, regardless of who pays the bills or whether he may additionally choose to do a little business there.[12] If someone's been granted the use and control of another person's place, and lives there as though he owns it, he bears the same privacy interest in that place as he would in any home.[13]/[14] Points of persuasion that will substantiate such a claim include the possession of a key, storage of personal property on the premises, eating and sleeping there, and full access to the entire home. They're the sorts of privileges that might ordinarily be accorded to "one of the family."

The casual visitor, to whom no such authority has been granted, doesn't enjoy a privacy interest in his host's place. Though he sleeps, eats, and has some belongings there, his status as a transient houseguest might be insufficient to invest him with an expectation of privacy. Where there's no semblance of privacy owing to the rapid turnover of visitors to a house, even a long-term visitor might not have a legitimate expectation of privacy there. Such a situation exists in a "drop house" where illegal aliens are temporarily sheltered.[15]

As in William Pitt's famous words at the beginning of this chapter, it's often implied that there's a magical quality inherent to the threshold of a man's "castle;" inside that boundary lies sanctuary, where the odious forces of despotism cannot go. The United States Supreme Court has, in fact, given support to this idea that the structural boundaries of a building represent lines of Fourth Amendment protection. In its keynote case on the subject, it declared that only a warrant or an exigency will justify the cops to enter a person's house without his permission.[16]

The requirement of a search warrant has been historically linked to criminal investigations, but a person's home is equally entitled to its protection when the authorities seek to enter for other reasons. City inspectors have tried to bully their way into the home without warrants by invoking local housing codes; if the citizen refused to let them in, they'd throw him in jail. The Supreme Court put a stop to this with the ruling that, unless they have a legitimate public health emergency, civil inspectors must have a search warrant to enter the home.[17] Unlike a crime, where probable cause is the basis for issuing the warrant, the public interest in health and safety only requires that there be "reasonable legislative or administrative standards" as the basis for such a warrant.

Such events as a fire[18] or a shootout[19] are understandable exigencies, but the police are also inclined to regard a nice juicy drug bust as an emergency, since the perpetrators are likely to flush the evidence as soon as they smell a cop.[20] The dilemma for the cops, however, is that they have no way of knowing from the outside of a building that such activities might be in progress inside.

A fourth justification for the cops to intrude, one which wasn't mentioned in the keynote *Payton* case, is the "incident to lawful arrest" excuse. The justifications for breaching the privacy of the home will be the subject of the following chapter.

The Fourth Amendment's protection of the house doesn't stop at the threshold; outside, for an indefinite distance surrounding the house, there exists a zone which carries much the same expectation of privacy as the house. The courts have created this concept over the years, and refer to this protected area as the "curtilage" of the dwelling. How far out it extends depends upon the layout of the property. It typically includes the area within a fenced yard,[21] and might include nearby buildings, such as a garage[22] or a barn.[23] Buildings as far as 80 yards away have been considered to lie within the curtilage of a house.[24] Factors which tend to embrace a structure within the curtilage include (1) proximity or annexation to the house, (2) structures suggesting propinquity and absence of barriers (such as a driveway between the house and building), (3) inclusion within the general enclosure surrounding the house, (4) habitual use for family purposes, and (5) indications that the owner sought to protect a privacy interest.[23]/[25] In layouts such as an apartment building, the concept of curtilage loses meaning; the area outside one tenant's home overlaps with that of other tenants, and a number of complications enter the picture. For this reason, some lower courts have disregarded the concept of curtilage, and instead hold that certain areas adjacent to the home are protected simply because a resident seeks to preserve a privacy interest in them, even though they may be accessible to the public. Where tenants keep a corridor private by locking its outer door, for example, they might thereby acquire Fourth Amendment protection for it.[26]

It's worth noting that a house guest, even one who has the full run of the place, might not have a recognized privacy interest in the curtilage.[13]

Beyond the curtilage of a house, a person's property loses most of its Fourth Amendment protection. After all, it must be remembered that the Fourth Amendment protects a person's privacy interests, not his possessory interests.[27] His open fields and the lands distant from his house have virtually no constitutional protection from search and seizure by the police.[26] It's true that a landowner has a certain degree of privacy protection by virtue of his right to keep others off his land,[2]/[29] but unless he can physically be there to turn them away, that right is likely to be meaningless. The cops can ignore his "no trespassing" signs, enter his land without a warrant, and take away evidence that they can use against him in court.[30] They can get away with all this because the exclusionary rule doesn't apply to evidence seized from "open fields," and any legal remedies that the owner may have against them for trespassing are purely illusory.[31] Just try to fight City Hall some time, and see how far you get. Furthermore, even if the cops are turned away on the ground, they can still fly over and use what they see from the air as the basis for a search warrant. Although one lower court recently expressed the assurance that "the Constitution does not require that one erect a stone bastion, or retreat to the cellar to exhibit a reasonable expectation of privacy,"[32] it's risky to place any confidence in the privacy of property outside the curtilage of the home. In the urban setting, structures such as the parking garage of a condominium have been held to be devoid of Fourth Amendment protection.[33]

Abandoned premises carry no legitimate expectation of privacy,[34] but ownership confers a certain amount of privacy interest by virtue of the owner's right to exclude other people from his property.[2] Vacant apartments within an active complex, for example, are not "abandoned premises," even though they may be in disrepair and standing open for anyone to see in.[35] The owner of such apartments is still legally entitled to a certain level of privacy for them (against warrantless entry, for example).

Although the Constitution specifically refers to "houses" in its Fourth Amendment wording, it's been generally accepted that the founders meant for this to include business property, too. Like privacy interests elsewhere, those concerned with a business may be contracted and expanded for different circumstances. A retailer, for example, is entitled to expect that his merchandise won't be subjected to wholesale search and seizure by police, even though it's on public display for customers.[36] Likewise, a bar owner who calls the police because of a shooting on the premises has a right to expect that his place won't be subjected to a warrantless search.[37]

A person's privacy interest in commercial property is largely determined by whether or not he has ownership rights to it,[38] but other factors can enter in and confer the interest upon an employee as well. Plans to assume ownership in the future, and having major control and responsibility in the business, are two such factors.[37] Legitimate expectations that one's belongings will be safe from search and seizure can even exist in a shared office, where a worker has neither proprietary rights nor exclusive control of the area; the non-public nature of the place is itself sometimes sufficient.[39]

The zones of Fourth Amendment protection on business property are roughly parallel to those of the home, except that any area where the public is allowed to go is naturally devoid of most privacy interests.[40] It's just as necessary for the police to have a warrant to search commercial premises as it is for them to search a house, and it doesn't matter whether they're doing a criminal investigation,[41] a city administrative inspection,[42] or a federal administrative inspection.[40] Probable cause for a civil administrative search can be based on either specific evidence of some existing violation or simply a showing that they have reasonable legislative or administrative standards for searching a particular place.[43] Just as for criminal investigators, it's no excuse for civil inspectors to claim that it's too inconvenient for them to get a warrant.[44]

Unlike the situation at home, the public nature of a place of business makes it unnecessary for the cops to have a warrant to arrest a person at work.[45] Also, a consequence of conducting certain types of business is that it's possible to become automatically subject to warrantless searches. Government contractors, for example, may be subjected to warrantless audits of their business records.[46] Pharmacists,[47] gun dealers,[48] and establishments that serve liquor[49] can expect warrantless inventories and searches of their merchandise. Mining operations may be inspected for safety conditions at any time without a warrant.[50]

As with the home, commercial buildings can have a recognized expectation of privacy in their curtilage.[29]

Whether he's at home, at work, or elsewhere, a person is constitutionally entitled to freedom from police espionage of his private life. Society recognizes that he has a reasonable expectation of privacy for such places as his house, a phone booth, and a taxicab,[1] and unauthorized police intrusion of these places with any kind of listening or surveillance device is illegal.[51]/[52] Moreover, a person has a right to expect privacy concerning all conversations that take place within his house, even when he's not present.[8] The one serious gap in a person's otherwise legitimate expectation of privacy is the possibility that a trusted friend could be an informer or an undercover cop, because a person has no expectation of privacy for statements that he makes in front of such vermin.[53] It's a sad commentary on society that, more often than not, there's a rat in friend's clothing nearby...

REFERENCES

1. *Katz v U.S.,* 389 US 347, 351-352, 88 SCt 507, 511 (1967)

2. *Rakas v Illinois,* 439 US 128, 143-144 n. 12, 99 SCt 421, 430-431 n. 12 (1978)

3. *U.S. v Kramer,* 711 F2d 789, 793 (7th Cir. 1983)

4. *U.S. v U.S. District Court,* 407 US 297, 313, 92 SCt 2125, 2134 (1972)

5. *Mapp v Ohio,* 367 US 643, 644-645, 81 SCt 1684, 1686 (1961)

6. *People v Sneed*, 32 Cal. App. 3d 535, 108 Cal. Rptr. 146 (Cal. Ct. App. 1973)

7. *Katz v U.S.*, 389 US at 359, 88 SCt at 515

8. *U.S. v Alderman*, 394 US 165, 176, 89 SCt 961, 968 (1969)

9. *U.S. v Lyons*, 706 F2d 321, 325-327 (U.S. App. D.C. 1983)

10. *Recznik v City of Lorraine*, 393 US 166, 168-169, 89 SCt 342, 344 (1968)

11. *Stoner v California*, 376 US 483, 490, 84 SCt 889, 893 (1964)

12. *Mowrer v State*, Indiana Ct. App., 4th Dist., 4/19/83

13. *U.S. v Torres*, 705 F2d 1287, 1295-1296 (11th Cir. 1983)

14. *U.S. v Jones*, 362 US 257, 259, 267, 80 SCt 725, 730, 734 (1960)

15. *U.S. v Briones-Garza*, 680 F2d 417, 420-421 (5th Cir. 1982)

16. *Payton v New York*, 445 US 573, 589-590, 100 SCt 1371, 1381-1382 (1980)

17. *Camara v Municipal Court*, 387 US 523, 538-540, 87 SCt 1727, 1736-1737 (1967)

18. *Michigan v Tyler*, 436 US 499, 509, 98 SCt 1942, 1950 (1978)

19. *Mincey v Arizona*, 437 US 385, 392, 98 SCt 2408, 2413 (1978)

20. *Ker v California*, 374 US 23, 37-41, 83 SCt 1623, 1632-1634 (1963)

21. *Hobson v U.S.*, 226 F2d 890, 894 (8th Cir. 1955)

22. *Taylor v U.S.*, 286 US 1, 52 SCt 466 (1932)

23. *Rosencranz v U.S.*, 356 F2d 310, 313 (1st Cir. 1966)

24. *Walker v U.S.*, 225 F2d 447, 448-449 (5th Cir. 1955)

25. *Wattenburg v U.S.*, 388 F2d 853, 857-858 (9th Cir. 1968)

26. *U.S. v Fluker*, 543 F2d 709, 716 (9th Cir. 1976)

27. *Warden v Hayden*, 387 US 294, 304, 87 SCt 1642, 1648 (1967)

28. *Hester v U.S.*, 265 US 57, 59, 44 SCt 445, 446 (1924)

29. *U.S. v Swart*, 679 F2d 698, 702 (7th Cir. 1982)

30. *Oliver v U.S.*, _ US,_ 104 SCt 1735, 1743 (1984)

31. *Mapp v Ohio*, 367 US at 670, 81 SCt at 1700, J. Douglas concurring

32. *Wheeler v State*, Texas Ct. Crim Appls., 9/29/83

33. *U.S. v Cruz Pagan*, 537 F2d 554, 558 (lst Cir. 1976)

34. *Abel v U.S.*, 362 US 217, 241, 80 SCt 683, 698 (1960)

35. *Wilson v Health Hospital Corp. of Marion City*, 620 F2d 1201, 1213 (7th Cir. 1980)

36. *Lo-Ji Inc. v New York*, 442 US 319, 329, 99 SCt 2319, 2326 (1979)

37. *State v Young*, 135 Ariz. 437, 440-441, 661 P2d 1138, 1141-1142 (Ariz. App. 1982)

38. *Brown v U.S.*, 411 US 223, 229, 93 SCt 1565, 1569 (1973)

39. *Mancusi v DeForte*, 392 US 364, 367-369, 88 SCt 2120, 2123-2124 (1968)

40. *Marshall v Barlow's*, 436 US 307, 315, 98 SCt 1816, 1822 (1978)

41. *U.S. v Lefkowitz*, 285 US 452, 52 SCt 420 (1932)

42. *See v City of Seattle*, 387 US 541, 543-544, 87 SCt 1737, 1739-1740 (1967)

43. *Marshall v Barlow's*, 436 US at 320, 98 SCt at 1824

44. *U.S. v Johnson*, 333 US 10, 15, 68 SCt 367, 369 (1948)

45. *U.S. v Blalock*, 578 F2d 245, 248 (9th Cir. 1978)

46. *Zap v U.S.*, 328 US 624, 628, 66 SCt 1277, 1279 (1946)

47. Title 21 U.S.C. Section 880 (c)

48. *U.S. v Biswell*, 406 US 311, 316, 92 SCt 1593, 1596 (1972)

49. *Colonnade Corp. v U.S.*, 397 US 72, 76-77, 90 SCt 774, 777 (1970)

50. *Donovan v Dewey*, 452 US 594, 603, 101 SCt 2534, 2540 (1981)

51. *Silverman v U.S.*, 365 US 509, 511, 81 SCt 679, 682 (1961)
52. *U.S. v Karo*, _ US, _ 104 SCt 3296, 3304 (1984)
53. *Hoffa v U.S.*, 385 US 293, 311, 87 SCt 408, 418 (1966)

Chapter 10

BREACHING THE CASTLE GATE

"The king's keys unlock all doors."

Justice Byron R. White dissenting in *Payton v New York*, 445 US 573, 604, 100 SCt 1371, 1389 (1980).

Having measured the extent of the wall of constitutional protection that surrounds the house, let's look at the ways in which the cops can break through it. On a basic level, the search and seizure issue for the house is similar to that for the person, with the gaps in its constitutional armor being the same ones of consent, warrant, exigency, and arrest. One major difference, however, is that there's no justification for an "intermediate intrusion" into a house based on reasonable articulable suspicion — the police aren't entitled to enter and conduct a "protective" search of a house the way they do a *Terry* frisk of a person.[1]

As with all police intrusions, the easiest way in is by consent, and nobody has more authority to grant it than the owner. When it's coerced at gunpoint, however, it hardly qualifies as legitimate consent.[2] Another eventuality that might invalidate a suspect's consent to search is a violation of his right to an attorney. An arrested person can legitimately give his consent without the benefit of counsel, but once he invokes his right to see an attorney, the law says that the cops must stop all questioning[3] — and that includes requests for consent to search.[4] Any grant of consent that somebody gives after asking for and being denied legal counsel might be regarded as the product of coercion; unless the suspect retracts and waives his request for counsel, his consent is questionable. By retracting and waiving his request, the fellow demonstrates that it's his own considered decision to permit the search of his house without first consulting his attorney.

The cops can sometimes get a third party to let them into a suspect's house, and that counts as valid consent if he has the authority to give it. A parent has that authority when it comes to granting consent to search his minor child's room.[5] A person's roommate has the authority because of mutual rights to the premises.[6] When the cops mistakenly take their consent from someone who isn't entitled to give it, however, it can spoil the legality of their search. Consider, for example, the case of a grandparent who consented to a warrantless search of her nineteen-year-old grandson's room. The cops mistakenly believed that her parental custody status and her ownership of the house entitled her to grant the consent; the young man had been paying rent and maintaining his *exclusive* use of the room, however, and the court ruled that the old lady had no right to give such consent.[7] It can sometimes be a close question, depending on the facts of each case, but the main consideration is whether or not the third party is violating the suspect's legitimate expectation of privacy by granting the consent for police to enter. It's long been settled that people such as landlords and hotel clerks are not entitled to give the police permission to enter a guest's room.[8]

The third way that the cops can acquire consent to enter their quarry's premises is indirectly through the use of guile and trickery. It's incredible how these hypocrites, who profess such indignation at the artistry of the con man, can freely employ all manner of deceit when it suits their own purposes. They've made betrayal their most important tool through the widespread use of snitches and undercover cops.[9]/[10] They use ruses such as the old "stranded motorist who needs to use the

- 138 -

phone" routine to trick their way into people's houses for covert investigational purposes.[11] They've even gone so far as to hire out as domestic servants; one of them worked as a handyman for six months in order to rifle the employer's home for evidence.[12] The Supreme Court ruled long ago that a pretext is just as unconstitutional as force or coercion for the purpose of gaining entrance to someone's house or office,[13] but the courts these days seem to regard it as merely an expression of constabulatory creativity. Once a rat gets inside a house by exploiting the uninformed consent of the householder, he's legally entitled to open the doors to all the rest of the cops outside — consent given to one cop is consent given to all of them.[14]/[15]

Lacking valid consent, a warrant's the best ticket for admission into a private house. The warrant stands for probable cause. It can be probable cause to search or probable cause to arrest; when they're out to make an arrest it doesn't really matter, because either type of warrant will legally get them past the front door. Even though it traditionally takes a search warrant to justify entering a house, it's been settled that an arrest warrant will do just as well when the suspect's in his own place.[16] At somebody else's house, where the arrestee has no privacy interest, they can still get away with having just an arrest warrant because (1) the unauthorized entry doesn't violate the visiting arrestee's rights, and (2) the arrest doesn't violate the householder's rights. Neither one has grounds to challenge the legality of the arrest.[17]/[18]

Of course, the *entry is* a significant violation of the *householder's* rights; police who intrude on the sanctity of a person's home with neither a search warrant nor the excuse of an exigency are simply not where they belong. Any incriminating evidence that the cops may fortuitously discover in such a situation is unusable against the householder because of the invalid entry.[19]

Police who want to make a warranted search of a particular house can often get the grounds for their warrant from what they see there. The only catch is that they have to do their snooping from a place where they have a right to be.[20]/[21]

The manner in which a warrant is executed may differ greatly from the traditional concept of a warranted search. The victim of a warranted bugging or wiretap, for example, won't even know of any warrant until sometime after-the-fact, when he's already sitting in jail, because the cops sneak in and plant their listening devices in complete secrecy.[22] Such warrants are, in effect, licenses to commit burglary. Another novel way of serving a warrant is by kicking the door in — the so-called "no-knock" entry. As will be discussed shortly, the cops are supposed to knock, identify themselves, and tell the occupant why they've come before they enter his house. In some states, however, they can actually get the court's advance permission to dispense with such nicities by having the magistrate issue "no-knock" warrants. They're usually used for drug busts, but the mere fact that drugs are involved isn't enough reason to issue one. In order to get such a warrant, there needs to be some specific reason to believe that evidence would otherwise be destroyed.[23]

While the citizen might expect them to properly produce their warrant for him to see when they come to make their search, the police around the country have come to depend more and more upon the use of verbal authorization over the telephone. The magistrate is supposed to record the phone conversation on tape for transcription, and the actual warrant shows up sometime later, after the search is over. Obviously, such an arrangement allows ample opportunity for the cops to fudge with their warrants. There are some places where the courts require that a warrant be physically on the scene before a house can be entered and searched.[24]

If the police have neither consent nor a warrant to justify their invasion of private ground, the existence of an exigency will always do. Even when they know that a felony's been committed, and have probable cause to go into a house after the evidence, there still has to be an emergency of some kind to justify doing it without a warrant.[25]/[26] Any situation where somebody's life appears to be in danger is justification for them to burst into a house to render "immediate aid."[27] When they're in hot pursuit of a suspect whom they've been chasing through the streets, they're entitled to follow him into a house without further adieu.[28]

These are the kinds of heroics that a cop dreams about — smashing dramatically through the door, gun in hand, just like his favorite TV detective — seizing immediate control of the place, and saving the day for all the grateful, adoring citizens whose very lives hang in the balance. Granting their characteristic psychological need to constantly reaffirm their machismo, it's no wonder that cops tend to eagerly grasp any opportunity that has the earmarks of an exigency in order for a chance to play Dick Tracy. The possibility that a criminal suspect might be about to run, destroy evidence, or endanger the public safety, are all exigent grounds for the police to enter a private building. They're often far less obvious than the "immediate aid" and "hot pursuit" exigencies, however, and consequently more difficult to be certain about. To restrain some of the zeal with which the cops would otherwise be freely breaking into homes under contrived "exigencies," the courts have adopted guidelines to assess whether or not a true crisis exists for each case. One such standard, which was set forth in the Dorman case, recommended that the police make a considered decision before each exigent entry based upon (1) the gravity of the offense (especially whether it involved violence), (2) the suspect's likelihood of being armed, (3) the existence of probable cause, (4) strong reason to believe that the suspect is inside the building, (5) the likelihood of his escape if he isn't swiftly apprehended, (6) the peacefulness of the proposed entry, and (7) the time (day or night) of the proposed entry.[29] Other courts have recognized that it's probably asking too much to expect a cop to provide the level of brainpower needed to apply the *Dorman* standard; they instead merely ask that there be reasonable grounds to believe that "if an immediate arrest were not made, the accused would be able to destroy evidence, flee, or... endanger the safety or property of others."[30]/[31]

In addition to police and fire emergencies, it's possible for a public health problem to be of such compelling proportions that it justifies an exigent entry of private property.[32] Such measures might be necessary in order to halt the distribution of unwholesome food or the spread of disease.

A critical point to realize is that all these warrantless exigencies will legally place the public officials in a position from which they can see things which are ordinarily private. Whether they're uniformed policemen, firemen, city housing inspectors, or public health officials, they're still basically cops; they're all likely to react to the discovery of contraband or other incriminating evidence by kicking off an immediate investigation. Just because their exigency justifies them to enter a house, it doesn't give them a license to go rummaging about; they're only supposed to be there for the purpose of handling the exigency. Should they inadvertently come across some incriminating evidence during the course of their work, however, they're just as entitled to seize it as if they had a search warrant for it.[33] Worst of all, it doesn't matter who or what the cops are after when they enter a house; the evidence that they find there in "plain view" is incriminating to the occupants. Unlike the situation where they enter on the authority of a warrant for the arrest of a visitor,[19] the cops who enter under exigent circumstances *can* use that "plain view" evidence against the householder.[33]

In addition to justifying a warrantless entry, an exigency can sometimes justify the temporary warrantless seizure of a place — or in police parlance, "securing the premises." When they think they have incriminating evidence inside and don't want to risk having someone remove or destroy it, they'll seal off access to it and stand guard over it until such time as they have their search warrant. Then they can go in and legally seize whatever it is they're after. It ought to be illegal for the cops to deny a person access to his own house, yet the Supreme Court has taken a permissive attitude toward this policy, holding that a warrantless seizure of premises is reasonable even if a warrantless search is not.[34] Other courts have rationalized the securing of premises either by claiming that it was justified by an exigency or that it played no part in actually acquiring the evidence.[35] Thus, by one rationale or another, the cops invariably get away with their warrantless securing of premises.

Another special form of intrusion that's related to exigency is the "no-knock" entry. There's no advantage like the element of surprise, and cops have been using it to get the drop on outlaws ever since Alley Oop first kicked in the front door to Somebody's cave. Breaking down the door to a man's house began to be frowned upon as individual rights came to acquire some recognition during the fifteenth century,[37] and in 1948 the United States Congress enacted a statute dictating that a cop who's executing a search warrant may break open a door only if, after notifying the occupant of his authority and his purpose, he's still denied admittance.[38] The purpose of such a rule is to (1) reduce the likelihood of violence from situations where the police mistakenly break into the wrong house, (2) prevent needless damage to private property, (3) show respect for the privacy of the home, and (4) give the occupant a brief opportunity to straighten up his "personal affairs" before the cops enter.[39]

The Supreme Court has given its approval to this knock-and-announce rule, though granting that there still may be times when the people inside wouldn't need to be given a notice of authority and purpose because they already know it.[40] It also says that the police should follow the knock-and-announce rule even when there's no need to use force to get in (as when the door is unlocked, or when they have a passkey).[41] It doesn't say that the cops can't make exceptions to the rule, or use ruses to trick their way into a place. The recognized exceptions to the knock-and-announce rule are when (1) there's nobody there to refuse admittance and they have to let themselves in, (2) the people inside already know of the officers' authority and purpose, (3) someone inside is in immediate physical peril, (4) the people inside are busy destroying evidence or making a getaway, and (5) the cops are afraid that it might be dangerous to themselves to announce their authority and purpose.[39] If the police think that the totality of circumstances in a situation add up to one of these exceptions, they're entitled to go ahead and do a no-knock entry.[42]

Though the words of the statute specify only search warrants, it's been accepted that the knock-and-announce rule applies equally to the execution of arrest warrants.[39] It shouldn't be assumed that this rule affords the occupant any substantial measure of time, however; the cops are likely to knock the door down if it isn't opened within 15 seconds,[43] and that's hardly enough time to pull up your pants, much less "clean up" the place.

The fourth way in which the cops can penetrate the constitutional "force field" of a house is through the use of a lawful arrest which began outside it. Just as a person may be searched incident to lawful arrest, so may a house be entered under analogous reasoning. It's settled law that, with probable cause, the cops can arrest a person in public without a warrant.[44] By stretching the grasp of that doctrine a bit, the Supreme Court has made it apply as well to a suspect who's standing in public view from the threshold of his house.[45] Thus, even though he's standing within the constitutionally-protected confines of his home, he's subject to "public arrest" because he's visible to the cops and because they can claim that as the beginning of their arrest. Should he slam the door on them, they're justified in breaking in because (1) the arrest has already begun, so they're entitled to enter incident to lawful arrest, and (2) evasive behavior would suggest an intent to escape or destroy evidence, and that turns the situation into an exigency. As the Court states, "a suspect may not defeat an arrest which has been set in motion in a public place... by the expedient of escaping to a private place."[45] Although the original case concerned a suspect who was actually standing in her open doorway, lower courts have twisted the logic of this holding even further by applying it to cases where the suspect was well inside and only opened his door a crack.[46]

If a person has already been placed under arrest out in public, and is foolish enough to bring the cops back to his house, there too is an opportunity for them to legitimately enter his place; a cop is entitled to remain at the side of his arrestee at all times, so if he lets the chump go into his house, the cop's entitled to tag along too.[47]

The right of the police to search goes along with their right to enter a place incident to lawful arrest, and it literally hangs like a black cloud over the head of the suspect. If he's in his front yard when they arrest him, their search must be restricted to that area; if he's inside his house, they're justified to search the entire room. Wherever he happens to be, they're entitled to search the area around him for as far as he might possibly grab; all other distinctions of distance, location, etc. are meaningless.[48] Assuming that their search is being conducted in a properly limited fashion, they can also seize anything that lies in plain view beyond the suspect's grabbable range.[33]

The analogy with a search of the person incident to lawful arrest doesn't hold up to the extent of permitting an "inventory search" of his house when he's arrested there. An inventory search of those possessions that go along with him to the stationhouse is standard policy.[49] But the cops can't use that rationale as an excuse to gather up items from personal premises such as his hotel room.[50]

The foregoing has been a discussion of the ways in which police can defeat the legitimate Fourth Amendment protections that we enjoy for our houses. There are, however, further intrusions on our privacy that the police can make without even concerning themselves about our rights. These are the intrusions into aspects of our privacy which the Constitution doesn't protect. Take garbage, for example (yes, please... *take* my garbage!)[51] If you want to keep something secret you can always destroy it, but the Constitution doesn't protect the privacy of the things you throw away. Even if the cops trespass into the curtilage surrounding your house in order to pick up your garbage, it still doesn't violate your rights to peace and quiet, relaxation, and public esteem. As far as the courts are concerned, such an intrusion is not a violation of the Fourth Amendment.[52]

Likewise, the use of modern technology to snoop on a person's activities isn't always unconstitutional just because it impinges in some way on his home. The phone company has a technique called the "pen register," whereby it can centrally accumulate a record of all telephone numbers that are dialed from a given house. We all know (or should know) that the phone company is in bed with the government, and that any information we feed into it will be freely passed on to the police. It's therefore been ruled that a person has no legitimate expectation of privacy in the telephone numbers that he dials from his own house; the Constitution simply doesn't protect that aspect of privacy.[53] Similarly, the location of a person's house by means of an electronic transmitter that the cops secretly attach to his car is no violation of his Fourth Amendment rights.[54] Such a device doesn't provide any information that couldn't be seen by an observer from public land, and a person has no right to expect any privacy concerning his movements on public thoroughfares. The beeper simply makes it possible for Big Brother to keep his eye on us a little more closely — and that's not so unreasonable, is it? After all, it *is* 1984...

REFERENCES

1. *State v Davis,* 295 Or. 227, 666 P2d 802, 811-812 (Or. 1983)

2. *People v Challoner,* Cal. Ct. App., 2d Dist., 10/21/82

3. *Edwards v Arizona,* 451 US 478, 485, 101 SCt 1880, 1885 (1981)

4. *U.S. v McCraney,* 705 F2d 449 (5th Cir. 1983) (no published opinion; see *Criminal Law Reporter* 33 CrL 2131-2132)

5. *In Interest of Salyer,* 44 Ill. App. 3d 854, 3 Ill. Dec. 648, 358 NE2d 1333 (1977)

6. *U.S. v Matlock,* 415 US 164, 170-171, 94 SCt 988, 993 (1974)

7. *State v Carsey,* 295 Or. 32, 664 P2d 1085-1086 (Or. 1983)

8. *Stoner v California,* 376 US 483, 489-490, 84 SCt 889, 893 (1964)

9. *Hoffa v U.S.,* 385 US 293, 311, 87 SCt 408,418 (1966)

10. *Lewis v U.S.,* 385 US 206, 209-210, 87 SCt 424, 426-427 (1966)

11. *State v Ahart,* Iowa Sup. Ct., 9/29/82

12. *Baldwin v U.S.,* 450 US 1045, 101 SCt 1767 (1981), Memorandum Decision, J. Marshall dissenting

13. *Gouled v U.S.*, 255 US 298, 305-306, 41 SCt 261, 263-264 (1921)

14. *U.S. v Schuster*, 684 F2d 744, 748 (11th Cir. 1982)

15. *State v Cantrell*, Fla. Ct. App., 2d Dist., 1/19/83

16. *Payton v New York*, 445 US 573, 602-603, 100 SCt 1371, 1388 (1980)

17. *U.S. v Buckner*, 717 F2d 297, 300 (6th Cir. 1983)

18. *U.S. v Underwood*, 717 F2d 482, 484 (9th Cir. 1983)

19. *Steagald v U.S.*, 451 US 204, 222, 101 SCt 1642, 1652-1653 (1981)

20. *Wilson v Health & Hospital Corp. of Marion City*, 620 F2d 1201, 1209-1210 (7th Cir. 1980)

21. *U.S. v Knotts*, 460 US 276, 103 SCt 1081, 1086 (1983)

22. *Dalia v U.S.*, 441 US 238, 256-259, 99 SCt 1682, 1693 (1979)

23. *Commonwealth v Scalise*, Mass. Sup. Jud. Ct., 9/15/82

24. *Riley v State*, Florida Ct. App., 3d Dist., 3/29/83

25. *Payton v New York*, 445 US at 590, 100 SCt at 1382

26. *Coolidge v New Hampshire*, 403 US 443, 468, 91 SCt 2022, 2039 (1971)

27. *Mincey v Arizona*, 437 US 385, 392, 98 SCt 2408, 2413 (1978)

28. *Warden v Hayden*, 387 US 294, 298-299, 87 SCt 1642, 1646 (1967)

29. *Dorman v U.S.*, 435 F2d 385, 392-393 (U.S. App. D.C. 1970)

30. *State v Canby*, 252 SE2d 164, 167 (W. Va. 1979)

31. *State v Guertin*, Conn. Sup. Ct., 6/21/83

32. *Camara v Municipal Court*, 387 US 523, 539, 87 SCt 1727, 1736 (1967)

33. *Coolidge v New Hampshire*, 403 US at 465-466 n. 24, 91 SCt at 2037-2038 n. 24

34. *U.S. v Segura*, _US,_ 104 SCt 3380, 3388-3390 (1984)

35. *U.S. v Allard,* 634 F2d 1182, 1186-1187 (9th Cir. 1980)

36. *U.S. v Lomas,* 706 F2d 886, 894, 896-897 (9th Cir. 1983)

37. *Miller v U.S.,* 357 US 301, 307, 78 SCt 1190, 1194 (1958)

38. Title 18 U.S.C. Section 3109

39. *U.S. v Kane,* 637 F2d 974, 977-978 (3d Cir. 1981)

40. *Miller v U.S.,* 357 US at 310, 78 SCt at 1196

41. *Sabbath v U.S.,* 391 US 585, 590, 88 SCt 1755, 1758 (1968)

42. *U.S. v Nolan,* 718 F2d 589, 599 (3d Cir. 1983)

43. *U.S. v Cruz,* 265 FSupp 15, 23-24 (W.D. Tex. 1967)

44. *U.S. v Watson,* 423 US 411, 423, 96 SCt 820, 827-828 (1976)

45. *U.S. v Santana,* 427 US 38, 42-43, 96 SCt 2406, 2409-2410 (1976)

46. *People v Levan,* N.Y., Sup. Ct., App. Div., 1st Dept., 2/10/83

47. *Washington v Chrisman,* 455 US 1, 9, 102 SCt 812, 817-818 (1982)

48. *Chimel v California,* 395 US 752, 766, 89 SCt 2034, 2041-2042 (1969)

49. *Illinois V Lafayette,* 462 US __, 103 SCt 2605, 2609 (1983)

50. *U.S. v Lyons,* 706 F2d 321, 333 (U.S. App. D.C. 1983)

51. Youngman, Henny, Caesar's Palace, Las Vegas, Nevada (1983)

52. *U.S. v Kramer,* 711 F2d 789, 792-794 (7th Cir. 1983)

53. *Smith v Maryland,* 442 US 735, 742-744, 99 SCt 2577, 2581-2582 (1979)

54. *U.S. v Knotts,* 460 US 276, 103 SCt at 1086-1087

Chapter 11

BELONGINGS

"The great end for which men entered into society was to secure their property. That right is preserved sacred and incommunicable in all instances where it has not been taken away or abridged by some public law for the good of the whole... every invasion of private property, be it ever so minute, is a trespass."

Lord Camden, *Entick v Carrington and Three other King's Messengers*, 19 How. St. Tr. 1029 (1765)

Now that we know what to expect from the law concerning the privacy of our "persons" and our "houses," let's conclude our survey of the Fourth Amendment by discussing its protection of our "papers and effects." In the last chapter it was disclosed that a person can have no expectation of privacy in his garbage,[1] but there are also other personal property contexts where one's privacy interest melts away.

When the cops have previously discovered contraband inside an item, and secretly follow it to its destination, they're conducting what's called a "controlled delivery." If they can catch the owner with the incriminating item shortly thereafter, they're entitled to freely open it, "discover" the contraband inside, and bust him for possession; their prior knowledge of the item's contents neutralizes the owner's legitimate expectation of privacy in it.[2]

While possession may be nine tenths of the law, that remaining tenth must represent the privacy interest, because a person who's in possession of another's property, but not delegated the full use and control of it, has no constitutional right to object to its being searched. Consider, for instance, a man who's standing guard over a truck full of weed but has neither the title nor the ignition key to it. Although he's been entrusted with the duty to keep undesirables away from it, the law says that his lack of either ownership or exclusive control of it leaves him without standing to object to an illegal search and seizure. Thus, the court can find him guilty of possession, but not entitled to the protection of the Fourth Amendment.[3]

Ownership of a thing doesn't always guarantee a privacy interest in it, either. The person who places his property in someone else's house or car does so at the risk of its being seized in a police search and used as evidence against him, because he has no standing to object to searches of someone else's premises.[4]/[5] This is also true for those papers of a person which are held by third parties such as his banker,[6] accountant,[7] or lawyer.[8] Similarly, a person forfeits his privacy interest when he loans out his car,[9] airplane,[10] or other such vehicle to other people; if they get busted carrying dope in it, the absent owner has no standing to object to the search of the vehicle, and will in all probability lose it in forfeiture to the government.

It would appear, then, that before a person can assert a right to privacy for a vehicle, he should be (1) in complete control of it (or preferably, the legal owner), (2) physically present at the time of the search, and (3) take reasonable measures to protect his avowed privacy interest. An interesting case in point was that of a fellow named Perez, who contracted with a Mexican national to drive a load of heroin into the U.S. Perez stashed the stuff in the gas tank, and paid for the services of the driver and his truck through another Mexican. Then, he and two other associates tailed the truck to its destination in central Arizona. Unbeknown to them, the entire odyssey had been under constant air and land surveillance by the cops, who finally got impatient and conducted a warrantless search and seizure without probable cause. The interesting thing about the case is that the federal Court of Appeals ruled in favor of Perez — since he (1) had a "formalized arrangement" with the

Mexican to be his "mule," (2) took precautions to assure privacy by following behind, and (3) was himself present at the time of the search, Perez was entitled to a legitimate expectation of privacy in the truck![11]

There are various circumstances under which the cops may intrude upon a citizen's personal property without even demonstrating reasonable suspicion. In public places, for example, people's luggage might be subjected to sniffing by drug detection dogs,[12] and baggage handlers are even justified in helping them to get a good smell by compressing the bags and forcing air out, a process known as "prepping."[13] In the public school setting, wall lockers and publically-parked cars may be subject to such dog sniffs.[14]/[15] Since the dogs are merely tasting the air around the outside of the object, there's some question as to whether the dog sniff really even constitutes a "search" in the constitutional sense.[12] The indiscriminate use of sniff dogs to check out people's property in public places hasn't been authorized by the federal courts in all parts of the country,[16] but with the "conservative" trend in government these days it's probably safe to assume that it soon will be.

When a bag has unquestionably been abandoned, the police are free to search inside it and use its contents as evidence against whomever the finger may point.[17] They're also free to go snooping if they have the consent of the joint user of an article;[18] consent of the owner himself might be automatic if it happens to be a condition of his parole agreement.[19]

The discretion to freely search personal property is enjoyed with especially wide latitude by the various types of federal cops that are concerned with the national borders. Any kind of property that enters the country from abroad, be it a letter or an ocean liner, is subject to as thorough a search as the feds may wish to conduct; no further justification is needed beyond the fact that it is entering national territory.[20] This wide degree of discretion, however, is confined to affairs at the border, or at its "functional equivalents" such as airports where people first disembark upon entering the U.S.

On major highways leading in from the national frontiers, the U.S. Border Patrol operates fixed checkpoints, some of them located more than fifty miles inland. Their main purpose is to detect illegal aliens, and they're entitled to stop motorists, check for proof of citizenship, ask questions, and peek inside the cars.[21] There's no need for them to have any individualized suspicion in order to make these brief checks,[22] but unless they pick up suspicious signals during the process they aren't entitled to do any real search of a vehicle. The scope of these routine inspections is supposed to be limited to only checking for *people*.[23]

Since water travel is impossible for them to control by means of fixed checkpoints or "functional border equivalents," the seagoing feds have authorization to freely conduct roving searches of any vessels within twelve miles of American shoreline. As with the border searches and the alien searches at fixed checkpoints removed from the border, they don't need to have any particularized suspicion in order to board a vessel and search it.[24]/[25]

If the cops do have reasonable articulable suspicion that a crime has been committed, they're entitled to do a "protective" search of the suspect's belongings in the same way that they frisk his person.

A closed container, such as a purse, a suitcase, or even an envelope, carries the inherent implication of privacy by virtue of the fact that it *is* closed from view. Such an expectation of privacy is one that's recognized by society, and a cop's decision to violate it on the basis of mere suspicion should be justified by weighing the sufficiency of three criteria: (1) the public necessity of it, (2) the efficacy of such a search, and (3) the degree of intrusion involved in the proposed search.[26] If there isn't a compelling enough public interest in making such a search, the first criterion isn't met; the danger posed by a concealed weapon would usually be sufficient in this regard, whereas the prospect of turning up a few joints probably wouldn't. If the proposed search doesn't offer the promise of effectively *fulfilling* that public interest, it fails to meet the second criterion. As much as the cops would love to stalk around at rock concerts searching purses for liquor and drugs, the hopelessness of stemming the "drug menace" through such a measure renders it unreasonable under this second criterion. If the search involves a more drastic intrusion than would seem reasonable under the circumstances, it fails to satisfy the third criterion.

Grounds for the reasonable suspicion necessary to search a person's things might come from anywhere — even an anonymous phone tip.[27] The scope of the consequent search, however, should be limited by the nature of its purpose; on a "protective" search for weapons, for example, it wouldn't be reasonable for the police to inspect the contents of an envelope.[28]

Short of actually searching inside a closed container, the cops can legitimately detain it for a time while they attempt to either satisfy their suspicion through some nonintrusive means or obtain a judicial search warrant. It's noteworthy that the law enforcement interest in a detention of property focuses more on detecting contraband than it does on protecting the officer from the threat of a hidden weapon, which was originally the justification for intrusions based on reasonable articulable suspicion.[29] Such a detention is a temporary deprivation of the owner's property interest, and is therefore considered an intrusion in the constitutional sense. The Supreme Court has held that such investigative detentions are only reasonable when the cops make it quick and use the *least intrusive* methods available to investigate the item within a *brief* period of time.[30]

As an intrusion, the detention of personalty consists of two phases — the seizure and the investigation. Seizure of the article from a third party, to whom the owner voluntarily relinquished custody of it, represents an intrusion of a milder *nature* than seizure from the owner himself.[31] Examples of such third parties include transportation personnel and postal employees. The *extent* of the seizure, as measured in units of time, can vary from brief, permissible detention to those lasting over ninety minutes, which suggest a failure of the cops to act diligently, and are therefore impermissible.[32] Similarly, the nature and extent of the *investigation* to which they subject the item — fluoroscopy, dog sniff, or some other limited technique — is also pertinent. Thus, if the cops have reason to suspect that a citizen's personalty contains something illegal, they can seize it and hold onto it for whatever *brief* period of time it takes them to satisfy themselves by a *limited* investigation.[31] Part and parcel to the reasonableness of these property detentions is the condition that the owner be free to leave if he chooses.[33]

Vehicles, too, may be subject to cursory searches based upon reasonable articulable suspicion, but it has to be *particularized* suspicion directed at specific cars; area-sweep tactics that pick out cars at random are not considered reasonable.[34] Just as with other forms of personal property, the cops can get their suspicion either directly by their own observations[35]/[36] or indirectly through information from a snitch.[37]/[38] When a vehicle is in the vicinity of one of the national borders, the feds have a right to stop and search it at any time and place if they become reasonably suspicious.[39] In addition to things like erratic or evasive driving, which would give any cop reasonable suspicion, the Border Patrol will pick up on such factors as known recent illegal border crossings, proximity to the border, and the unusual pattern of traffic on a particular road. They'll be suspicious of cars that appear to be heavily loaded, and certain types of vehicles, such as trucks, vans, and station wagons with large hidden compartments suitable for hiding aliens. The nature of the passengers is also likely to arouse their suspicion; an extraordinary number of them, the appearance of someone attempting to hide, or the characteristic modes of dress and haircuts that Mexican nationals wear, are all adequate grounds for stopping and searching the car.[39]

State and local police may also conduct roving vehicle checks without probable cause, but their administrative concerns are unlikely to result in actual searches. Their interest in enforcing traffic laws will be reflected by a concern with licenses, registrations, truck weights, and the like.[40] If a person's driving is satisfactory, his vehicle is in proper mechanical condition, his papers are in order, and there's no obvious cause for suspicion (such as the odor of alcohol or marijuana, or evidence of a crime lying in plain view) there's no justification for them to search his car.

The intensity of a vehicle search based on reasonable suspicion is supposed to be less aggressive than would be justified by probable cause, although the distinction is likely to be meaningless if the evidence isn't carefully hidden. It may be reasonable to search a closed container inside the passenger compartment if the circumstances suggest a danger that calls for a "protective" search.[41] Unless some compelling exigency exists, such as the threat of an explosion in public, it wouldn't be reasonable to enter the locked trunk without probable cause.[42] State courts have reasoned similarly in declaring that a policeman may not enter under the hood or the locked interior of a citizen's car without probable cause.[43]/[44] It seems contradictory to the popular tone of the law, then, that the Supreme Court should approve as it does of the secret attachment of automobile tracking devices — a significant intrusion — on the basis of mere suspicion.[45]

With probable cause, the police can legitimately conduct an extensive array of search and seizure activity on people's effects. The use of a judicial search warrant enables them to carry it out with the official blessing of the court, although it limits the search and seizure to just those things which are specified, or "particularized,"in the warrant. With an eye to preventing the kind of general search that the British military used to conduct during colonial times, the Supreme Court has declared that nothing should be left to the discretion of the officer executing the warrant.[46]/[47] Particularity requirements don't prevent the cops from seizing unexpected contraband which turns up "in plain view" during a warranted search, but it does prevent them from searching where the warrant doesn't specify. A warrant to search a specific address will therefore not provide for a search of the owner's car if it's parked away from the premises.[48]

In two major respects, the automobile is unique as an item of personalty: (1) it's likely to be evasive of police efforts to detain it, and (2) it has a diminished expectation of privacy. On the first score, the Supreme Court long ago established the concept of an "automobile exception" to the warrant requirement.[49] The reasoning is that, when the cops stop a car on probable cause, if they leave it long enough to get a search warrant it might not be there when they get back. On the other hand, if they take it with them, they're depriving the owner of his transportation. The less intrusive option, the Court reasoned, is to allow the cops to search vehicles on the spot when they have probable cause to do so. That way, if they score a bust, they can arrest the occupant and impound the car; if they come up dry, they can simply let him be on his way. The same reasoning, incidentally, applies to wagons, boats, and other mobile conveyances.[49]

Regarding the second aspect, there seem to be five reasons for the lowered expectation of privacy in a vehicle: (1) it seldom serves as a residence, (2) it seldom serves as a repository for personal effects, (3) it travels in plain view on public thoroughfares, (4) it requires extensive state licensing and registration, and (5) it's often inspected and taken into custody for public safety.[50] The courts are quick to fall back on this reasoning in order to justify warrantless auto searches. There's a smaller expectation of privacy attached to an automobile than to luggage,[50] and it's far smaller than that which one enjoys for his person or his house.[51] Even when the vehicle functions incidentally as a dwelling (e.g. a sleeper van) it's accorded a low rating on the privacy scale.[52] The expectation of privacy for an airplane is probably about the same as for an automobile.[53]

The prime rationale for warrantless automobile searches has traditionally been the element of exigency — either the fear that someone would drive the car away[49]/[54] or the danger posed by the object of the search itself, such as a gun.[55] The lack of exigency has in the past led the High Court to reject the application of the automobile exception.[56] but recent holdings have given the police complete discretion in this regard. It's now okay for them to conduct a warrantless search of *any* part of a vehicle, including any closed containers inside it, as long as they have probable cause to search in those particular places.[57] Moreover, they can wait until later to perform their warrantless searches in the convenience of the police compound if they choose, because the probable cause remains just as valid there as it is on the scene.[58]/[59] Those feds that run the fixed inland checkpoints and inland roving patrols are authorized to search vehicles only upon probable cause.[60]/[61] For them, however, probable cause is likely to consist of much the same criteria as those mentioned above for reasonable suspicion (i.e. appearances, responses, nature of the vehicle, etc.).[60]

Concomitant with a lawful arrest (which is itself necessarily based upon probable cause) the police are entitled to conduct a search and seizure of any personal property in the immediate grabbable area of the arrestee;[62] that includes closed containers,[62]/[63] papers,[64] and vehicles,[65] even the more private ones that serve as homes.[52] The lowered expectation of privacy attached to the interior of an automobile is diminished even further by the occupant's arrest, but it's important to note that this rationale itself has limits — the "bright line rule of *Belton"* defines them. The Supreme Court authored this rule in order to make it simple for a cop to decide how far he can extend a search incident to lawful arrest. Basically, it says that such searches may include the entire passenger compartment of a vehicle, including any closed containers inside it, but not the trunk.[65] The glove compartment is considered a "closed container," and the implication is that it's searchable even if locked.[65]/[66] Note that this rule is unconcerned with the concept of probable cause, and is purely related to the search of the grabbable area *inside* the car of an *arrested* person.[65] Thus, it recently happened that the police stopped a car in order to arrest the driver, and one of the passengers promptly alighted with his briefcase and walked away. Although the cops immediately hailed him back and exposed evidence of drug trafficking in his briefcase, the federal appeals court ruled that the search of the bag was unconstitutional under the *Belton* rule; the man had not been *arrested,* and his bag was not *inside* the car when they arrested the others, so the search was invalid![67]

It should be emphasized that the search incident to lawful arrest is an *affirmative right* of the police whenever they make an arrest, irrespective of the nature or locations of the items; they're entitled to go through *everything* that's conceivably within reach.[68] It doesn't even matter that the arrestee may be completely *unable* to reach things within the "grabbable" area; even when the cops themselves are holding the items,[69]/[70] or the arrestee is hog-tied, overpowered, and hopelessly separated from them,[71]/[72] they're still considered to be searchable simply because they *are* within the grabbable area. The nature of the crime which prompts the arrest is also irrelevant; an arrest for using a revoked driver's license entitles them to conduct the same search as one for murder.[68]

A search incident to lawful arrest must necessarily be conducted at the same time and place as the arrest or it isn't truly "incident" to it. The cops can't use this excuse to justify the search of a container or vehicle which takes place sometime later.[73]/[74]

Just as the authority of a lawful arrest gives cops the right to search nearby personalty for weapons and evidence, so does the responsibility of custody give them the right to search any personalty which they hold in storage. This type of intrusion is called an "inventory search," and it represents a very real threat to privacy because there are numerous fortuities by which a person's property can fall into police hands.

Any time a person is arrested away from his home he's likely to have effects, and often a vehicle, in his possession at the time. Upon his being booked in at the police station, all these things are inventoried — that is, they are individually examined and described on a list. This is an administrative step which is designed to fulfil several functions: (1) it gives the cops an opportunity to rummage through their prisoner's things in the privacy and convenience of the station house rather than in view of the public; (2) it protects the owner's property interests by providing an accounting of each item entrusted to police custody; (3) it deters disgruntled citizens from making false claims against the police for theft of their property; (4) it gives the cops a measure of control against the introduction of weapons, drugs, and other security threats into the jailhouse or auto compound; (5) it aids the cops in establishing an arrestee's identity; and (6) in the case of an abandoned vehicle, it gives them an opportunity to ascertain if it's been stolen.[75]/[76]

Automobiles are frequently impounded by the cops, often for unforeseeable reasons. The arrest of a car's occupant[77] or its use in the commission of a crime (whereby it comes to be referred to as an "instrument of crime")[78] are both justifications for the seizure of a vehicle. When a car is involved in a traffic accident which calls for the preservation of evidence, or when an abandoned, disabled, or illegally parked vehicle obstructs the flow of traffic in some way and isn't attended by a qualified driver who can remove it, impoundment can occur.[76]/[79]

During the course of an inventory search, closed containers may be opened in order to make an accurate accounting of their contents.[75] The passenger section of a vehicle[76] and the back part of a camper[79] may be entered whether locked or not, and any unlocked compartments (such as the glove compartment and trunk) may be searched.[76] There's still a degree of controversy over whether it's reasonable to searched a *locked* compartment. The Tenth Federal Circuit, which covers the states of Colorado, Kansas, New Mexico, Oklahoma, Utah, and Wyoming, holds that the police may indeed go into a locked trunk during an inventory search;[77] the Eighth Circuit, which consists of Arkansas, Iowa, Minnesota, Missouri, Nebraska, and the Dakotas, holds that they may not.[80] A consideration which might influence this decision is whether damage must be done in order to open a locked compartment; if so, then it's likely to be an impermissible intrusion for the police to make.[81]

The obvious danger from these inventory searches is that, in the course of their "caretaking functions," the cops will discover evidence that can be used against the owner. Even though it may have been carefully hidden, it will fall into "plain view" once the cops do their inventory search.[78] All altruistic rhetoric aside, their real interest in doing inventory searches is to ferret out evidence, not only for the principal crime being charged, but for unrelated ones as well. It's a free chance for the cops to go fishing in what would otherwise be protected waters, and often results in new criminal charges being brought.[82]/[83]

There are a couple of exceptions to property which must be subjected to an inventory search. It was mentioned in the last chapter that a person's belongings in his hotel room are not subject to police impoundment upon his arrest. The hotel room is considered his "house" even if the cops themselves paid the bill, and the things in a person's house cannot be subjected to search and seizure except by warrant or one of the established exceptions to the warrant requirement. If they aren't impounded, the citizen's things can't be subjected to an inventory search.[84] Another exception is one which may be provided by state law, whereby a person who's taken into temporary protective custody does not have his effects searched. Alaska has such a law, and when the cops there pick up a drunk and put him in the cooler to "sleep it off" he isn't subjected to the usual inventory search. Where there is no specific law to that effect, however, such detainees who are not under formal arrest will have their property searched like anybody else.[85]

"Papers" is a term which is mentioned in the Fourth Amendment as a form of personalty deserving of its protection against unreasonable search and seizure, and it's generally considered to include letters, documents, checks, records, books, and the like. Because they are physical items, they're considered on one hand as "goods and chattels."[86] They differ from other types of property, however, in that their essence as tools of communication allows for their use as testimonial evidence against the owner. The Fifth Amendment, which will be discussed more thoroughly in the following chapter, says that no one should be forced to testify against himself. When a person writes his private thoughts down he risks this very danger, because the cops, who care very little for notions of fair play, will seize such papers and use his own written words to convict him. One's papers, therefore, have the distinction of being dually protected under the Fourth and Fifth Amendments. This privacy aspect as to the contents of papers is exemplified by the federal court holding that, once the government has finished an investigation of a person, it must return to him not only the originals of any papers that were seized, but all copies that were made as well.[87]

Papers can be taken from a person in two ways: the court can order him to voluntarily submit them himself, a process called "subpoena," or the cops can go out and seize them like any other article. Authority for the seizure of records can stem from prior agreement, such as that which a person makes when he accepts a government contract,[88] or it can be based upon a judicial search warrant[89] or one of the established exceptions to the warrant requirement, such as the incident-to-lawful-arrest exception.[64] The Supreme Court has held that less stringent particularity is acceptable in the warranted record searches of white-collar crime investigations, since they tend to be complicated.[90] Like other property, however, papers are protected from search and seizure which doesn't conform to at least a vestige of constitutionality.[91]

If, during the course of investigating a person, the cops want some relevant papers which are in the hands of a third party such as his banker, accountant, or lawyer, they can use the subpoena to get them.[6]/[7]/[8] In order for them to use the subpoena to compel the suspect himself to give up his papers, however, the records sought must be ones which are required by law to be kept. Various occupations are required by statute to keep certain business records, and since there's no legitimate expectation of privacy for these, a person can be compelled to surrender them upon subpoena.[92] Other papers — the ones that are supposed to be "private" — must be seized if the cops want them. A person's Fifth Amendment privilege only relieves him of having to *produce* his papers; most of the constitutional protection of them comes from the Fourth Amendment, and that doesn't always prevent their *production* by someone else.[89]

If the police can't legally do their own seizure, a civilian who has access to the evidence can sometimes be used to unofficially make the snatch for them; evidence that a *civilian* turns up for the police is always usable, regardless of whether he may have violated somebody's constitutional rights to get it.[93] This is something which must be anticipated and guarded against for all types of belongings — papers in your desk, packages you have shipped, things you put into storage — some meddlesome clerk or handler can break in, dig around, and ultimately expose your private affairs to the police, and there's no constitutional protection from the use of such evidence against you.

REFERENCES

1. *U.S. v Kramer*, 711 F2d 789, 792 (7th Cir. 1983)

2. *Illinois v Andreas*, 463 US __, 103 SCt 3319, 3323 (1983)

3. *U.S. v Torres*, 705 F2d 1287, 1292 (11th Cir. 1983)

4. *Rakas v Illinois*, 439 US 128, 148-149, 99 SCt 421, 433 (1978)

5. *U.S. v Salvucci*, 448 US 83, 91-92, 100 SCt 2547, 2552-2553 (1980)

6. *U.S. v Miller*, 425 US 435, 444, 96 SCt 1619, 1624 (1976)

7. *Couch v U.S.*, 409 US 322, 333-335, 93 SCt 611, 618-619 (1973)

8. *Fisher v U.S.*, 425 US 391, 403, 96 SCt 1569, 1577 (1976)

9. *U.S. v One 1977 Mercedes Benz*, 708 F2d 444, 449 (9th Cir. 1983)

10. *U.S. v Dyar*, 574 F2d 1385, 1390 (5th Cir. 1978)

11. *U.S. v Perez*, 689 F2d 1336, 1338 (9th Cir. 1982)

12. *U.S. v Goldstein*, 635 F2d 356, 361 (5th Cir. 1981)

13. *U.S. v Viera*, 644 F2d 509, 510-511 (5th Cir. 1981)

14. *Horton v Goose Creek Independent School District*, 690 F2d 470, 477, 488 (5th Cir. 1982)

15. *Zamora v Pomeroy*, 639 F2d 662, 663-664 (10th Cir. 1981)

16. *U.S. v Beale*, 674 F2d 1327, 1335-1336 (9th Cir. 1982)

17. *U.S. v Tolbert,* 692 F2d 1041, 1045 (6th Cir. 1982)

18. *Frazier v Cupp,* 394 US 731, 740, 89 SCt 1420, 1425 (1969)

19. *Owens v Kelley,* 681 F2d 1362, 1366-1368 (11th Cir. 1982)

20. *U.S. v Ramsey,* 431 US 606, 616, 97 SCt 1972, 1978-1979 (1977)

21. *U.S. v Martinez-Fuerte,* 428 US 543, 558, 96 SCt 3074, 3083 (1976)

22. *Id.,* 428 US at 562, 96 SCt at 3085

23. *Id.,* 428 US at 566-567, 96 SCt at 3087

24. *U.S. v Villamonte-Marquez,* 462 US __, 103 SCt 2573, 2582 (1983)

25. *U.S. v Hidalgo-Gato,* 703 F2d 1267, 1272-1273 (11th Cir. 1983)

26. *Collier v Miller,* 414 FSupp 1357, 1361-1364 (S.D. Tex. 1976)

27. *U.S. v Mason,* D.C. Ct. App., 9/9/82

28. *U.S. v Thompson,* 597 F2d 187, 191 (9th Cir. 1979)

29. *U.S. v Place,* 462 US __, 103 SCt 2637, 2642-2643 (1983)

30. *U.S. v Royer,* 460 US __, 103 SCt 1319, 1325

31. *Id.,* 103 SCt at 2643-2644

32. *Id.,* 103 SCt at 2645-2646

33. *U.S. v Walraff,* 705 F2d 980, 990 (8th Cir. 1983)

34. *U.S. v Best,* 563 FSupp 1075, 1080 (D.D.C. 1983)

35. *Michigan v Long,* 463 US __, 103 SCt 3469, 3473 (1983)

36. *People v Lewis,* 659 P2d 676, 678 (Colo. 1983)

37. *Adams v Williams,* 407 US 143, 144-145, 92 SCt 1921, 1922 (1972)

38. *State v Holbrook,* 33 Wash. App. 692, 657 P2d 797, 798 (Wash. App. 1983)

39. *U.S. v Brignoni-Ponce,* 422 US 876, 884-885, 95 SCt 2574, 2582 (1975)

40. *Id.,* 422 US at 883 n. 8, 95 SCt at 2581 n. 8

41. *State v Luxem,* S.D. Sup. Ct., 9/8/82

42. *People v Clements,* 661 P2d 267, 272 (Colo. 1983)

43. *State v Moore,* 659 P2d 70, 72 (Hawaii 1983)

44. *State v Simpson,* 95 Wash.2d 170, 622 P2d 1199, 1210 (1980)

45. *U.S. v Knotts,* 460 US 276, 103 SCt 1081, 1086 (1983)

46. *Marron v U.S.,* 275 US 192, 196, 48 SCt 74, 76 (1927)

47. *Lo-Ji Inc. v New York,* 442 US 319, 325-326, 99 SCt 2319, 2324 (1979)

48. *Landers v State,* Georgia Sup. Ct., 4/5/83

49. *U.S. v Carroll,* 267 US 132, 153, 45 SCt 280, 285 (1925)

50. *U.S. v Chadwick,* 433 US 1, 12-13, 97 SCt 2476, 2484 (1977)

51. *Almeida-Sanchez v U.S.,* 413 US 266, 279, 93 SCt 2535, 2542 (1973)

52. *People v Chestnut,* Cal. Ct. App., 3d Dist., 1/20/83

53. *U.S. v Nigro,* 727 F2d 100, 106-107 (6th Cir. 1984)

54. *Cardwell v Lewis,* 417 US 583, 594-595, 94 SCt 2464, 2471 (1974)

55. *Cady v Dombrowski,* 413 US 433, 447, 93 SCt 2523, 2531 (1973)

56. *Coolidge v New Hampshire,* 403 US 450, 461-462, 91 SCt 2022, 2035-2036 (1971)

57. *U.S. v Ross,* 456 US 798, 102 SCt 2157, 2172 (1982)

58. *Chambers v Maroney,* 399 US 37, 51-52, 90 SCt 1975, 1981 (1970)

59. *Texas v White,* 423 US 67, 68, 96 SCt 304, 305 (1975)

60. *U.S. v Ortiz,* 422 US 891, 896-897, 95 SCt 2585, 2589 (1975)

61. *Almeida-Sanchez v U.S.,* 413 US at 273, 93 SCt at 2539-2540

62. *Chimel v California,* 395 US 752, 766, 89 SCt 2034, 2041-2042 (1969)

63. *U.S. v Robinson,* 414 US 218, 236, 94 SCt 467, 477 (1973)

64. *Marron v U.S.,* 275 US at 199, 48 SCt at 77

65. *New York v Belton,* 453 US 454, 460-461, 101 SCt 2860, 2864 (1981)

66. *Id.,* 453 US at 472, 101 SCt at 2870, J. White dissenting

67. *U.S. v Vaughan,* 718 F2d 332, 334 (9th Cir. 1983)

68. *U.S. v Robinson,* 414 US at 234-235, 94 SCt at 476

69. *Savoie v State,* Fla. Sup. Ct., 11/10/82

70. *U.S. v Kaye,* 492 F2d 744, 746 (6th Cir. 1974)

71. *People-v-Levan,* N.Y. Sup. Ct., App. Div., 1st Dept., 2/10/83

72. *State v Caraher,* 293 Or. 741, 653 P2d 942, 943, 952 (Or. 1982)

73. *U.S. v Monclavo-Cruz,* 662 F2d 1285, 1290 (9th Cir. 1981)

74. *Preston v U.S.,* 376 US 364, 367-368, 84 SCt 881, 883 (1964)

75. *Illinois v Lafayette,* 462 US _, 103 SCt 2605, 2609-2610 (1983)

76. *South Dakota v Opperman,* 428 US 364, 368-369, 96 SCt 3092, 3097 (1976)

77. *U.S. v Martin,* 566 F2d 1143, 1145 (10th Cir. 1977)

78. *Harris v U.S.,* 390 US 234, 235, 88 SCt 992, 993 (1968)

79. *U.S. v Maier,* 691 F2d 421, 424-425 (8th Cir. 1982)

80. *U.S. v Wilson,* 636 F2d 1163, 1165 (8th Cir. 1980)

81. *State v Cabage,* Tenn. Sup. Ct., 3/21/83

82. *U.S. v Jenkins,* 496 F2d 56, 73-74 (2d Cir. 1974)

83. *People v Richards,* Ill. Sup. Ct., 1/24/83

84. *U.S. v Lyons,* 706 F2d 321, 333-334 (U.S. App. D.C. 1983)

85. *U.S. v Gallop,* 606 F2d 836, 839-840 (9th Cir. 1979)

86. *Boyd v U.S.*, 116 US 616, 6 SCt 524, 531 (1886)

87. *Sovereign News Co. v U.S.*, 690 F2d 569, 577-578 (6th Cir. 1982)

88. *Zap v U.S.*, 328 US 624, 629, 66 SCt 1277, 1279-1280 (1946)

89. *Andresen v Maryland*, 427 US 463, 474, 96 SCt 2737, 2745 (1976)

90. *Id.*, 427 US at 480 n. 10, 96 SCt at 2748-2749 n. 10

91. *Mancusi v DeForte*, 392 US 364, 369, 88 SCt 2120, 2124 (1968)

92. *Shapiro v U.S.*, 335 US 1, 34, 68 SCt 1375, 1393 (1948)

93. *U.S. v Jacobsen*, 466 US __, 104 SCt 1652 1656-1657 (1984)

Part III

THE FIFTH

Chapter 12

THE PRIVACY OF WORDS

"No person... shall be compelled in any criminal case to be a witness against himself... "

The United States Constitution, Amendment V (1787)

In the foregoing chapters we've shown how the Fourth Amendment guarantees a measure of privacy for the physical aspects of our lives. There are, however, other avenues by which the government invades our privacy — those of our thoughts and our words. Just as it can use physical evidence such as fingerprints and contraband, so can it use testimony as evidence to convict a person. "Testimony" consists of a person (the "witness") telling the court ("testifying") what happened. It can be a pretty damaging type of evidence when the testimony suggests guilt, but it's virtually conclusive when the defendant himself provides it.

For as long as the trial has been used to justify punishment, the confession has been a mainstay of the prosecutor's "proof." The ruler can more easily maintain his credibility with the populace if he can get his victims to accuse themselves — that way he doesn't look so much like an oppressor. It was thus that the flowering of a complete technology in confessionary inducements was seen in the Europe of Medieval and Renaissance times. As Justice Black has colorfully written, "the rack, the thumbscrew, the wheel, solitary confinement, protracted questioning and cross questioning and other ingenious forms of entrapment of the helpless or unpopular had left their wake of mutilated bodies and shattered minds along the way to the cross, the guillotine, the stake and the hangman's noose. And they who have suffered most from secret and dictatorial proceedings have almost always been the poor, the ignorant, the numerically weak, the friendless, and the powerless."[1]

Coupled with its undeniable effectiveness as a way of getting things done, compelled confession has a major drawback in its lack of truthfulness. A skillful tormentor can make a person tell things he didn't even know, and that leaves much to be desired by the serious seeker of truth. Moreover, it encourages the natural laziness of a class of individuals already impoverished in ambition and intelligence. As one cop admitted, "it is far pleasanter to sit comfortably in the shade rubbing red pepper into a poor devil's eyes than to go about in the sun hunting up evidence."[2]

The Founding Fathers didn't believe such policies to be a satisfactory substitute for justice, so they specifically declared in the Fifth Amendment that nobody should be forced to bear witness against himself. Their reasons for making this law underscore our most basic concepts of justice and may be summarized as follows:[3] (1) It's unfair to make a person choose between contempt (refusal to answer), perjury (lying), and self-accusation; the court can punish him for any of the three choices, and none of them is both honorable and sensible according to traditional values; (2) The accusatorial system of criminal justice is preferable to the inquisitorial system. The first way, a person is told exactly what it is that he's accused of, and he has a chance to prove his innocence. By the inquisitorial system, however, they probe into an unlimited range of issues and prosecute on whatever turns up. It provides no firm charge that a person can confront and defeat; (3) There's a fear, justified by the lessons of history, that cops will resort to inhumane methods in order to get incriminating statements from their suspects. The incentive for that sort of conduct is removed by prohibiting them from using such evidence; (4) Fair play demands that, except for good cause, the big Frankenstein of government should leave the individual alone... and if it does become necessary to get on his case, the *government* should bear the burden of proving his guilt; (5) Every human being is morally entitled to have a unique personality guided by free will and self-interest, and it's considered unreasonable for any authority to force him to act in a self-destructive manner. Moreover, he needs and deserves at least a small measure of privacy for his thoughts in order to maintain order and stability of mind. Respect for the inviolability of the individual's personality and critical sphere of privacy is at the very heart of Fifth Amendment philosophy; (6) There's a distrust in the truthfulness of self-deprecatory statements. Self-destruction is irrational, and suggests that extraordinary pressures may have been brought to bear upon such an individual. Truth is likely to be disregarded in the effort to escape pressures of this magnitude; and finally, (7) There's a realization that the privilege against self-incrimination protects the innocent as well as sheltering the guilty. It's worth losing many guilty convictions in order to prevent the travesty of a single innocent one.

Forced confessions and any other statements that a person makes under duress are invalid as evidence against him in court, and at trial the defendant has a right to "take the Fifth" and "refuse to answer on the grounds that it may tend to incriminate" him. Compulsory self-incrimination is therefore similar in some ways to evidence which has been acquired by illegal search and seizure. The latter, being a violation of the Fourth, is suppressible from court under the exclusionary rule; the former, being a violation of the Fifth, is suppressible under a privilege of silence.

That the Fourth and Fifth Amendments are closely related — indeed, even functionally intertwined — has been pointed out by the Supreme Court on numerous occasions. Their complementary functions can be viewed as a concerted effort to confer upon the individual citizen a large area of privacy in his life, with room for personal conscience and human dignity.[4]/[5] It's been described as "the right to be let alone — the most comprehensive of rights and the most valued by civilized man."[6] This relationship between the two amendments was, in fact, considered to represent a compelling constitutional basis for adopting the exclusionary rule as standard policy.[7]

It was briefly pointed out in the last chapter that one's personal papers are a type of property by which this close relationship between Fourth and Fifth Amendments can be illustrated. As physical items, they're subject to the protection of the Fourth; as testimonial representations of one's thoughts, they're protected by the Fifth. To the extent that all unreasonable governmental intrusions upon a person's privacy are actually an endeavor to compel him to give up evidence against himself, the whole concept of search and seizure is really a Fifth Amendment issue.[6]/[8] When the cops come poking around in a man's property, asking questions, and placing restrictions on his freedom, they're seeking to force him to give them some kind of evidence which they can use against him. Setting aside all the euphemistic rhetoric about "legitimate authority" and "societal interests," these intrusions are really nothing more than a form of coercion backed up by the artillery, the troops, and the organizational machinery they have at their disposal. Were it not for their military strength, the police would be far less successful than they are at prying incriminating evidence out of the hands and mouths of their suspects.

The privacy of one's statements is constitutionally guaranteed only to the extent that (1) it's recognized by society as legitimate, and (2) the speaker tries to keep it private.[9] Broadly speaking, then, we can think of statements (both spoken and written) as falling into two categories: those which are privileged, and hence protected under the Fifth Amendment, and those which are not.

Privileged statements may consist of (1) one's own spoken statements under certain circumstances, (2) certain papers within one's possession, and (3) certain third-party testimony.

In the first category the most important group of statements includes those which are elicited through custodial interrogation without the suspect's waiver of his right to be silent or his right to counsel. If that sounds like a mouthful of legal double talk, don't feel alone; even the courts are confused about the fine points of that one. It'll become clear in the next chapter, which is devoted primarily to that subject, so it needs only a passing mention for now.

The other group of statements that the speaker has a right to expect won't be used as evidence against him consists of those which have been overheard by the police through illegal electronic surveillance. Federal law says that the cops can't bug or wiretap a private conversation without either a warrant or the consent of one of the conversants.[10] This means that (1) if they don't have a valid warrant for eavesdropping on a particular conversation, and (2) if none of the people talking happens to be an undercover cop, the statements made during the conversation can't be used as criminal evidence against any of them. This is a statutory law, and unlike the state of affairs with a purely constitutional violation, *all* the parties to an illegally monitored conversation are potentially eligible to challenge it in court. That they didn't own the place that was bugged, or weren't the ones being charged with a crime, doesn't preclude their right to challenge the evidence.[11]/[12]

In the category of privileged written statements, it's generally recognized that some element of a *personal* nature must attach. When they're one's own papers this condition is more easily met, but the distinction between "personal" and "official" is still made. Business records that a sole proprietor or practitioner keeps for his own exclusive use are usually considered personal enough to qualify for privileged status. Non-business economic records, such as cancelled personal checks and tax records, are also privileged provided that they haven't been disclosed to other people. Once something has been shown around, it loses most of its expectation of privacy for legal purposes. Even though a personal letter is by nature given disclosure to at least one other person, the law still recognizes it as private if it has received only limited exposure. A personal diary is unquestionably a privileged writing.[13]

When someone is holding papers which don't belong to him, there's some possibility that these too might be privileged from disclosure; he must show that he has them in a purely personal, non-official capacity.[14] Remember, however, that the "privileged" status of personal papers refers only to their immunity from *subpoena;* as physical articles, even the most intimate of them can be entered into evidence if the cops can somehow *independently* get their hands on them (i.e. officially seizing them, having a third party sneak them out, etc.).[15]

The third category of privileged communications consists of that testimony which other people bear as a result of their role in certain confidential relationships. The law generally considers the courts to be presumptively entitled to hear "every man's evidence,"[16] and shows no sympathy at all for an individual's preference not to testify against a friend. It's a major part of the grand scheme of government control over the masses; keep them in line by dividing loyalties so that every individual can be used as an informer against the next.[17] There are, however, a few relationships that even the government is prepared to recognize as being so important that they shouldn't be threatened by the prospect of broken confidence. Provided that (1) a relationship is worthy of being fostered by society, (2) it's dependent for its continued existence upon confidentiality, (3) the nature of its communications is indeed confidential, and (4) damage to the relationship by a breach of confidence would outweigh the societal benefits from it, the courts are prepared to recognize a privilege against requiring the parties to testify against each other.[18] Such privileged standing for third-party testimony isn't absolute; it's governed by previous court decisions, and doled out "in light of reason and experience."[19] If a court is convinced that societal interests are compelling enough, as in a case of child abuse, it might decline to recognize certain testimonial privileges.[20] On the other hand, courts can also create new, previously unrecognized ones if they see fit.[21]

The best known of these is the spousal privilege, whereby neither partner in a marriage can be forced to testify against the other. It's the currently active state of the marriage which makes the privilege valid, so it covers any testimony that a spouse is capable of giving, even that pertaining to events which took place prior to marrying. Being a *privilege*, however, it's only claimable by the spouse who's the potential witness; the other one doesn't have a standing to object if his (or her) partner decides to rat.[22]

Some courts have found the parent-child relationship to be at least as deserving of a privilege as the spousal one.[23] There's no question that the healthiness of this relationship is fundamental to the very fabric of society. Nevertheless, there are some courts which will jail a child who refuses to testify against her parents.[24] Such proceedings bring to mind the well-known story of Pavlik Morozov, the youngster who became a Soviet national hero by snitching off his parents to Stalin's secret police.[23]

Another well-recognized context of privileged communications is the clergy-penitent relationship; what a person tells his priest in the confessional is supposed to remain strictly between himself and Le Bon Dieu.[25]/[26]

Similarly, if one's spiritual salubrity demands a privilege against disclosure of what he tells his priest, so does his mental well-being demand it for the disclosures he makes to his analyst. Of all the different types of doctor-patient relationships, that with the psychotherapist is the only one which carries a universally-recognized privilege of confidentiality[27]/[28] In order to merit the testimonial privilege, it should be a true doctor-patient relationship as judged by the standard conduct of examination, diagnosis, treatment, and follow-up visits.[20] Some courts have additionally recognized certain quasi-psychotherapeutic relationships as bearing a testimonial privilege. Examples of these include the relationships between a client (or student) and his marriage counselor, social worker, teacher, guidance counselor, or school psychologist.[27]

The attorney-client relationship is likely to produce plenty of information which the client expects to be kept secret. Indeed, due process of law demands that he be able to confidently disclose anything to his lawyer that may be pertinent to planning his legal defense. The belief that *nothing* between a client and his attorney can be divulged is a popular *misconception,* however. Those communications which are generally recognized as privileged include (1) confidential disclosures, (2) the attorney's "work product," and (3) certain papers belonging to the client.

Confidential disclosures which are made to a lawyer in order to obtain legal assistance are among the most sacred of all privileged communications, and are recognized as such by either statute or common law in all jurisdictions of the United States.[29] Without the public's reliance on this tenet, many people would be afraid to fill their lawyers in on important incriminating facts, and adequate legal defense would be impossible.[30]

"Work product" refers to any writings (e.g. work notes) which an attorney makes in the process of preparing his client's case. It reflects his thoughts on the case, as well as the results of his interviews and investigations, and is accorded a privileged status, although not as inviolate as that of the client's confidential disclosures.[31]

When a person turns over to his lawyer papers which are testimonial in nature (and therefore priviliged against being subpoenaed from his own hands), they carry with them that same privilege while they're in the custody of the lawyer. The courts can no more order the lawyer to hand them over than they could order the client to do so.[30]

Having thus outlined the different categories of privileged communications, we might simplistically dismiss the subject of non-privileged communications as being "everything else." That would leave the story half-untold, however, because much of what's discussed below represents closely drawn exceptions to those categories of privileged statements we've just discussed. Moreover, there are many interpersonal relationships and situations of daily living which the average person is likely to assume are private, but which actually have no expectation of privacy at all. Since the whole object of this book is to point out these legal snares that the cops are so fond of setting, it would be negligent not to devote some detailed discussion to non-privileged statements.

One's own spoken statements are nearly always devoid of any privilege; after all, people don't usually say things that they don't intend others to hear — and if they intend them to be heard, the statements are hardly "secret." The spontaneous volunteering of information is usually sufficient to guarantee that it can be used against the blabbermouth in court.[32] It doesn't matter in the least that a person might intend for his statements to be kept in strictest confidence by a trusted friend, because it's a hard fact of life that one's best friend can turn out to be a snitching dog.[33] Often, the cops will insinuate an undercover agent into a group for the purpose of trapping them into incriminating themselves. Statements which are gathered in this way are usable as evidence, regardless of whether the agent may be "wired" for electronic transmission of the conversation.[34] As was pointed out earlier, the federal anti-bugging laws permit them to burglarize people's conversations as long as one of the conversants (the cop) has "given consent."[10] In the Eleventh Circuit (Alabama, Florida and Georgia) the courts even permit police to freely plant listening devices in their suspects' *rooms*; thus, they can send in an agent who isn't "wired" and still get the conversation on tape.[35] The agent doesn't risk being caught wearing a wire, and the suspects aren't aware that they're "on the air" unless they do an electronic "sweep" of the room and discover the bug. In using such strategy the cops are relying upon their statutory right to bug conversations where one of their agents is a participant. The potential for them to activate such warrantless bugs in the *absence* of their undercover agent raises strong Fourth Amendment questions, however (C.f. Chapter 9). It's for this reason that the First Circuit (Maine, Massachusetts, New Hampshire, Rhode Island, and Puerto Rico) has ruled against such practices.[36]

In places where a person has no legitimate expectation of privacy, such as a police squad car[37] or a prison visiting room,[38] the courts have held that passive listening devices may be used, and the conversations which they happen to pick up are admissible as evidence. Where such bugging is conducted as a general security measure, rather than a surreptitious investigative technique, it's been considered justifiable.

Papers which aren't personal in nature don't qualify for a privilege against subpoena. Business records which are required by law to be kept — sales invoices, etc. by which the government seeks to keep tabs on the flow of commerce — might even be said to have public aspects to them, and carry an implicit duty of disclosure.[39] When one takes custody of an organization's papers in an official capacity, those too must be surrendered upon subpoena. A corporate officer, for example, can't expect to withhold his company's records from the police by taking them home with him; even if they do implicate him personally in some crime, he holds them in an official rather than a personal capacity, and must surrender them upon a court order.[14]

Third-party testimony, the backbone of courtroom evidence, is rarely privileged; the spousal, clerical, psychotherapeutical, and attorney-client privileges are about the only ones which can be expected as a matter of course, and some aspects even of these aren't afforded the privilege.

The psychotherapist, for example, is not given a privilege against testifying about a person with whom he had no true doctor-patient relationship. A brief visit to his office for a conversation about one of his patients, or to pick up a prescription for some Ludes, doesn't qualify as a bona fide psychotherapeutic relationship.[20]/[40] Pretrial evaluations of a suspect by state-appointed mental health professionals are likewise devoid of the privilege; their professional titles shouldn't belie the fact that they're acting as cops in the adversary process, not as doctors who have their patients' interests at heart.[41] There are some quasi-therapeutic aspects of counselling services which the courts are also unlikely to recognize a privilege for, such as that of draft counselor.[25]

Of the attorney-client relationship, which the average person naively assumes to be a form of sanctuary, there's a surprisingly large range of communications which carry no privilege against disclosure. Non-confidential statements, for example, are subject to the same disclosure by a lawyer as they would be if made to anyone.[42]/[43] Even *confidential* disclosures, which should by rights be inviolate, are subject to release under certain circumstances.[44] The latest code of ethics adopted by the American Bar Association says that an attorney can snitch off his client concerning things which were told to him in confidence if it's necessary in order to prevent the client from committing a crime which might cause bodily harm to someone. Furthermore, if he needs to divulge a client's secrets in order to get himself off the hook, he can do that, too. Such unpleasant situations as a legal controversy with a client, a client's allegations of professional misconduct by the lawyer, and civil or criminal action against the client which might suck the lawyer in as a codefendent, are all grounds for an attorney to wiggle out of his obligation of confidentiality.

Any papers that a lawyer holds for his client, which are impersonal enough to be subpoenaed from the client himself, can likewise be subpoenaed from the lawyer.[42] So can the lawyer's "work product" papers if the court deems it necessary because it can't get the data from any other source.[31]

The attorney-client relationship is not legally recognized when the "attorney" isn't authorized to practice law. Lay people such as draft counselors and probation officers frequently counsel others in matters pertaining to the law, but there's no testimonial privilege attached to such relationships.[25]/[45]

The doctor-patient relationship has been listed here instead of with the privileged communications because (except for psychotherapists) doctors aren't universally invested with a testimonial privilege concerning their patients. Some state statutes do provide for it, but neither common law nor federal law recognizes the privilege,[28]/[40] and it's probably safer not to expect it. Patient files,[40] as well as the names of patients who attend particular types of clinics,[28]/[46] have been subpoenaed over the objections of the doctors in charge of them.

Notwithstanding the courageous resolution displayed over the years by members of the press who went to jail rather than give up the identity of their informants, a reporter-informant privilege is still not recognized by the courts.[47] Confidential business relationships, such as those between a client and his banker or accountant, are likewise unprotected by testimonial privilege.[48]/[49]

We've been speaking here about privacy expectations concerning the statements that people make, but there's another category of evidence that involves no testimonial "statements" at all, yet demands varying degrees of compliance which border on self-incrimination. This is the so-called "nontestimonial evidence" that a suspect is forced to give against himself by performing certain acts or surrendering samples from his body. The Fifth Amendment doesn't protect a person against this type of seizure,[50] but the Fourth and Fourteenth Amendments do to a certain extent. The Fourteenth, which purports to guarantee that the legal process will be applied fairly and evenly to each suspect, is brought into this issue by the need to curb the overzealous actions of the cops. These fools see themselves as crusaders on a holy mission against the odious forces of the Devil, and their concern for the Devil's rights (if any) tends to be quickly outweighed by their eagerness to get evidence of his guilt. The nature and degree of the physical intrusion, as well as a consideration for due process in conducting it, is the focus of the Fourteenth Amendment concern over the gathering of this kind of evidence.[51] The lack of suspect participation required for the delivery of the evidence is the focus of attention where the courts have played down its testimonial nature and denied its entitlement to Fifth Amendment protection.[52]

Examples of such "nontestimonial evidence" include posing before witnesses (the "identification lineup"), speaking aloud for them,[53] modeling incriminating clothing,[54] and giving samples of one's handwriting for comparison analysis.[55]/[56] Of a less participatory nature are such things as the taking of fingerprints, photographs, measurements, and samples of body tissue (e.g. blood).[50] None of these types of evidence are considered to be "testimonial" in the sense of providing a confession, but there's no question that, in providing them, the suspect is helping to cops to convict him. In some states the refusal to submit nontestimonial evidence can even be held as an *assumption of guilt;* a motorist in South Dakota, for example, can be convicted of drunk driving on the basis of his *refusal* to give the cops a blood sample for alcohol testing![57] If the refusal to give evidence can itself be evidence, one wonders how long it will be in this country before the failure to confess will be considered to be a confession...

REFERENCES

1. *Chambers v Florida*, 309 US 227, 237-238, 60 SCt 472, 477 (1940)

2. 1 Stephen (Sir James Fitzjames Stephen), *A History of the Criminal Law of England*, note 442 (1883)

3. *Murphy v Waterfront Commission of New York Harbor*, 378 US 52, 55, 84 SCt 1594, 1596-1597 (1964)

4. *U.S. v Feldman*, 322 US 487, 489-490, 64 SCt 1082, 1083 (1944)

5. *Frank v Maryland*, 359 US 360, 376, 79 SCt 804, 814 (1959), J. Douglas dissenting

6. *Olmstead v U.S.*, 277 US 438, 473, 48 SCt 564, 570 (1928), J. Brandeis dissenting

7. *Mapp v Ohio*, 367, US 643, 662, 81 SCt 1684, 1695 (1961), J Black concurring

8. *Boyd v U.S.*, 116 US 616, 633, 6 SCt 524, 534 (1886)

9. *U.S. v Katz*, 389 US 347, 351, 88 SCt 507, 511 (1967)

10. Title III of the Omnibus Crime Control and Safe Streets Act of 1968, Title 18 U.S.C. Sections 2510 et seq.

11. *Alderman v U.S.*, 394 US 165, 179-180 n. 11, 89 SCt 961, 969-970 n. 11 (1969)

12. *U.S. v Dorfman*, 690 F2d 1230, 1235 (7th Cir. 1982)

13. *Fisher v U.S.*, 425 US 391, 426-427, 96 SCt 1569, 1589 (1976)

14. *U.S. v White*, 322 US 694, 699, 64 SCt 1248, 1251 (1944)

15. *Andresen v Maryland*, 427 US 463, 472-473, 96 SCt 2737, 2744-2745 (1976)

16. *U.S. v Bryan*, 339 US 323, 331, 70 SCt 724, 730 (1950)

17. *Roberts v U.S.*, 445 US 552, 557-558, 100 SCt 1358, 1362-1363 (1980)

18. *In re Agosto*, 553 FSupp 1298, 1308 (D. Nev. 1983)

19. *Trammel v U.S.*, 445 US 40, 47, 100 SCt 906, 910 (1980)

20. *People v Stritzinger*, Cal. Ct. App., 2d Dist., 10/29/82

21. *In re Agosto*, 553 FSupp at 1324

22. *Trammel v U.S.*, 445 US at 53, 100 SCt at 914

23. *In re Agosto*, 553 FSupp at 1325

24. *In re Grand Jury Proceedings*, 647 F2d 511, 512-513 (5th Cir. 1981)

25. *In re Verplank*, 329 FSupp 433, 436-437 (C.D. Cal. 1971)

26. *U.S. v Nixon*, 418 US 683, 709, 94 SCt 3090, 3108 (1974)

27. *In re Agosto*, 553 FSupp at 1303

28. *In re Verplank*, 329 FSupp at 438

29. *In re Agosto*, 553 FSupp at 1306-1307

30. *Fisher v U.S.*, 425 US at 403-404, 96 SCt at 1577-1578

31. *Upjohn v U.S.*, 449 US 383, 401-402, 101 SCt 677, 688-689 (1981)

32. *Miranda v Arizona*, 384 US 436, 478, 86 SCt 1602, 1630 (1966)

33. *U.S. v Hoffa*, 385 US 293, 302-303, 87 SCt 408, 413-414 (1966)

34. *U.S. v White*, 401 US 745, 751-752, 91 SCt 1122, 1126 (1971)

35. *U.S. v Yonn*, 702 F2d 1341, 1347 (11th Cir. 1983)

36. *U.S. v Padilla*, 520 F2d 526, 528 (1st Cir. 1975)

37. *People v Seaton*, Cal. Ct. App., 3d Dist., 1/17/83

38. *U.S. v Hearst*, 563 F2d 1331, 1344, 1348 (9th Cir. 1977)

39. *U.S. v Shapiro*, 335 US 1, 34-35, 68 SCt 1375, 1393 (1948)

40. *In re Doe*, 711 F2d 1187, 1193 (2d Cir. 1983)

41. *State v Holland,* 98 Wash.2d 507, 656 P2d 1056, 1063-1064 (Wash. 1983)

42. *Fisher v U.S.,* 425 US at 403, 96 SCt at 1577

43. *In re Agosto,* 553 FSupp at 1312

44. *American Bar Association (A.B.A.) Model Rules of Professional Conduct,* Rule 1.6: Confidentiality of Information (1983)

45. *Fare v Michael C.,* 439 US 1310, 1315, 99 SCt 3, 6 (1978)

46. *People v Florendo,* Ill. Sup. Ct., 1/24/83

47. *Branzburg v Hayes,* 408 US 665, 706-708, 92 SCt 2646, 2669-2670 (1972)

48. *U.S. v Payner,* 447 US 727, 732 n. 4, 100 SCt 2439, 2444 n. 4 (1980)

49. *U.S. v Couch,* 409 US 322, 335, 93 SCt 611, 619 (1973)

50. *Schmerber v California,* 384 US 757, 761, 86 SCt 1826, 1830-1831 (1966)

51. *Roschin v California,* 342 US 165, 172-173, 72 SCt 205, 209-210 (1952)

52. *Schmerber v California,* 384 US at 765, 86 SCt at 1832-1833

53. *U.S. v Wade,* 388 US 218, 222-223, 87 SCt 1926, 1930 (1967)

54. *Holt v U.S.,* 218 US 245, 252, 31 SCt 2, 6 (1910)

55. *Gilbert v California,* 388 US 263, 266-267, 87 SCt 1951, 1953 (1967)

56. *U.S. v Hawkins,* 501 F2d 1029, 1032 (9th Cir. 1974)

57. *South Dakota v Neville,* __ US, __ 103 SCt 916, 918 (1983)

Chapter 13

MIRANDA AND THE SEIZURE OF WORDS

"In all criminal prosecutions, the accused shall enjoy the right... to have the Assistance of Counsel for his defense."

The United States Constitution, Amendment VI (1787)

In the United States, the Fifth Amendment says that a person's words — what we've referred to as "testimonial evidence" — may not be squeezed out of him and used to convict him of a crime.[1] This testimonial evidence consists of everything which we've discussed in the last chapter under the broad category of "privileged statements," and additionally includes any kind of test results based upon physiological responses (as lie detector results are).[2]

Volunteered statements, however, can be used by the cops in a variety of ways. First, the statement itself can be used as *evidence* against the speaker; careless remarks which imply that the person *knows* something about a crime can be used in court as evidence that he was, in fact, *involved* in it. Second, a statement can be used as a *lead* toward finding other evidence against the speaker. Since a person has no expectation of privacy in a statement that he spontaneously blurts out, the inculpatory evidence which his remark points the cops to is not "fruit of the poisonous tree" (C.f. Chapter 5), and can be used against him. Third, a person's volunteered statements can be used to *"impeach"* his credibility at trial; when he attempts to give testimony that supports his innocence, and it doesn't jive with the earlier volunteered statements he's made, the prosecutor can bring out the statements in order to show the jury that he's a liar.

In some instances, even that which a person doesn't say — his silence — can be used against him to impeach (discredit) his testimony or enhance the punishment he gets upon conviction. Like a volunteered statement, silence is not forced; and it's the element of *force* which invokes the spirit of the Fifth Amendment.

In analyzing the admissibility of a person's statements as evidence against him, it's useful to identify the precise time at which he becomes a defendant. Up until that point, he's simply another citizen who may happen to be questioned as part of a criminal investigation.

During this early investigatory phase, a person's failure to come forward with information about a crime can constitute material for the impeachment of his testimony at trial. Consider, for example, a man who kills in self-defense but attempts to escape notice by keeping quiet about it. When he's eventually identified and brought to trial, the prosecutor can destroy the credibility of his claim to self-defense by pointing out that his silence was inconsistent with conduct expected of an innocent man.[3]

Statements which are foolishly volunteered during the investigatory phase can be used as primary evidence against the speaker. Because of the *Miranda* Rule, which will be discussed shortly, it's usually necessary for the cops to warn a suspect that his statements can be used against him; if they fail to give the warning they can't use the statements. In the investigatory phase, however, the person hasn't been accused yet, and the warning isn't required. It doesn't matter that they may have focused their attention on a particular person, because it's still just an investigation.[4] Anybody gullible enough to even *talk* to a criminal investigator, much less volunteer statements to him, risks having his words used as evidence against him at trial... the lack of *Miranda* warnings notwithstanding.[5]

Once a person has been marked for prosecution and taken into police custody he has entered the "adversary" phase of the criminal process; he's officially "in trouble." The adversary phase begins the moment a person is either indicted or arrested, whichever comes first.[6] The term "adversary" means "opponent" or "enemy," and that's a pretty good assessment of the relationship between the government and a criminal suspect. Any illusions of cordiality that may have existed previously should be dispelled with the onset of the adversary phase; it's all-out war from then on.

For this reason, the early adversary phase is an especially critical period for the suspect; the cops will do anything they can to solidify the evidence against him. Much of their activity in this regard is cloaked under the guise of legitimate procedure, so the average person wouldn't even suspect that he's being taken advantage of. It isn't until he gets into court that he realizes that those friendly cops who drove him back to town had successfully baited him for statements implying guilt, that his identification lineup was a prejudicial farce, and that his "homey" in the county jail cell was really a paid informer assigned to get disclosures from him. Such slimy police tactics have led the Supreme Court to rule that a person should be allowed to have his lawyer's assistance at any proceedings during the adversary phase — lineups, interrogation, psychological evaluations, etc.[7] With the suspect's lawyer there to look out for his interests, the cops have to stay relatively honest, and the suspect is guarded against the unwitting release of damaging evidence from his own lips.

"... the efficiency of the rack and the thumb-screw can be matched, given the proper subject, by more sophisticated modes of 'persuasion.'"

Chief Justice Earl Warren in *Blackburn v Alabama*, 361 US 199, 206, 80 SCt 274, 279 (1960)

Infused with the conviction that it's sound police work to use a little pressure to get the truth out of a suspect, the boys in blue have developed over the years a whole technology of interrogation methods designed to physically and psychologically exhaust the will to resist.[8] In the old days they'd isolate the suspect in a windowless room where there would be no witnesses except the police interrogators themselves. The suspect would be seated in the center of the room, often with a low-hanging light directed on him, and the cops would alternately fire questions at him and slap him around to keep his attention. These "third degree" sessions might go on for days, usually with denial of food and sleep. Sometimes they'd even threaten to kill the suspect if he didn't confess. Since these kinds of tactics were too close to torture, the police were eventually forced to modify the interrogation process by refraining from beating the suspect and allowing him to eat and sleep at intervals. Psychological ploys, rather than terror, became the principal "swords of truth."

The atmosphere of police domination, the isolation from supportive family and friends, and the aura of confidence in the suspect's guilt remained as the framework for the interrogation process, and a variety of tricks were devised to capitalize on the suspect's insecurity in this setting. Most of them rely on a suspect's lack of critical perception concerning inference and deduction — the very skills that a lawyer is expert in.

They might pose the assumption of guilt as a fact, and sucker the suspect into explaining his reasons (Example: "We already have proof that you're guilty, Al, but we'd just like to confirm some of the details about *why* you did it... "). Similarly, they might coax out an explanation by minimizing the moral seriousness of the crime and casting blame on the victim or on society (Example: "it wasn't *your* fault you did it, Bob; anybody would have gotten angry in that kind of situation. Besides, the son-ofabitch was asking for it. Everybody knows what a scumbag he is..."). Another ploy they can use is to give false legal advice. For example, the cop might create the illusion of fairness by showing the suspect that he's willing to allow him to stay silent, but then put the scare in about how bad it will look later if he doesn't talk, and how innocent people don't have anything to hide. If the police can offer the suspect a defense explanation long enough to coax an admission out of him, they can then come back around with some controverting circum-stantial evidence that might rattle him enough to tell the whole story (Example: "Okay, Chuck, we can maybe buy your story about shooting this dude in self-defense, because he did have a gun... but now, how are we going to explain the fact that you went over to his place carrying a gun *yourself?*").

Some interrogative ploys involve staging an act in order to set up the suspect to make an incriminating statement. A phony identification lineup might be conducted, for example, where the suspect is falsely picked out for a crime he didn't do; the threat of a frameup might thereby induce him to cooperate with interrogators. Alternatively, they might confront him with the news that his partner had talked and put the blame on him — or that his fingerprints were found at the scene of the crime. Though untrue, such stories might upset a person enough to make him crack. The most famous of these theatrical-type ploys is the "Mutt and Jeff" or "Good cop-Bad cop" act. The bad cop pounds his chest, acts deranged, and generally intimidates the suspect, whereupon the good cop intercedes and, having won the suspect's trust and gratitude, proceeds to take a statement. If the suspect starts to clam up, the good cop will threaten to turn him back over to the bad cop, who's "not such a nice guy."

Sometimes the cops would simply let the suspect's imagination go to work for them; leaving him sitting naked in an interrogation room is likely to prime all manner of suspicions and fears about what's going to happen next. If all their tricks fail, the cops can still attempt to impress the suspect with their inexorable will to get the truth. They'll dismiss and discourage any explanations of innocence, doggedly maintaining that the suspect is guilty, and that they won't relent until he "comes clean."

It was against the background of such interrogation practices that in 1966 the U.S. Supreme Court created its famous *Miranda* Rule — a procedural safe-guard designed to assure that every criminal suspect will at least be aware that he has some rights. The Rule says that, before the cops can question somebody who's in custody, they have to tell him about his rights against self-incrimination under the Fifth and Sixth Amendments.[9] Most cops aren't bright enough to remember them, so they carry around little printed cards from which they can "read him his rights."

There are four basic elements to these *Miranda* warnings: (1) You have the right to remain silent; (2) Anything you say can and will used as evidence against you; (3) You have the right to have an attorney present during questioning; and (4) If you can't afford an attorney you have the right to have a free appointed one. The exact words may differ slightly, but the cops are obligated to get across the general idea of each of these four warnings before they question an arrestee. The only exception to the Rule is that failure to give the fourth warning has been excused in a few cases where there was no doubt that the suspect had his own attorney and ample funds.[10]/[11]/[12]

As we've stated, the *Miranda* warnings don't have to be given to everybody the cops talk to; it's only when "custodial interrogation" is about to occur that they're absolutely required. "Custodial" refers to being under arrest, or something of the sort. It might begin when a suspect is accused of the crime,[13] when guns are drawn,[14] or when any other such event puts the suspect under police custody or significantly restricts his freedom.[9] An arrest on a misdemeanor charge, such as a traffic violation, demands a recitation of the *Miranda* warnings as surely as does a felony arrest.[15] If the suspect is a prisoner who's already locked up for something else, the situation becomes "custodial" when any *change* in his surroundings *adds* an additional imposition against his freedom of action — such as being interviewed by a police investigator.[16] An investigator must give a prisoner *Miranda* warnings, regardless of the reason for his being in custody, and regardless of the fact that it may not initially be a criminal investigation.[17] Thus, even a pretrial proceeding which involves testimonial questioning (e.g. a psychological evaluation) demands that *Miranda* warnings be given first.[18]

Many situations which the public commonly assumes are "custodial" are really merely investigative inquiries and don't require that *Miranda* warnings be given. On-the-scene questioning, where the cops are trying to get facts to determine whether a crime has been committed, is one such setting.[19] Interviews which are voluntarily conducted — such as when someone invites tax investigators into his home for talks, or when he goes down to the police station on his own for a discussion with a detective — also fall into this category, even though the person may already be singled out as the primary suspect.[4/20] Blocking the exit of a person's car doesn't mean that he's under arrest,[14] and just because questioning happens to take place in a police station it doesn't mean that the person isn't free to leave.[20/21] Oddly enough, even witnessing before a grand jury isn't considered a custodial situation, and as in these other situations, no *Miranda* warnings are required.[22]

Being in custody is the threshold condition needed for compulsory *Miranda* warnings, but it's also necessary that there indeed be some sort of "interrogation" — either express questioning or the functional equivalent of it. Even *actions* on the part of the police which they should know would be likely to elicit an incriminating response can be considered a form of interrogation.[23] An example would be the placement of a paid informant into a prisoner's cell with the objective of picking up information from him. Even if the cops explicitly tell their snitch to merely *listen* for things, there's a probability that he'll be actively drilling for information in the hope of being better rewarded. The cops ought to realize that this might occur, and that makes the whole scheme a form of interrogation which is illegal without *Miranda* warnings.

Accusation[13] and giving a speech which appeals to the sentiments[24] are both ways of provoking a suspect's response without actually asking a question; they too are forms of interrogation. Some questions are inevitably part of the normal routine of booking an arrestee into jail — one's name, address, etc. These kinds of questions are not "interrogation," but anything else — questions about one's personal property, for example — would be.[25]

It can often be a very fine line that distinguishes between interrogation and mere conversation. A quip, for example, or comments between officers which aren't directed at the suspect, generally wouldn't be considered interrogation.[23]/[26] Neither would it be interrogation when a policeman attempts to clarify what the suspect means by his equivocal response to the *Miranda* warnings. Naturally, a person must understand what they mean or the warnings would be pointless. If a cop isn't sure whether the suspect understands, wants a lawyer, or what, then he's entitled to ask enough questions to clear up any misunderstanding; this isn't considered interrogation.[27]

Though the *Miranda* Rule is unquestionably a mighty bulwark for the citizen, particularly the poor or uneducated one, it's regarded by law-and-order buffs as a symbol of judicial coddling of the criminal.[28] Within the conservative government of today there are powerful currents at work seeking an opportunity to do away with it.

Once a person has been given the *Miranda* warnings, and understands them, there are three possible responses that he can make: (1) he can invoke his constitutional rights, (2) he can waive them, or (3) he can do neither (what we shall refer to here as a "non-waiver"). The *Miranda* Rule speaks of two basic rights — that of being silent and that of having an attorney. Thus, we must consider separately the consequences of invoking or waiving each of these rights.

When a person invokes his right to silence — when he tells the cop that he doesn't wish to talk — all interrogation must cease immediately.[5] Any questions they ask after that are improper according to the *Miranda* Rule, and they can't use the answers as evidence. The cops don't have to tell the defendant that he can shut up their questioning this way, but they are obligated to respect his wishes and stop promptly upon his request.[29] It isn't clear how long they have to wait before they can try starting up interrogation again after being turned down,[30]/[31] but it would definitely be illegal for them to badger somebody after he had plainly said he didn't want to talk. When the subject of their inquiry is a *new* crime, however — different from the one the suspect invoked his silence on — they can reinitiate interrogation immediately (after giving a new set of *Miranda* warnings, of course).[32]

When a person invokes his right to have an attorney present, this too has the effect of immediately turning off all interrogation.[33] The cops don't have to provide an attorney immediately — they can delay it for a while if they want to do some more field investigation first — but they can't do any interrogation in the meantime.[34] Unlike the situation with an invocation of silence, it's quite settled that after invoking the right to counsel the cops can't come back later and attempt to reinitiate interrogation unless either (1) they furnish a lawyer, or (2) the defendent himself initiates further communication, effectively opening the door for their questions.[33] Merely asking for his lunch doesn't constitute the initiation of communications we're talking about here; the suspect has to show a willingness to start up a discussion *about the investigation,* and he also has to *knowingly waive* his right to an attorney.[35]

Should the cops wish to reinitiate interrogation concerning a new, unrelated crime, it's not as simple a matter as with the invocation of silence. Some courts have allowed it,[36]/[37] while others have not.[38]/[39] The problem doesn't usually occur when the new crime is being investigated by the same bunch of cops who gave the initial *Miranda* warnings; they already know about the suspect's request for a lawyer, so they (properly) leave him alone. It's when cops from a different jurisdiction come in and start interrogation about a new crime that the potential for a *Miranda* violation exists. The question is basically one of responsibility; should cops be responsible for ascertaining whether or not a prisoner has already invoked his right to counsel before attempting to interrogate him about a new crime? It's another grey area in the law which could go either way in court.

Another effect of invoking one's right to counsel is that any subsequent consent that he gives them without having his lawyer present becomes invalid. Should the police act upon such invalid consent — to search his home, for example — none of the evidence they find can be used in court. Only by first *withdrawing* his request for counsel, and then waiving the right, can his consent be made valid.[40]

Somewhere between the definite invocation and the definite waiver of one's *Miranda* rights there exists what we might call a "non-waiver." Its effect is to prevent the assumption of a waiver, and in doing so it tends to keep the person's rights alive. Silence is a non-waiver. When a person fails to ask for a lawyer, or refuses to sign the waiver form which the cops often present after they give *Miranda* warnings, it doesn't mean that he has given up his rights; he has simply remained silent on the issue.[41]/[42]/[43] Likewise, an equivocal response is also a non-waiver. When a cop gives the *Miranda* warnings and his suspect says "I think I should call my lawyer," it leaves open the question of exactly what the guy really wants to do. A normal human being would interpret such a statement as being an invocation of the right to counsel, but alas — cops and judges are neither normal nor human. If the person speculates about whether he should have a lawyer, rather than coming right out and demanding one, he's making a non-waiver, and the police are justified in asking more questions in order to clarify his wishes. Something like "Do you want to talk about it?" would be proper under the circumstances, and not at all violative of the *Miranda* Rule.[27]

Waiver of one's rights means that the person knowingly gives them up; he realizes he's entitled to them, and nevertheless wishes to cast them aside. It has sagely been said that there's no such thing as an intelligent, voluntary waiver of Fifth Amendment rights[44] (indeed, this author would expand that claim to include the other amendments as well). Waiver of one's right against self-incrimination, however, is especially irrational; it's far easier to imagine an intelligent decision to commit suicide than an intelligent decision to deliver oneself into the hands of hostile mental defectives.

The cops would claim that confession is good for the soul, and that the relief it affords the guilty conscience is compensation for the consequent punishment. There's much that doesn't go into a person's "intelligent" decision to waive his right to silence, however. When the cops attempt to convince a suspect that he should "make a clean breast of things," they don't tell him what all the consequences will be. They don't tell him that it'll cost him all his savings and everything he owns to pay the legal fees; that it'll kill whatever professional, occupational, or business opportunities he's managed to build during this lifetime; that it'll destroy his marriage, deprive his children, and wreak untold mental hurt upon those he loves; that it'll consign him to an endless succession of insults, deprivations, and torment at the hands of inferiors and petty tyrants; that it may result in his death or loss of health; and that, if he does finally get out alive, he'll always be stigmatized within society and deprived of many opportunities that are open to "decent" people (viz. those without a prison record). If all the consequences of conviction could be impressed upon a person, and if his state of mind at the time were objective enough to allow him to logically reason things out, perhaps an "intelligent" waiver could be achieved. Short of that, however, a waiver of constitutional rights is at best an uninformed, irrational mistake.

Ordinarily a waiver has to be stated explicitly, and its validity is heightened if it can be put into writing.[27] It is possible, however, for a waiver to be made without directly saying so. This can occur when a person *understands* that he's being asked to waive his rights, and then goes ahead and starts talking with the apparent intent of making a waiver.[45]

A waiver isn't irreversible. Any time a person wants to invoke his right to have an attorney present or his right to silence, all he has to do is say so; the interrogation must stop immediately, and the cops can't ask any more questions until he gives them permission.[5] The cops don't have to tell a person that he has the power to turn them on and off at will, but they're certainly required under the *Miranda* Rule to abide by his wishes.[28]

After a person waives his right to be silent and does a little talking to the police, his failure to disclose other pertinent information might be interpreted as a form of dishonesty. It's as though they expect a guy to go ahead and confess everything once he breaks his silence. Holding his tongue about certain incriminating matters cannot be used as *evidence* against him, but it can be used to *impeach* his credibility if he testifies[46] — it's one more reason not to waive the right in the first place.

What we've been discussing — custodial interrogation — doesn't account for some of what a suspect says while he's in custody. Statements made to persons *other* than official American police officers can be used as direct evidence in court. Off-duty cops who are moonlighting as security guards or store detectives are not considered "official" police; unless they're working in concert with regular on-duty police officers, and at their request, they have the same official status as civilians. That means they don't have to give *Miranda* warnings or otherwise defer to a person's constitutional rights.[47] The same is true in regard to police of foreign countries; Canadian, Mexican, or any other police that an American may happen to fall prey to, owe him nothing in terms of constitutional rights.[48]/[49] Friends and relatives who come to visit the suspect in jail are similarly free of official restrictions.[50] Anything that any of these people happens to pry out of a suspect is evidence for the prosecutor's case-in-chief. The only way a defendant can object to the use of such statements against him is if he can show that the cops deliberately set up a situation that was likely to induce them.[51]

Another exception to the use of improperly gotten statements is when the cops use them not as evidence, but as *leads* to evidence. If the statements turn them onto a third party who can offer the police testimony against the suspect, they can often get away with using such testimony in court. They can overcome the suspect's objection to using such "fruit of the poisonous tree" by showing that the statements he made were voluntary, even if they were in violation of the *Miranda* Rule.[52]/[53]

Improperly acquired statements can also be used against a defendant to *impeach* his testimony at trial. All they have to do is show that the statement was made voluntarily, which presumably makes it trustworthy by legal standards.[54] This impeachment angle gives the cops a tremendous advantage in court because it allows them to slip in their illegally acquired material — not only statements that were taken in violation of the *Miranda* Rule, but even physical evidence which was taken in violation of the Fourth Amendment[55] — and when the jury hears it, it's just as damaging as if it were being presented as direct evidence. The cops can't use improperly acquired evidence in their case-in-chief, so the defendant can avoid being confronted by it if he simply refuses to testify; they can't impeach his testimony if he doesn't give any. Unfortunately, this robs him of the opportunity to take the stand and declare his innocence, so it comes down to a decision of trial strategy — whether to take the stand and be impeached or sacrifice the opportunity to testify in one's own behalf.

Involuntary statements, such as those which have been wrenched from a suspect by "third-degree" tactics, are not considered trustworthy by legal standards, and can't even be used as impeachment material.[56] Statements which have been taken from a person in violation of his right to counsel, written ones as well as oral ones, are likewise barred from such use.[57]

Regardless of whether one is being held in custody or is on release pending trial, there are several ground rules which govern the taking of statements. They're based upon the Fifth and Sixth Amendment principles that we've discussed already, but deserve to be treated separately because they may come into to play at times when a defendant may not be in custody (as opposed to the *Miranda* Rule).

First of all, silence — what a person *doesn't* say prior to trial — can be used to impeach his testimony if *Miranda* warnings hadn't been given at the time.[58] It's as though a person has an obligation to come forward and tell everything he knows at the earliest opportunity except when he's been given *Miranda* warnings. It's a very artificial assumption, and one which is totally in favor of the cops, because it gives them something to use later against people who were involved in a crime but weren't identified right away as suspects. The absurd implication that it makes is that every good little citizen should go running to the nearest constable as soon as he knows something that might be useful, even if he tends to put himself into hot water in the process.

If the *Miranda* warnings are given, however, it puts things in a whole different perspective; nobody can be faulted for keeping his silence after the police have specifically given him the option, and the silence cannot thereafter be used to impeach his testimony.[59]

Silence can also be used against a person by the judge at sentencing time. On the same theory as mentioned above — that it's the duty of every citizen to be a rat for the government — they can enhance a person's punishment and give him more prison time on the basis of his refusal to inform on his partners. The only way he can get out from under this bit of judicial extortion is to claim his privilege against self-incrimination at the time of the trial.[60]

Statements which have been taken from a defendant, though proper by Fifth Amendment standards, are not usable as evidence against him when they result from an illegal arrest. In other words, if the cops barge in and violate a person's Fourth Amendment rights in the process of arresting him, they can't expect to clean it up by reading him his *Miranda* warnings afterward; they've blown the whole scene, and nothing the arrestee says at that time can be used as evidence against him because it's all "fruit of the poisonous tree."[61] An illustration of this principle can be seen in the case of a seventeen-year-old boy whose will was overborne by a fifty-three-year old cop. Without probable cause to arrest him, the cop went to his home and accused him saying, "I'm here to pick you up." The kid demurely went along, and under police interrogation he eventually made a confession.

Since the confession was obtained "properly," with *Miranda* warnings and all, it held up initially in court and resulted in conviction. On appeal, however, it was tossed out because the initial improper arrest spoiled the confession, which was a direct causal result of it.[62]

Though they can't use the statements themselves as evidence in such cases, the cops have been able to salvage some usefulness out of them as leads to other evidence which they could use. All they have to do then is claim that they were about to discover the new evidence anyway through independent police work.[63]

Statements which a suspect is induced to make without his lawyer being present are also inadmissible as evidence. This rule was originally created by the Supreme Court in order to foil some of the police shenanigans that used to take place before the *Miranda* Rule came out. Not only was it deemed improper to deny a suspect the assistance of counsel while he's being questioned by the police,[64] but it was also held to be improper for them to bait him for admissions with an undercover informant in the absence of counsel.[65] Later, the use of psychological ploys — e.g. preying upon emotion, religiousness, feeble-mindedness, etc. — was also condemned when plied to a suspect with no access to counsel.[24] More recently, even the creation by police of a situation which is likely to induce a suspect to make incriminating statements outside the presence of his lawyer, has been declared improper.[51]

There are several exceptions to the rule against using statements acquired in the denied absence of counsel. For one, a spontaneously volunteered statement can generally be used under any circumstances.[31] Careless remarks that people occasionally spit out without thinking, or in the heat of emotion, tend to fall into this category. Statements that a person thoughtlessly blurts out during a time when he's free of restraint,[66] or in a place where he shouldn't expect privacy,[36] are as much "volunteered" as those which are deliberately directed to the police.

Another exception is the use of statements which a suspect makes in the process of committing an ongoing crime.[67]/[68] Some guys can't seem to lay low even while the heat's on, and when they're overheard making plans for some new crime during the adversary phase of a previous one, these statements are usable as evidence, with or without the attorney's presence. Such statements are likely to be overheard by police surveillance as the suspect attempts to continue his dope business or arrange for a witness to be eliminated.

A further exception occurs in cases where the cop needs to do some emergency interrogation in order to head off a disaster or neutralize a threat to his own safety or that of the public. *Miranda* warnings are thus unnecessary when there's a bomb ticking away or a loaded gun lying around; the immediate concern of neutralizing the danger overrides the need for procedural niceties. If the suspect is gullible enough to talk to the cops or show them what they're looking for, his good citizenship is certain to be rewarded by the use of his statements against him at trial.[69]/[70]

Prior to trial there are various kinds of proceedings which are held in order to answer preliminary questions about the defendant, such as his identification by eyewitnesses, or his sanity. As we've already established, these proceedings offer plenty of opportunities for the cops to stack the deck, so it's crucial that a person have a little help from his lawyer on these occasions. A defendant is absolutely entitled to have counsel present during such events as his identification lineup.[71] While a lawyer isn't usually allowed to *attend* psychological examinations, his client is entitled to his assistance in *preparation* for them.[72]

At a suppression hearing, where the judge decides whether or not he's going to allow particular pieces of evidence to be used in a trial, it's sometimes necessary for a defendant to make an admission in order to get the standing to object to the evidence. For example, if he doesn't want the police to use his illegally seized bag of dope as evidence against him, he might first have to admit that it belongs to him so he can assert his right to object to its seizure, and thereby get the evidence suppressed... but if he does cop to owning it, he's admitting his own guilt. It would be a *Catch-22* dilemma for the defendant if it weren't for a Supreme Court ruling that prohibits such admissions from being used as evidence. Provided that a person files an appropriate objection, anything he admits to in order to get evidence dropped at a suppression hearing is inadmissible itself as evidence.[73]

In pre-trial proceedings where a defendant is evaluated by state-employed mental health workers, his statements are barred from being used as evidence for the case-in-chief. They *can* be used against him to impeach his testimony, however, and that's one reason why prior preparation by counsel is important.[74]/[75]

The ultimate forum for a person's statements is the courtroom, where their impact is made and their substance recorded for posterity. The importance of one's words is probably no greater at any time or place than in there. Conversely, the integrity of one's silence is nowhere more significant than at trial; so valuable is this right that it's improper for a defendant's silence at trial to even be *mentioned* before the jury, much less used to discredit him.[2]/[76]/[77] The right to be silent isn't an inalienable one, however; when it serves the designs of the government, a person can be squeezed like a lemon for his testimony. In the next chapter we'll see just how it's done.

REFERENCES

1. *Fisher v U.S.*, 425 US 391, 408, 96 SCt 1569, 1579 (1976)

2. *Counselman v Hitchcock*, 142 US 547, 562, 12 SCt 195, 198 (1892)

3. *Jenkins v Anderson*, 447 US 231, 238, 100 SCt 2124, 2129 (1980)

4. *Beckwith v U.S.*, 425 US 341, 347, 96 SCt 1612, 1616 (1976)

5. *Miranda v Arizona*, 384 US 436, 478, 86 SCt 1602, 1630 (1966)

6. *Spano v New York*, 360 US 315, 327, 79 SCt 1202, 1209 (1959), J. Stewart concurring

7. *U.S. v Wade*, 388 US 218, 225, 87 SCt 1926, 1931 (1967)

8. *Miranda v Arizona*, 384 US at 454-456, 86 SCt at 1617

9. *Id.*, 384 US at 444-445, 461, 86 SCt at 1612-1613

10. *U.S. v Messina*, 388 F2d 393, 395 (2d Cir. 1968)

11. *U.S. v Cullinan*, 396 FSupp 516, 517-518 (D. Ill. 1975)

12. *Miranda v Arizona*, 384 US at 473 n. 43, 86 SCt at 1627 n. 43

13. *U.S. v Jordan*, 557 F2d 1081, 1083-1084 (5th Cir. 1977)

14. *U.S. v Jimenez*, 602 F2d 139, 143-144 (7th Cir. 1979)

15. *Berkemer v McCarty*, _ US _, 104 SCt 3138, 3151 (1984)

16. *Cervantes v Walker*, 589 F2d 424, 428 (9th Cir. 1978)

17. *Mathis v U.S.*, 391 US 1, 4-5, 88 SCt 1503, 1505 (1968)

18. *Estelle v Smith*, 451 US 454, 469, 101 SCt 1866, 1876 (1981)

19. *Cervantes v Walker*, 589 F2d at 427

20. *Oregon v Mathiason*, 429 US 492, 495, 97 SCt 711, 714 (1977)

21. *U.S. v Luther,* 521 F2d 408, 410 (9th Cir. 1975)

22. *U.S. v Washington,* 431 US 181, 186, 97 SCt 1814, 1818 (1977)

23. *Rhode Island v Innis,* 446 US 291, 300-302, 100 SCt 1682, 1689-1690 (1980)

24. *Brewer v Williams,* 430 US 387, 400-401, 97 SCt 1232, 1240-1241 (1977)

25. *U.S. v Downing,* 665 F2d 404, 406 (1st Cir. 1981)

26. *State v Ladd,* N.C. Sup. Ct., 5/3/83

27. *Cannady v State,* Fla. Sup. Ct., 2/24/83

28. Lederer, *Miranda v Arizona — The Law Today,* 78 Mil. L. Rev. 107, 162 (1978)

29. *The Supreme Court, 1965 Term,* 80 Harv. L. Rev. 91, 205 (1966)

30. Stone, *The Miranda Doctrine in the Burger Court,* Sup. Ct. Rev. 99, 129-137 (1977)

31. Lederer at 155-157

32. *Michigan v Mosley,* 423 US 96, 105-106, 96 SCt 321, 327 (1975)

33. *Edwards v Arizona,* 451 US 477, 484-485, 101 SCt 1880, 1885 (1981)

34. *Miranda v Arizona,* 384 US at 474, 86 SCt at 1628

35. *Oregon v Bradshaw,* _ US _, 103 SCt 2830, 2834-2835 (1983)

36. *Offut v State,* Md. Ct. Special App., 7/7/83

37. *McFadden v Commonwealth,* Va. Sup. Ct., 3/11/83

38. *State v Routhier,* 137 Ariz. 90, 669 P2d 68, 75-76 (Ariz. 1983)

39. *Karr v Wolff,* 556 F2d 760, 765 (N.D. Ill. 1983)

40. *U.S. v McCraney,* 705 F2d 449 (5th Cir. 1983) (No published opinion; see 33 CrL 2131)

41. *Carnley v Cochran,* 369 US 506, 516, 82 SCt 884, 890 (1962)

42. *U.S. v DiGiacomo*, 579 F2d 1211, 1215 (10th Cir. 1978)

43. *Pallotta v U.S.*, 404 F2d 1035, 1038 (1st Cir. 1968)

44. Kuh, *Symposium: Interrogation of Criminal Defendants — Some Views on Miranda v Arizona*, 35 Fordham L. Rev. 169, 233 (1966)

45. *North Carolina v Butler*, 441 US 369, 373, 99 SCt 1755, 1757 (1979)

46. *Anderson v Charles*, 447 US 404, 408, 100 SCt 2180, 2182 (1980)

47. *City of Grand Rapids v Impens*, Mich. Sup. Ct., 12/7/82

48. *U.S. v Nagelberg*, 434 F2d 585, 587 n. 1 (2d Cir. 1970)

49. *U.S. v Chavarria*, 443 F2d 904, 905 (9th Cir. 1971)

50. *State v Loyd*, La. Sup. Ct., 11/29/82

51. *U.S. v Henry*, 447 US 264, 274, 100 SCt 2183, 2189 (1980)

52. *Michigan v Tucker*, 417 US 433, 444-446, 94 SCt 2357, 2364 (1974)

53. *U.S. ex rel Hudson v Cannon*, 529 F2d 890, 894-895 (7th Cir. 1976)

54. *Harris v New York*, 401 US 222, 224-225, 91 SCt 643, 645 (1971)

55. *U.S. v Havens*, 446 US 620, 627-628, 100 SCt 1912, 1916-1917 (1980)

56. *Mincey v Arizona*, 437 US 385, 399-402, 98 SCt 2408, 2417-2418 (1978)

57. *Bishop v Rose*, 701 F2d 1150, 1157 (6th Cir. 1983)

58. *Fletcher v Weir*, 455 US 603, 102 SCt 1309 (1982)

59. *Doyle v Ohio*, 426 US 610, 618-619, 96 SCt 2240, 2245 (1976)

60. *Roberts v U.S.*, 445 US 552, 556-559, 100 SCt 1358, 1362-1364 (1980)

61. *Taylor v Alabama*, 457 US 687, 102 SCt 2664, 2668 (1982)

62. *State v Freeman*, N.C. Sup. Ct., 1/11/83

63. *U.S. v Brookins,* 614 F2d 1037, 1042 n. 2 (5th Cir. 1980)

64. *Escobedo v Illinois,* 378 US 478, 490-491, 84 SCt 1758, 1765 (1964)

65. *Massiah v U.S.,* 377 US 201, 206, 84 SCt 1199, 1203 (1964)

66. *Barfield v Alabama,* 552 F2d 1114, 1118 (5th Cir. 1977)

67. *U.S. v Lisenby,* 716 F2d 1355, 1359 (11th Cir. 1983)

68. *U.S. v Moschiano,* 695 F2d 236, 241 (7th Cir. 1982)

69. *Clonk v State,* Ind. Ct. App., 1st Dist., 1/11/83

70. *New York v Quarles,* _ US _, 104 SCt 2626, 2633 (1984)

71. *U.S. v Wade,* 388 US at 236-237, 87 SCt at 1937

72. *Estelle v Smith,* 451 US at 470-471, 101 SCt at 1877

73. *Simmons v U.S.,* 390 US 377, 390, 394, 88 SCt 967, 974, 976 (1968)

74. *State v Holland,* 98 Wash.2d 507, 656 P2d 1056, 1063-1064 (Wash. 1983)

75. *State v Davis,* 82 Wash.2d 790, 514 P2d 149, 151 (Wash. 1973)

76. *De Luna v U.S.,* 308 F2d 140, 154 (5th Cir. 1962)

77. *Griffin v California,* 380 US 609, 615, 85 SCt 1229, 1233 (1965)

Chapter 14

THE SQUEEZE

"...society is entitled to every man's evidence...
Limitations are properly placed upon the operation of this general principle only to the very
limited extent that permitting a refusal to
testify or excluding relevant evidence has a
public good transcending the normal predominant principle of utilizing all rational means for
ascertaining truth."

Justice Felix Frankfurter dissenting in *Rios v U.S.*
and *Elkins v U.S.*, 364 US 206, 234, 80 SCt 1431,
1454 (1960)

Detective work can accomplish a great deal for the
police, but there's a point, particularly in conspiracy and
organized crime cases, where the cops need somebody
who will name names and tell secrets. Many cases, in fact,
would be unsolvable without a snitch to roll over and
"turn State's evidence." Whether he's the one who
initially brings a case to their attention, or merely
provides them with information or testimony during
subsequent phases of investigation and prosecution, the
snitch is an invaluable tool of the cops. Rare is the prisoner whose prosecution didn't involve at least one of
them somewhere along the line.

It occasionally happens, however, that a person who
has useful information also has a measure of integrity as
well; despite their usual "good citizenship" appeals, he
refuses to become a rat for the cops. Morally speaking,
this is a person's rightful prerogative. He's fundamentally
entitled to his own personality and conscience, and his
primary obligation is to be true to himself. if his personal
code dictates that he not betray a friend (or a stranger,
for that matter) it should be his decision to make. *Legally*
speaking, however, this is not the case. The government
couldn't care less about a person's integrity, his conscience, or his personal interests. Its sole concern is to

maintain *control,* and at both state and federal levels there are well-developed systems of laws designed to rob the individual of his free will and force him to perform at the government's bidding.

By either verbal order or written subpoena, a court can order a person to testify or submit personal papers into evidence.[1] If he refuses outright the court can hold him in "civil contempt," which means that he goes straight to jail and stays there until he decides to be good and talk.[2] In the case of a federal grand jury, that might be up to eighteen months because that's how long each jury term lasts. Assuming that they're still interested in his testimony, he doesn't get off the hook when the term ends; they simply empanel a new jury, and if the person still refuses to talk it's back to the pokey again.

One thing about civil contempt is that the person being held under it can get out at any time by giving up and agreeing to talk — in fact, that's the whole idea. If the judge gets *really* pissed-off, though, he can hold the witness in "criminal contempt" and give him a fixed prison sentence, perhaps as much as five years. That's only likely to happen if the fellow repeatedly snubs the court's orders, makes a scene in the courtroom, or offers impertinent suggestions of novel places for the judge to store his gavel.[3]/[4]

As we've learned in the last two chapters, a person has a constitutional right to refuse to incriminate himself, and this operates very well as an excuse not to testify or present papers. When one does so, however, it doesn't necessarily put an end to the matter. What it does is force the police to decide which they want more — the witness' testimony or his conviction. If the answer is the latter they're stuck with his silence, and they'll have to do the best they can to convict him on the basis of independent evidence. If they opt for the testimony, however, they can overrule his use of the Fifth by granting him immunity from prosecution.

It often occurs that the cops stand to get the goods on a more important crime figure, or perhaps several of them, if they can put the squeeze on one key witness. In such cases it's worth the risk of losing a conviction of the witness in order to get the "bigger fish." What the feds do is offer the witness "use and derivative use immunity," or simply "use immunity," concerning his testimony.[5] This means that his testimony can never be used in any way against him in an American criminal prosecution. Even other evidence, which is later revealed because of leads from the immunized testimony, is barred from such use. This use immunity is purported to be a substitute for Fifth Amendment protection, but as we'll see later, it's a preposterous fraud and hardly equivalent to the right of silence.

Some state laws provide for a still broader form of protection called "transactional immunity," which guarantees that the witness won't be prosecuted for the crimes he testifies about.[6] No such assurance accompanies a grant of use immunity, which only guarantees the witness that his *own* testimony won't be turned against him.[7] Whether immunity is granted by state or federal authority, it's supposed to be recognized by the courts of both jurisdictions.[8]/[9] The feds, however, are likely to recognize only the federal minimum extent of immunity (i.e. use immunity) when greater degrees of protection have been promised by a state.[8]/[10]

Only the prosecutor can offer a grant of immunity to a witness; the judge can't do it, and the witness can't invoke it for himself.[11]/[12] This is so because it's really nothing but a device of the police; they can employ it when *they* need to extract testimony to use against someone, but they don't have to offer it when it doesn't serve their interests. Thus, a defendant will usually be out of luck if he needs the testimony of a recalcitrant witness in order to support his defense; a prosecutor isn't likely to extend a grant of immunity in order to help out the defendant.[12]/[13]/[14]

Use immunity is touted by the government as being a fair substitute for the citizen's Fifth Amendment right against self-incrimination,[15] but in truth it's one of the biggest lies that's ever been foisted upon the American public. Use immunity isn't even an adequate guarantee that the witness' own testimony won't be used against him, because it's often a simple matter for the cops to use it as leads to other evidence, which they can claim to have found through "independent police work." They probably have a thousand ways of setting up such scenarios.

Apart from the prospect of police misconduct, however, all grants of immunity suffer from a fatal inadequacy — they only provide protection against *domestic criminal prosecution.* The government would ask us to pretend that an American criminal prosecution is the only harmful consequence that can come from testifying, and it just isn't so. There are a number of other consequences, some of them more of a threat than the government's prosecution, and none of them are prevented by these phony grants of immunity.

First of all, immunity from a state or from the federal government isn't worth a plug nickel in the courts of other nations, yet any admissions that a person makes *can* be used by them as evidence. Defendants have attempted to use this point to argue against compelled testimony under the grant of immunity, but federal courts have held that, unless a given case presents (1) a real danger (i.e. possibility) of prosecution under foreign law, and (2) the fear (i.e. probability) that foreign prosecution will indeed follow, an immunized witness must talk.[16]/[17] Where these foreign dangers are clearly demonstrable, however, a court might recognize the privilege of silence for *specific* questions before a grand jury, despite the extension of immunity.[18]

Second, people who live in glass houses shouldn't throw stones; one who has been snitched on is often in a pretty good position to dredge up a little dirt himself.

The use immunity statute prohibits the cops from taking testimony from a person who has been fingered and then using it as evidence against the immunized snitch. It doesn't prevent the betrayed party from giving the cops all sorts of information and leads, however, which they can launder into usable evidence through "independent police work." The need for revenge is strong and once the snitching starts it isn't long before the snitches are in turn being snitched on by the snitchees.[19]

Third, there's a danger to the physical safety of an informant (and his family) which no amount of immunity can neutralize. Depending upon who the snitch offends, his chances of long-term survival can vary between good and zero; governmental witness protection programs aren't all they're cracked up to be. It's impossible to measure the risk because it depends as much on the avenger's level of determination as it does on anything the snitch can do. The courts have naively held that, unless a witness is subjected to either (1) a specific threat or incident of violence, or (2) denial of some means of escape (such as police protection), the threat to his safety isn't sufficient to merit a privilege of silence.[20] Generally speaking, the fear of reprisals isn't accepted by the courts as an excuse for not testifying[21]... but then, what do they care?

Fourth, a grant of immunity doesn't protect a person from the use of his testimony against him in professional disciplinary proceedings.[11] To a lawyer, that might eventuate in disbarment — to a doctor, the loss of his license to practice medicine. After investing a fortune and the better part of one's lifetime in acquiring the training and experience necessary for such a career, it's no small consequence to have it suddenly foreclosed and be thus deprived of the means of earning a living.

Fifth, a grant of immunity doesn't protect a person from the use of his testimony against him in a civil court action.[22] Thus, a witness could find himself confronted by his own admissions in a liability suit, a divorce action, a tax hearing, or some other civil proceeding after supposedly being "protected" by a grant of immunity.

Sixth, religious convictions under currently established forms of belief haven't been recognized by the courts as constituting a justification for refusal to testify.[23]/[24] If a person's religious laws are broken or his spiritual sensibilities offended by being forced into the role of a Judas, it's just one more instance where the immunity statute doesn't measure up to the privilege of silence.

Seventh, immunity from prosecution totally fails to insulate the witness from the infamy that he can suffer because of his testimony. A guy's family and friends are usually willing to give him the benefit of a doubt, but once he testifies and makes the admissions himself, even *their* loyalties can wear thin. Most of the self-righteous hypocrites that make up society are inclined to believe the worst about a person anyway, so his admissions in testimony merely confirm what they'd suspected all along. Nevertheless, the added burden of opprobrium and prejudice can cause unnecessary hardships in many spheres of everyday life; social acceptance, job opportunities, and union membership are only a few of such areas that are likely to be adversely affected.[25] There's reason to believe that the authors of the Constitution intended to prevent this when they drafted the Fifth Amendment,[26] but judicial statists have unfortunately managed to erode away most of our protections against infamy.

Lastly, a grant of immunity can never restore a person's dignity and self-respect — qualities which he necessarily sacrifices when he becomes a snitch. Whatever euphemism he may apply to the role — witness, informant, spy, police auxiliary — he's still the lowest form of scum in the lake of humanity. If he's so lacking of integrity and manhood that he can't appreciate that fact, then he's truly suited to the role, and will never be troubled by the realization of what he is. For a person who lives by his conscience and personal integrity, however, the unwilling compulsion to give testimony can be a devastating assault upon the personality.

> "As for that Oath that was put upon me, I did refuse to take it as a sinful and unlawful oath, and by the strength of my God enabling me, I will never take it, though I be pulled in pieces by wild horses, as the ancient Christians were by the bloody tyrants of the Primitive Church."
>
> John Lilburn, *The Trial of Lilburn and Wharton,* 3 Howell's State Trials 1315, 1332 (1637)

In John Lilburn's time, the Court of Star Chamber was the inquisitional body by which the government extracted confessions and information from English citizens; the royal judges ran the show, and the "oath ex officio" was the procedural tool that was used to legally force people to talk. Witnesses would be given the oath, subjected to all lines of inquiry, and ultimately found guilty of one thing or another on the basis of their own testimony.[27] In our time, here in the United States, the grand jury has taken over this role; prosecutors call the shots now, and the grant of immunity has taken the place of the oath ex officio, but in effect we see pretty much the same grim picture that seventeenth-century Englishmen saw — a tribunal which is unhindered by the requirements of due process and discretionarily run by power-hungry bureaucrats, with the wherewithal to coerce people into talking against their wishes.

The grand jury hasn't always been a tool of the State;[28] early on in the history of this country it served to protect the rights of the *individual* by insulating him from arbitrary prosecution. It was a panel of impartial citizens which stood between prosecutor and suspect in order to pass judgment on the sufficiency of grounds for a criminal prosecution. Its purpose was to protect the individual from police harassment and ensure that he wouldn't be jeopardized by unfounded charges from personal enemies or an overreaching prosecutor.

Thanks to judicial and legislative legerdemain, the grand jury has long since ceased to be the friend of the individual, and instead operates today as an instrument of the police. Unaware of their independent power and responsibility, grand jurors are programmed to blandly go along with whatever the prosecutor tells them, rubber-stamping his proposals like so many smiling robots. Instead of sitting for the purpose of judging the *sufficiency* of the prosecutor's case, the grand jury sits now to legitimize a form of *interrogation* by which the cops flush out new evidence against a suspect by extorting people's testimony under threat of imprisonment.

Briefly, it works like this: Folks who are suspected of knowing something useful are commanded to appear before the grand jury and give testimony. If they don't show up, or if they refuse to testify, they're cited for civil contempt and thrown into jail until they decide to cooperate. If a witness takes the Fifth, the prosecutor grants him use immunity, thereby extinguishing his right to be silent. Refusal to answer, a pretense of forgetfulness, or any response other than a straight answer will then be grounds for a contempt citation and jail. If he gets caught in a lie it constitutes the felony of perjury, which also means prison. Any way you look at it, it's either snitch or the slammer.

Unlike a trial, where evidence must meet standards of "competency" and "materiality" in order to be heard, the grand jury is an evidentiary free-for-all.[29] Competency is a quality of testimony which attaches by virtue of having come from firsthand knowledge; it also assumes that the Constitution wasn't violated in the process of getting it.[30] Roughly, it stands for the reliability of the evidence. In grand jury proceedings all sorts of incompetent evidence can be thrown in by the prosecutor: tidbits acquired through violations of the Fourth[31] and

Fifth[32] Amendments... even statements elicited by torture.[33] They don't even need to inquire into the validity of their sources of evidence.[34] Materiality is the tendency of evidence to establish some fact at issue in a case. Roughly, it stands for the importance or necessity of a given piece of evidence. In grand jury proceedings, materiality issues, such as the question of whether a given piece of testimony is necessary, impose no restriction on the freedom of the prosecutor; virtually anything is admissible.[35] On top of everything else, they don't even allow a witness' lawyer to be in the grand jury room during his testimony.[36] When they put the squeeze on, they try to make *sure* that the sucker doesn't get an even break.

With such an elaborate scheme worked out, and all the guns on their side, it would appear unlikely that a person could defeat it in a head-on encounter. Indeed, once a witness is sworn in and given immunity, there are only a couple of exceptions that can be claimed. One of these is the communications privilege for confidential disclosures that have been made to the witness by his spouse, his legal client, or his patient. It has been possible for the cops to defeat this gambit, too; an affidavit of immunity indemnifying the wife can be issued in order to compel a husband to relate disclosures she made to him in confidence.[37]

Another exception is when the cops have used illegal electronic surveillance in order to get the basis for their line of inquiry.[38] Once it becomes evident from their questions that they've been doing a little shady wiretapping, the witness can refuse to give any more testimony. He must actually *allege* that a violation has occurred, however, and should be able to substantiate his charge; merely questioning whether it may have happened isn't good enough.[39] The next step for the cops in such a case, assuming that they want to deny the charge, is to go collect affidavits from the twenty-odd government agencies that might have had spooks out in the field planting bugs and doing wiretaps. Unlikely as it is that any of them will admit to being guilty, an adequate inquiry into the matter is the least that's required of the cops in order to refute the charge.[40] In the meantime, the grand jury has to be put on "hold," and there remains the possibility that proof of illegal surveillance will turn up and vindicate the witness' claim. It can definitely put a stick into their spokes for at least a little while.

Of course, if a potential witness is judged to be mentally incompetent to testify, the prosecutor can't bring him before the grand jury in the first place. Incompetence means more than just having psychiatric problems; if the mere presence of a mental defect automatically rendered a person incompetent, the government would never be able to get a single politician before the grand jury. Actually, there's no correlation between the issues of mental disease and legal efficacy.[41] Even a lunatic confined to a mental institution can legally be a competent witness,[42]/[43] and so can somebody who's on drugs.[44] It isn't really necessary for a person to even have an understanding of the proceedings he's testifying at.[42] All these considerations are within the scope of responsibility of the jurors to assess as to *credibility* and the amount of *weight* to be given to the testimony.

Competency, on the other hand, is a *threshold* determination that the court has to make before a witness can even be allowed to appear.[42]/[45] It's based upon a three-fold set of conclusions drawn by an appointed psychologist who has thoroughly examined the witness. The questions which must be answered are the following: (1) Does the witness have sufficient understanding to realize the obligation of taking an oath? (2) Is he capable of giving a correct account of things which he has seen or heard? And, (3) will his physical or mental health be imperiled by compelling him to testify? The first two questions explore concerns about the ability of the witness to tell the truth. while the third one contemplates the likelihood that compelling him to testify might inspire him to commit suicide.

The psychological examination that a person might typically be subjected to for the determination of competency consists of three parts: (1) psychological testing, (2) the psychologist-witness interview, and (3) the psychologist's interviews with the witness' relatives, counsel, the prosecutor, etc.[42]

Psychological testing involves all those little games and multiple-choice questionnaires that are supposed to reveal how one's mind works. It typically includes the Rorschach ink blot test, the Thematic Apperception Test (TAT), the Wechsler Adult Intelligence Scale (WAIS) I.Q. test, the Minnesota Multiphasic Personality Inventory (MMPI) test, the four sentence completion test, and the house-tree-person test.

The most critical part of the examination is probably the psychologist's personal interview. These guys watch *everything*, and they note how the subject's initial reactions compare with those later on in the interview. People who really are "incompetent" don't tend to get better in their performance and sociability as the interview progresses, whereas those who are faking or just a little squirrely tend to loosen up, relax, and generally improve after a while. The psychologist takes note of his subject's alertness and general affect as well as his responsiveness to questioning and sense of humor. He sizes up the witness' overall appearance of health, and attempts to assess how well his memory functions.

There are a number of ways in which people have *un*successfully tried to avoid having to testify before the grand jury, some of which have already been mentioned. Being the very measures that most people tend to think of first, they deserve to be summarized here in order to emphasize their uselessness.

First of all, the rules of evidence and due process don't carry any weight before a grand jury. Things like the adequacy or competency of evidence and the improper constitution of the jury are therefore useless as the basis of a challenge to subpoena.[46]/[47]

Second, the fear of danger from reprisals is not an acceptable excuse for avoiding an order to testify.[14]/[48] The cops figure that their protection is an adequate remedy for such concerns.

Religious views, while guaranteed under the First Amendment, have been recognized in this context only to the extent of justifying temporary postponement of grand jury testimony, as when it must be rescheduled so as not to take place on a holy day.[49] Those who have tried to excuse themselves altogether on the basis of religious convictions have not been successful.[23]/[24]

Medical unfitness is likewise only useful as a means of delaying the testimony. Even then, however, it's necessary that the medical advice which the witness is relying upon is (1) not categorically wrong, and (2) is similar to advice which might be popularly available from other doctors. The courts take a dim view of sham medical excuses.[50]

The convenient "inability to remember" is generally recognized as a lame excuse, and not worthy of belief.[51] Perjury, of course, is a crime by itself; the courts don't condone it as a means of avoiding the obligation to tell the truth, even when confusion arises because of language difficulties and misunderstandings.[52] When a witness perjures himself out of fear which is based on a *specific* threat or incident, or on the failure of the police to afford protection, it might be a defensible offense; but a *general* fear for one's safety doesn't justify an act of perjury.[20]

REFERENCES

1. *Jencks v U.S.*, 353 US 657, 668-669, 77 SCt 1007, 1013 (1957)

2. Title 28 U.S.C. Section 1826

3. *Green v U.S.*, 356 US 165, 183, 78 SCt 632, 643 (1958)

4. *U.S. v Brummitt*, 665 F2d 521, 526-527 (5th Cir. 1981)

5. Title 18 U.S.C. Sections 6001 et seq.

6. *Grochulski v Henderson*, 637 F2d 50, 52 (2d Cir. 1980)

7. *U.S. v Rocco*, 587 F2d 144, 147 n. 9 (3d Cir. 1978)

8. *In re Bianchi*, 542 F2d 98, 101 (1st Cir. 1976)

9. *Murphy v Waterfront Commission of New York Harbor*, 378 US 52, 79, 84 SCt 1594, 1609 (1964)

10. *U.S. v Quatermain*, 467 FSupp 782, 788 (E.D. Pa. 1979)

11. *In re Daley*, 549 F2d 469, 479-480 (7th Cir. 1977)

12. *U.S. v Lenz*, 616 F2d 960, 962 (6th Cir. 1980)

13. *U.S. v Thevis*, 665 F2d 616, 639-640 (5th Cir. 1982)

14. *In re Kilgo*, 484 F2d 1215, 1222 (4th Cir. 1973)

15. *Kastigar v U.S.*, 406 US 441, 461-462, 92 SCt 1653, 1665-1666 (1972)

16. *In re Quinn*, 525 F2d 222, 223 (1st Cir. 1975)

17. *U.S. v Yanagita*, 552 F2d 940, 947 (2d Cir. 1977)

18. *Mishima v U.S.*, 507 FSupp 131, 135 (D. Alaska 1981)

19. *U.S. v Quatermain*, 467 FSupp at 789

20. *U.S. v Housand*, 550 F2d 818, 824-825 (2d Cir. 1977)

21. *In re Kilgo*, 484 F2d at 1221

22. *U.S. v Cappetto*, 502 F2d 1351, 1359 (7th Cir. 1974)

23. *U.S. v Martin*, 525 F2d 703, 710 n. 11 (2d Cir. 1975)

24. *U.S. v Huss*, 482 F2d 38, 51 (2d Cir. 1973)

25. *Ullman v U.S.*, 350 US 422, 430-431, 76 SCt 497, 502 (1956)

26. *Id.*, 350 US at 449-454, 76 SCt at 512-515, J. Douglas dissenting

27. Harris, Richard, *Freedom Spent*, Little, Brown & Co., Boston, 1976, pp. 350-355

28. Wright, Federal Practice and Procedure: Criminal 2d Section 101

29. *Costello v U.S.*, 350 US 359, 364, 76 SCt 406, 409 (1956)

30. 31 C.J.S. Evidence, Section 2; 31A C.J.S. Evidence, Sections 186-187

31. *U.S. v Calandra*, 414 US 338, 354, 94 SCt 613, 623 (1974)

32. *U.S. v Blue*, 384 US 251, 254-255, 86 SCt 1416, 1419 (1966)

33. *In re Weir*, 495 F2d 879, 881 (9th Cir. 1974)

34. *Lawn v U.S.*, 355 US 339, 348-350, 78 SCt 311, 317-318 (1958)

35. *In re Kilgo*, 484 F2d at 1218, 1219

36. *U.S. v Mandujano*, 425 US 564, 581, 96 SCt 1768, 1779 (1976)

37. *In re Snoonian*, 502 F2d 110, 112 (lst Cir. 1974)

38. *Gelbard v U.S.*, 408 us 41, 46, 92 SCt 2357, 2360 (1972)

39. *In re Millow*, 529 F2d 770, 774-775 (2d Cir. 1976)

40. *In re Quinn*, 525 F2d at 224-226

41. *In re Loughran*, 276 FSupp 393, 416 (C.D. Cal. 1967)

42. *Id.* at 429

43. *Shuler v Wainwright*, 491 F2d 1213, 1223 (5th Cir. 1974)

44. *U.S. v Banks*, 520 F2d 627, 631 (7th Cir. 1975)

45. *U.S. v Benn*, 476 F2d 1127, 1130 (U.S.App. D.C. 1973)

46. *U.S. v Calandra*, 414 US at 344-345, 94 SCt at 618

47. *U.S. v Fitch*, 472 F2d 548, 549 (9th Cir. 1973)

48. *U.S. v Patrick*, 542 F2d 381, 388 (7th Cir. 1976)

49. *Smilow v U.S.*, 465 F2d 802, 804 (2d Cir. 1972)

50. *U.S. v Lansky*, 496 F2d 1063, 1071-1072 (5th Cir. 1974)

51. *Langella v Commissioner of Corrections, State of New York*, 545 F2d 818, 823 (2d Cir. 1976)

52. *U.S. v Wong*, 431 US 174, 176, 180, 97 SCt 1823, 1824-1825, 1827 (1977)

Part IV

FACTS OF LIFE

Chapter 15

DIRTY TRICKS

"Loose talk about war against crime too easily infuses the administration of justice with the psychology and morals of war... Of course criminal prosecution is more than a game. But in any event it should not be deemed to be a dirty game in which 'the dirty business' of criminals is out-witted by 'the dirty business' of law officers."

Justice Felix Frankfurter dissenting in *On Lee v U.S.*, 343 US 747, 758, 72 SCt 967, 974 (1952)

It comes as a natural expectation that, if the government is going to preach morality through its laws, it should exemplify those same moral principles in its own dealings. After all, what's good for the goose is good for the gander. Much of this expectation arises from the popular notion that the government is fundamentally good, a misconception that's grafted onto our minds from early childhood. Having absorbed enough James Bond-G-Man-Texas Ranger-war hero stories, a person can begin to believe that the only thing separating him from sudden death at the hands of thugs and foreigners is his trusty government. The faith in government is further cemented by the impact of its many programs upon our daily lives. Perils are presumably everywhere, so we need a legion of bureaucratic agencies to watch out for us — ones like the F.D.A., H.U.D., and F.D.I.C. If you lose your job, the unemployment agency finds you another one and pays you a stipend in the meantime. If you can't work for some reason, the welfare agency comes to the rescue. When you retire, the Social Security Administration kicks out some cash every month while Medicare pays the doctor bills. What a wonderful, maternal institution our government is! Surely *Mother* wouldn't lie or cheat, would she?

You'd better believe she would. As we discussed in Chapters 1-4, the criminal justice system is an economic enterprise, not a charity devoted to good works. Those who fill its ranks seriously believe that they're pursuing a career in a legitimate profession, and they approach their work with the same competitive spirit that the businessman approaches his. Instead of measuring success in terms of sales volume, however, cops measure it in numbers of busts, and prosecutors in terms of conviction rates. Like the businessman, the cop strives for results; how he gets them is often of little concern to him.

This is an important point to realize because cops don't feel the need to follow the same rules that apply to everyone else. For the very reason that cops *are* its servants, the government has given them extraordinary powers and privileges — license to do things that would be crimes if done by anybody else. Within broad limits they're permitted to ignore standard concepts of fairness, official regulations,[1] and even statutes.[2]

They enjoy this generous freedom of action because the decision-makers — the legislators and judges — have decided that catching lawbreakers is more important than maintaining a code of integrity. They don't see the System as a game of chess with the cops being checkmated for failing to play by the rules, and the outlaw going free as a reward for winning.[3] As Supreme Court Chief Justice Warren Burger has confessed, "the sporting theory of criminal justice... has been experiencing a decline in our jurisprudence."[4] Instead, the government views the law breaker as a threat to its authority, hence its existence, and that merits top priority action. The government would prefer to keep its image of honor and fairness in the eyes of the public, but not at the cost of losing authority. At the same time, it must temper its aspirations of absolute control with enough restraint to avoid shocking the public "conscience" and thereby destroying its credibility.[5] In seeking to strike this balance, the government has drawn those constitutional limits that we've discussed in previous chapters and has carved out the permissible limits for the "dirty tricks" which are discussed in this chapter.

"Dirty tricks" is a general term referring to techniques of deception — the tools of the spy and the con man. For purposes of the discussion at hand, it's useful to consider them as falling into three basic categories, according to whether they impinge on Fourth Amendment, Fifth Amendment, or Due Process rights.

THE RUSE

"Some trickery is here. Trojans, do not trust in the horse. Whatever it may be, I fear the Greeks, even when they bring gifts."

Virgil, *The Aeneid: Book II*, lines 68-70 (19 B.C.)

In order to defeat a suspect's legitimate expectation of privacy, which is ordinarily protected by the Fourth Amendment, the police frequently find it helpful to create ruses. A ruse is some sort of false pretense which is calculated to fool the suspect into willingly giving his consent to something. The idea is to create a cordial, or at least neutral, atmosphere of openness and trust. Such an ambience would usually be impossible if the suspect knew that he were dealing with the cops, so they masquerade as passers-by, customers, or even partners-in-crime, in order to gain acceptance. Thus disguised, they gain access to places and events which would never have been open to them otherwise — and it's all done without a fight.

The most commonly used ruse is the undercover agent. He might be a cop who's on a specific assignment to infiltrate a criminal enterprise, or just a local stool pigeon who keeps his eyes and ears open for the police.

Sometimes the cops use ordinary citizens as decoys in their ruses,[6] especially junkies, people who've been busted, guys with a score to settle, and police groupies. The decoy sucks the suspect in because of his authenticity as a user of drugs or whatever other type of illegal goods or services the cops are after. Typically, the decoy will get the suspect to do the deal in the presence of an undercover cop so the testimonial evidence will hold up better in court. Since cops tend to have an authoritative bearing about them that they find difficult to hide, they're usually cast into the role of dealer, hit man, or other macho-type character.

The most elaborate ruses are the "sting" type operations which have been fashionable in recent years. They're based on the "big store" concept that was developed by the great American con artists of the early 1900's and depicted in the movie *The Sting*. An illegal enterprise is set up and staffed by undercover cops who continue to run the business over a prolonged period of time under the guise of being outlaws. All the time, however, they're developing records on the real outlaws who do business with them, and making movies and sound recordings of the transactions using hidden equipment. Fencing operations for stolen goods and bribery setups lend themselves well to such methods. Because of the extensive police involvement in the illegal activities that constitute these decoy and sting operations, there arises a question of whether they violate a person's due process rights under the Fifth Amendment; this will be dealt with below under the discussion of entrapment.

Many ruses are conducted simply to get inside the suspect's place in order to look around. The cops might suspect that evidence of some crime is present there, but without probable cause they can't legally force their way in. If they think the suspect might be likely to refuse them admittance as police, and probably destroy any evidence that he has inside, they'll conduct a ruse in order to trick their way in without letting on that they're cops. They might pose as prospective land buyers checking out the area, or perhaps as a motorist whose car has broken down and who needs to use the telephone to call for a mechanic. Once they get inside under such pretenses, anything they see in plain view becomes probable cause for them to get a search warrant. If the situation appears to be an exigency, they can go ahead and make the bust right there on the spot.

The cops are sometimes treading on thin ice with these ruses, because if they get too aggressive the courts are likely to declare a Fourth Amendment violation and apply the exclusionary rule in favor of the suspect. The Supreme Court ruled long ago that the police can't use fraud in order to get into a person's place for the purpose of conducting a warrantless *search*.[7] If they just "happen" to see the evidence in plain view while masquerading under false pretenses, that's okay; rifling the drawers, however, is verboten. Similarly, the use of either moral or legal compulsion in a ruse is likely to be regarded by the courts as a Fourth Amendment violation.[8] Moral compulsion, for example, exists when sympathy is invoked for a person who's suffering and in need of help.[9] Legal compulsion occurs when a cop falsely claims to have a valid search warrant, or pretends to be a gas company employee looking for a dangerous gas leak.[8] These kinds of ruses represent such compelling demands that no person would be reasonably justified in refusing them, and are therefore usually impermissible. The role of lover, however, is a fully permissible ruse, and cops have successfully exploited their suspects' romantic weaknesses on many occasions.[10]/[11]

Some ruses are conducted for the purpose of manipulating the suspect's behavior rather than invading his privacy. An example of this would be the techniques that airport cops use to cajole a suspect into waiting around while they develop the legal justification to arrest him. Since they can legally detain his luggage, they'll seize it and offer to provide him with a receipt for it. Or, if he doesn't have an ID card, they'll offer to run off a computer printout for him to use as identification. The offers of a receipt or an ID are ruses; they seem to be favors furnished for the suspect's benefit, but they're actually an attempt to lure him into a back office and delay his departure.[12]

THE PRETEXT

"How easy a thing it is to find a staff if a man be minded to beat a dog."

Thomas Becon, *Early Works: Preface* (1563)

Another type of dirty trick that the cops will play in order to beat the rules is to act on pretext. Unlike a ruse, a pretext doesn't depend upon the development of cordiality. It's nothing more nor less than a circumstance which is created to serve as an excuse for something else. They don't attempt to fool the suspect as to their identity because they don't need his consent. The pretext provides all the legal justification they need for what they do.

A common example of a pretext is the use of a local "stop and identify" ordinance. As we've discussed in Chapter 8, it's unconstitutional for the cops to stop people on the street and roust them for no reason. Sometimes they just don't like the looks of a person, however, and feel sure that they'd find something to charge him with if only they could shake him down. For this reason, some cities have enacted ordinances which entitle the cops to stop people on the street and demand proof of their identity. The cops can use the ordinance as a pretext in several ways. They scrutinize the suspect for anything suspicious while he's fumbling around after his ID, occasionally being thereby able to spot the bulge of a weapon, contraband, or suspicious behavior which will serve as justification for a frisk.

Having gotten an ID of some kind, they can then kill some more time running it through a computer check (if they have that capability at their disposal). Should the ID appear to be irregular, or if the computer check shows something wrong, they can run the suspect in and do their routine field and inventory searches in the process. If the person doesn't have an ID, the ordinance gives them an excuse to run him in for that. One way or another, they're probably going to get to do their search, which was the real purpose for all these shenanigans.

Another pretext is the old planned-incident-to-lawful-arrest search, which is usually used to find contraband. As will be recalled from Chapter 7, the police can search anywhere within reach of a person who's being arrested, and that includes his car or the entire room he happens to be in. Thus, if they suspect that a person might be likely to store contraband in a particular place, they'll plan a pretextual arrest to take place there in order to get an excuse to search it. If they already have cause to arrest, all they have to do is wait until the suspect gets into his car, or goes into his house, and then make the bust. [13] If they're after someone in particular but haven't been able to get the goods on him, sometimes they can dig up an outstanding arrest warrant on him for an old traffic violation,[14] failure to pay child support,[15] or some other penny ante charge. They'll hang onto the warrant like a gambling marker, then "cash it in" when they see the suspect go into his car or his house, depending on where they think they'll find the evidence they're looking for.

Although they're supposed to confine their search-incident-to-lawful-arrest to the room in which they make the arrest, the cops can get around that rule by means of another pretext — claiming that they fear there may be armed accomplices in other rooms.[16]/[17] That justifies them in going through the whole building, looking for the imaginary accomplices wherever they could be hiding, and casing the place out for evidence in "plain view" all the while. What it boils down to is a free general search.

Creating an exigency is another pretext that the police can use in order to get around the warrant requirement. Used in combination with the incident-to-lawful-arrest trick, it can be every bit as effective as a planned police raid — only they don't need the warrant. If the cops are after a dope distributor, for example, they can bait a junkie into unknowingly making a purchase from him with marked bills which they've supplied, then bust the junkie while still in the supplier's neighborhood. The exigency that has thus been created warrants an immediate arrest of the distributor, since it's assumed that he's bound to learn of his customer's arrest within minutes and attempt to destroy all the evidence. Incident to the arrest, of course, they get to do the search which turns up more dope and the marked bills. Busting the junkie in the supplier's immediate vicinity thus serves as a pretext for the emergency arrest and incident search of the supplier.[18]

Although the presence of a search warrant presumably confers a dimension of fairness to a search, it too can be adulterated by means of a pretext. An affidavit based upon an informant's testimony is sufficient probable cause to justify the issuance of a search warrant. If an unscrupulous cop should find some low-life willing to lie for him in the affidavit, he'd have himself a custom-made search warrant. Even if it could be proven that the claims in the affidavit were lies, the warrant would still be legal unless it could also be proven that the *cop himself* was involved in the lie.[19] That, of course, would never happen because the informant would become impossible to locate, and the cop would deny any knowledge of a lie. Thus, the fraudulent affidavit serves as the pretext to legally carry out a search that should never have been permitted.

Another way that the police can manipulate a search warrant through pretext is by having it specify something tiny as one of the objects of the search.[20] This gives them an excuse to pry into every jar and rat hole, no matter how small. It is, in other words, a pretext for conducting the sort of general search that the warrant requirement is supposed to prevent.

Sometimes it's useful for the police to separate a suspect from his family during the investigative phase; gullible family and friends will often give up incriminating evidence more readily when the suspect isn't around. This can be accomplished by getting him out of town on the pretext of some examination, such as a polygraph test. While the old man's gone, the cops can go over to his house and flim-flam his family into giving them evidence that they would otherwise have needed a warrant for.[21]

Not to be forgotten in our discussion of pretexts is the anonymous tip. Since the police eagerly solicit reports from the good citizens of the community regarding suspicious things they see, it isn't at all unusual for them to receive anonymous letters and telephone calls. A cop in the field can capitalize on this by sending in his own anonymous "citizen report" telling the central office anything he wants them to believe. Headquarters will then relay such "information" to officers in the field and advise them to make the appropriate investigation.

This technique is useful whenever the cops need to shake somebody down but don't have just cause to do so. Suppose that, by way of an illegal entry or wiretap, they learn that a suspect has possession of a large cache of drugs. They can't use such information as grounds for a search warrant, but it does tell them that a search would yield results. All they need is the justification to make the search. It's a simple enough matter to write an anonymous note describing the information and send it in to the police station as though it came from some dutiful citizen. With the inclusion of a few easily confirmable details, the note can be corroborated by some cursory police observations and thus rise to the level of probable cause — it becomes the basis for a legal search warrant.[22]

Similarly, if they suspect that a guy is holding drugs, but don't have justification to search him, they can get their justification by means of a quick anonymous phone call to the station. They merely describe their suspect, tell his location, and allege that he's carrying a concealed gun. Still maintaining visual contact of him, the cops will be all set to shake their suspect down when the bulletin comes back over the radio.[23]

Pretexts represent an attempt by the officer to circumvent the lawful procedures that he's sworn to uphold, and are therefore looked upon by the courts with greater disapproval than are ruses, which merely seek to fool the suspect. It's pretty difficult to prove that a cop has used a pretext, however, so it usually succeeds in its intended purpose.

DECEITFUL ACQUISITION OF STATEMENTS

"I, under fair pretence of friendly ends
And well-plac'd words of glozing courtesy
Baited with reasons not unplausible,
Wind me into the easy-hearted man,
And hug him into snares."

John Milton, *Comus*, line 160 (1634)

Just as they use dirty tricks to compromise a person's Fourth Amendment rights, so do they use them in getting around the Fifth. Most commonly it's a simple matter of exploiting people's misplaced confidence. The family and friends of an arrestee are often made the unwitting tools of the prosecutor by virtue of their naive hopes of leniency and willingness to believe in the fairness of the System. More often than is realized, a wily interrogator can successfully con his suspects loved ones into using their influence to coax an admission (or even a confession) from the addled fellow. Remember, it's *not* a constitutional violation for *family or friends* to "interrogate" a suspect after he has invoked his right to have counsel present.[24]

The probation or parole officer has a unique opportunity to take advantage of misplaced confidence, since many of his charges are likely to believe that they somehow owe him their candor. This sense of responsibility is likely to be even greater among those probationers and parolees who are enrolled in a special rehabilitation program, since they perceive their freedom to be contingent upon their fullest level of cooperation. The officer is thus in a position to trick his wards into making confidential disclosures to him which he can turn around and submit to the police as evidence toward new charges.[25]

In addition to the use of confidence, the cops can employ conversational tricks which are calculated to entice careless statements from a suspect's mouth. Many of these have been disclosed in Chapter 13 under the discussion of interrogation techniques. Seemingly insignificant statements can sometimes be as damaging as admissions,[26]/[27] and since everything a suspect says to the cops is recorded, it behooves them to provoke such statements whenever they can. Little comments which imply a knowledge of facts in a crime, or remarks suggesting a suspect's awareness of his rights and obligations, are often useful to the prosecution when it wants to apply legal technicalities against him later, such as his waiver of various rights.[28]

If their little attempts to bait comments fail, and it appears that they might come up without any material at all, they'll sometimes salvage a benefit from deliberately violating the *Miranda* Rule. Even though statements which a person makes as a result of such a violation are inadmissible as *evidence*, they *can* be used to *impeach* his testimony. Thus, if the cops can badger a suspect into losing his temper and making a few inculpatory remarks, they can hold it over his head in order to prevent him from taking the stand in his own defense.[29]

Probably the most egregious dirty trick of all in the Fifth Amendment context is the manipulation of the grand jury by the prosecution in order to turn it into an investigative tool. In a way, it's really a form of pretext by which a suspect's friends and relatives can be forced to inform on him — something which would be impossible by any other legitimate means. It's nothing less than an abuse which has been made legal for the exclusive benefit of the government.

ENTRAPMENT

"Artifice and stratagem may be employed to catch those engaged in criminal enterprises."

Chief Justice Charles Evans Hughes, *Sorrells v U.S.,* 287 US 435, 441, 53 SCt 210, 212 (1932)

There's a great deal of talk these days about "police entrapment," but most people have little understanding of what it means. Common sense suggests that it would be "entrapment" for the cops to represent themselves as lawbreakers in order to conduct an illegal undertaking by which they entice suspects to become partisans in the crime. Many people would even say that *any* police involvement in an illegal enterprise amounts to entrapment. These notions represent popularly held ideas of fairness, but they *don't* accurately state the law.

The concept of entrapment is based upon the idea that the government shouldn't induce innocent folks to commit crimes.[30] The "innocence" of the suspect is the key consideration. Obviously, if he's caught taking part in an illegal operation he isn't one hundred percent innocent, but whether or not he did the crime is not the question here. It's accepted from the outset that the suspect broke the law; it's the factors which *caused* him to do so that must be identified.

The law recognizes only three possibilities: either (1) the police cause the suspect to participate in the crime by planting the idea in his head and then goading him into it; (2) the suspect steps in on his own initiative, but the cops take such an active role that they virtually commit the crime for him; or (3) the suspect enters on his own initiative and utilizes the facilities and opportunities furnished by the police to commit a crime. The first situation is "entrapment," the second is "outrageous government involvement," and the third is tough luck.

It's usually impossible to prove to a certainty that the police did or did not put the idea of crime into a suspect's head. Therefore, it's customary to allow a jury to decide this question based upon facts.[31] The *predisposition* of the suspect to commit the particular crime in question is the main focus of attention. In a drug case the lack of predisposition might be suggested by such things as: (1) the absence of any effort to profit from the drug business, (2) the absence of other evidence of trafficking, (3) hesitancy to become involved, (4) an effort to kick the drug habit, and (5) the oldness or absence of prior drug convictions.[32] These kinds of facts tend to suggest that the suspect was not prone to commit the crime, and that the cops may have created it themselves. The lack of predisposition is the threshold condition that must be satisfied in order for a suspect to claim the defense of entrapment.[33]

Once that's been established, the degree of police involvement can be considered in order to determine whether or not entrapment did indeed occur. If we're considering a drug case, clues as to the extent of police involvement might be revealed by such conduct as: (1) the inducement of the suspect to return to using drugs, (2) the use of threats, repeated begging, or other forms of pressure to get him to do the crime, (3) appealing to his sympathy by feigning withdrawal symptoms, (4) originating the idea for the crime, (5) supplying facilities, labor, raw materials, equipment, capital, or the dope itself, (6) providing all the customers, and (7) the instigation of other arrests which are suggestive of entrapment.[30]/[34] A suspect can thus establish the conventional "subjective" entrapment defense by showing that (1) he was not predisposed toward committing the crime, and (2) the cops came along and made him do it.

It's important to realize that, when a person is pulled into an entrapment setup by somebody who isn't connected with the police, he technically hasn't been entrapped. Such an unfortunate twist of fate is known as "derivative entrapment," and it generally leaves the suspect without any right to make use of the entrapment defense.[35]/[36]

Some of the Supreme Court Justices have recognized the possibility of a second type of defense based upon an intolerable level of government involvement in an entrapment-type setup, even though the suspect is predisposed to committing the crime and therefore ineligible for the conventional entrapment defense. They call it the "objective," "outrageous government involvement," or "fundamental fairness" defense. Basically, it's for cases where the cops are extremely pushy and heavily involved in the creation of the crime. Those Federal Circuits where it's been recognized include the Second (Connecticut, New York and Vermont),[37] Third (Delaware, New Jersey and Pennsylvania),[36] Fifth (Louisiana, Mississippi and Texas),[38] and Ninth (Alaska, Arizona, California, Hawaii, Idaho, Montana, Nevada, Oregon and Washington).[39] It isn't often that anyone gets acquitted in federal court on the basis of the "outrageous involvement" defense, but it's gaining wider acceptance in the state courts, and enjoys a strong following in legal academic circles.[40] In at least one instance, a minimally involved suspect who was the victim of derivative entrapment was allowed to use this defense in lieu of the entrapment defense, to which he wasn't entitled.[36]

There's no constitutional right to be free of entrapment.[41]/[42] The legal reasoning behind the defenses of entrapment and outrageous government involvement is based upon a clause in the Fifth Amendment which says that no person shall "be deprived of life, liberty, or property, without due process of law." This "due process clause" imposes the obligation of a fundamental standard of fairness upon the operation of the law; it makes the police answerable to a universal sense of justice. Granted, it's a sense of justice conceived by judges and other hypocrites, but it nevertheless does set a limit to the extent of police knavery. The cops are permitted to *trap* suspects, but not to *entrap* them. They're given a broad margin of freedom in which to play sneaky tricks and set up all manner of ambushes, but they're not allowed to create crime and drive the innocent into it. As Justice Rehnquist put it, "Congress could not have intended criminal punishment for a defendant who has committed all the elements of a proscribed offense but was induced to commit them by the government."[43]

REFERENCES

1. *U.S. v Caceres,* 440 US 741, 757, 99 SCt 1465, 1474 (1979), J. Marshall dissenting

2. *Scott v U.S.,* 436 US 128, 143-144, 98 SCt 1717, 1726-1727 (1978), J. Brennan dissenting

3. *McGuire v U.S.,* 273 US 95, 99, 47 SCt 259, 60 (1927)

4. *Brewer v Williams,* 430 US 387, 417, 97 SCt 1232, 1248 (1977), C. J. Burger dissenting

5. *Roschin v California,* 342 US 165, 169, 72 SCt 205, 208 (1952)

6. *Benson v California,* 336 F2d 791, 792, 797 (9th Cir. 1964)

7. *Gouled v U.S.*, 255 US 298, 305-306, 41 SCt 261, 263-264 (1921)

8. *Guidry v State*, 671 P2d 1277, 1281 (Alaska 1983)

9. *Pascu v State*, 577 P2d 1064, 1067-1068 (Alaska 1978)

10. *U.S. v Hinkle*, 637 F2d 1154, 1158-1159 (7th Cir. 1981)

11. *U.S. v Carreon*, 626 F2d 528, 535 (7th Cir. 1980)

12. *U.S. v Wallraff*, 705 F2d 980, 986 (8th Cir. 1983)

13. *New York v Belton*, 453 US 454, 470, 101 SCt 2860, 2869 (1981), J. Brennan dissenting

14. *People v Holloway*, Michigan Sup. Ct., 12/23/82

15. *People v Zimmerman*, N.Y. Sup. Ct., Suffolk City, 1/14/83

16. *U.S. v Baker*, 577 F2d 1147, 1152 (4th Cir. 1978)

17. *U.S. v Gardner*, 627 F2d 906, 909-910 (9th Cir. 1980)

18. *U.S. v Santana*, 427 US 38, 48-49, 96 SCt 2406, 2412 (1976), J. Marshall dissenting

19. *Franks v Delaware*, 438 US 154, 171, 98 SCt 2674, 2684 (1978)

20. *Harris v U.S.*, 331 US 145, 188-189, 67 SCt 1098, 1116 (1947), J. Murphy dissenting

21. *Coolidge v New Hampshire*, 403 US 443, 446, 91 SCt 2022, 2027 (1971)

22. *Illinois v Gates*, 462 US __, 103 SCt 2317, 2325-2326 (1983)

23. *U.S. v Mason*, D.C. Ct. App., 9/9/82

24. *Taylor v Alabama*, 457 US 687, 102 SCt 2664, 2668 (1982)

25. *Minnesota v Murphy*, __ US, __ 103 SCt 1136, 1140-1141 (1984)

26. *Franks v Delaware*, 438 US at 156-157, 98 SCt at 2677

27. *U.S. v Jimenez*, 602 F2d 139, 141 (7th Cir. 1979)

28. *U.S. v Thomas*, 729 F2d 120 (2d Cir. 1984)

29. *Harris v New York*, 401 US 222, 224-225, 91 SCt 643, 645 (1971)

30. *Sherman v U.S.*, 356 US 369, 372-374, 78 SCt 819, 821-822 (1958)

31. *Id.*, 356 US at 380, 78 SCt at 824

32. *Id.*, 356 US at 375-376, 78 SCt at 822

33. *U.S. v Russell*, 411 US 423, 436, 93 SCt-1637, 1645 (1973)

34. *Greene v U.S.*, 454 F2d 783, 786-787 (9th Cir. 1971)

35. *U.S. v Shapiro*, 669 F2d 593, 597-598 (9th Cir. 1982)

36. *U.S. v Twigg*, 588 F2d 373, 381-382 (3d Cir. 1978)

37. *U.S. v Archer*, 484 F2d 670, 676-677 (2d Cir. 1973)

38. *U.S. v Oquendo*, 490 F2d 161, 163 (5th Cir. 1974)

39. *U.S. v Wylie*, 625 F2d 1371, 1377 (9th Cir. 1980)

40. *U.S. v Twigg*, 588 F2d at 383 n. 3

41. *U.S. v Russell*, 411 US at 430, 93 SCt at 1642

42. *Jones v Bombeck*, 375 F2d 737, 738 (3d Cir. 1967)

43. *U.S. v Russell*, 411 US at 435, 93 SCt at 1644

Chapter 16

THE AIRPORT

"With increasing recurrence, we have considered the delicate balance which must be struck
between the interest of the public in terminat-
ing narcotics smuggling and the individual's
right to live unburdened by unreasonable
intrusions on his privacy as we are called upon
to assess the constitutionality of a warrantless
"investigatory stop" of domestic air passengers
by Drug Enforcement Administration agents
struggling to stem the flood of dangerous
drugs."

Judge Irving R. Kaufman, *U.S. v Ramirez-
Cifuentes,* 682 F2d 337, 338 (2d Cir. 1982)

If you've ever been observant while passing through
an airport, you've probably noticed the impassive-
looking gentlemen in the J.C. Penney suits. They loiter
about as though waiting for a bus, when in fact they're
really waiting around to "make a bust." These detectives
have created a profession out of snooping on travelers
in the hope of ferreting out those who are secretly engaged in illegal activities. Today's highly mobile society
and the travel demands of the free enterprise system
have made the airport their ideal pool in which to "go
fishing."

Though far from being their only quarry, the drug
trafficker has proven to be the police's best customer at
the airport. So cozy is this relationship that the Drug Enforcement Administration (D.E.A.) has compiled a whole
list of characteristics just to detect possible traffickers
— the so-called "drug courier profile." Most of the
features on the profile are totally innocent by themselves, and easily fit many ordinary travelers who pass
through the airport. Several features together, however, are unlikely to be seen in the ordinary passenger.
The feds know from experience that, once they spot a
person who conforms to several of the points on their
profile, they will usually find drugs in his possession.

In order to exploit the use of as many auxiliary eyes and ears as possible, federal officers educate airline employees[1] and train officials[2] in the use of the profile. Some of the things that an agent would ordinarily miss are thus brought to light by a diligent ticket clerk or an attentive skycap. The profile used by such functionaries, however, is necessarily brief and simplistic. It will be more informative to consider the profile from the viewpoint of the narcotics agent, for whom it may be thought to exist in two stages: the initial impression and the investigation.

THE INITIAL IMPRESSION

Any psychologist will tell you that a wealth of information about a person can be had simply by watching him. The narcotics agent gains his initial impression by observing the appearance and behavior of the travelers. Of course, he pays special attention to those arriving on flights at off-peak hours,[3] and particularly those coming from "drug source cities," where couriers are likely to have picked up a load. Some of the principal "distribution centers" include Los Angeles, San Diego, El Paso, Miami, Ft. Lauderdale, San Juan, Chicago, Detroit, and New York. When such a flight comes into one of the other large metropolitan airports, there must certainly be a magically charged atmosphere akin to the Christmas Eve vigil of small children waiting up for Santa Claus.

Features of the general appearance that are typical for drug couriers include membership in the 25- to 35-year-old age group,[4] being a black female,[5] being of a racial extraction different from most of the people on the flight,[6] and traveling alone.[7] Clothing that's inappropriate for the weather[6] or for the particular flight[8] is a red flag to the narcotics agent; casual dress on a 3 p.m. businessman's flight, where everyone else is wearing a business suit, will quickly raise eyebrows. A distinctive piece of clothing, such as a colorful coat, will occasionally set off alarms when agents elsewhere have previously become interested in that individual and reported his description among their ranks.[3] A similar situation occurs when agents who have watched a person depart see him return the next day wearing the same clothes.[1]/[9] Carrying a shoulder bag is another point on the profile,[9] particularly if it's untagged, or if two traveling companions both carry them.[10] Unusual bulges or distortions of body shapes suggest contraband to even untrained eyes.

A person's luggage also constitutes part of his appearance, and there are several aspects that will render it suspicious to inquisitive police. Being without luggage altogether,[11] or having only a limited amount of it on a long trip that's supposed to be a vacation,[9] is a major tipoff. Suitcases that are noticeably empty[1] tend to catch the attention of the baggage clerks. New[12] or especially heavy-looking luggage (like American Tourister)[4] is also an eyecatcher, as are those tiny padlocks that some people put on their suitcases.[13] They may keep the lids from accidentally popping, but they also tend to set a nark's imagination popping. The way luggage is tagged is very significant; untagged pieces[13] or tags that are marked with only a last name and city of destination (instead of the complete set of information called for)[4] often betray their illegal contents.

There are many characteristic modes of behavior that the drug agents look for, beginning immediately with the sequence of deplaning. Couriers are typically among the first[14] or the last[10] to disembark, and it's particularly curious when one of the first and one of the last are later noted to be traveling companions.[6] Those who are traveling together often create an intrigue about it that gives them away. They may converse freely with one another outside the terminal, then separate and ignore each other once they come inside, conducting their limited conversations there in whispers.[10] There's a characteristic fashion of "single file progression" frequently seen, where one courier follows the other from several paces behind, always stopping and starting in concert with the leader.[10] Answering in his behalf one moment and avoiding him the next is another form of this repudiatory behavior of one courier with another.[13] The signalled nod,[14] of course, is a conspiratorial cliche that's familiar to anyone who's ever watched a George Raft movie.

By far and away, nervousness is the most important behavioral sign. Knowing that you're carrying a pound of coke right past The Man's nose is likely to make you a little jumpy, no matter how "cool" you are. Most couriers are sufficiently lacking in savoir faire that, even without police provocation, they'll exhibit some degree of hesitancy, cautiousness, or furtiveness.[15] "Scanning" behavior is easily spotted from afar, particularly when the person looks behind him over his shoulder. It's usually evident as the subject looks all around upon entering the terminal, sometimes even slowing down the flow of pedestrian traffic in his futile effort to spot police surveillance before it spots him.[16] Apprehensive people often "scan" as they enter or exit from a vehicle.[16] Just being overly conscious of nearby people is a recognizable sign of nervousness,[12] but looking directly at the agents, or worse — playing mutual-surveillance "cat and mouse" games with them — is an open invitation to official inquiry.[14]

Haste is a common ingredient, and is often evidenced by a person's fast pace[14] or by his dash to leave the terminal directly upon arrival.[7] An initially slow pace which subsequently quickens is similarly suspicious.[17] Acts of desperation, such as hailing a taxi in the rain rather than waiting in the sheltered taxi stand,[16] blatantly advertises a trafficker's anxiety to get away quickly. Most couriers are not met by anyone at the airport,[1] and consequently tend to make a beeline for the phone upon arrival,[11] often making several calls.[8]

Time-killing is likely to arouse the suspicion of police when a person walks at a conspicuously slow pace,[18] repeatedly stops at water fountains,[17] goes into rest-rooms without using the facilities,[15] hangs around the magazine stand without looking at the wares,[10] or waits at the baggage carousel without picking up any luggage.[13] If he shows special care in handling one of his bags compared with the others, that too is noteworthy.[16] Of course, the most suspicious behavior of all is seen when a subject resorts to deliberate evasive action.[10]

Some profile matches are hustled to the attention of the narcotics agent by dutiful airline employees, as already mentioned. Such tips are often the only introductory clues to a fruitful "bust," and are therefore a significant part of the agent's initial impression. A customer can expect to get some scrutiny if he purchases his ticket at the desk;[3] when he does so immediately prior to departure,[3] or even on the same day,[13] it's certain to be noticed by some would-be gendarme. Paying in cash,[11] especially from a large roll of bills[6] of small denomination[11] or large denomination[19] is said to be highly characteristic. Since drug couriers often change flights en-route in the mistaken notion that they are thereby shaking off surveillance,[18] ticket agents turn this tactic against them by immediately reporting such requests.

THE INVESTIGATION

Once a detective has picked up enough suspicious signals from his initial impression of a traveler, he'll feel justified to poke his nose into the matter a little further by making a few inquiries. This is the second, or investigative, phase of the profile. It usually begins when the agent saunters up to his quarry with an authoritative flash of the credentials and requests permission to "ask a few questions." Knowing that most people with something to hide will immediately become uneasy when they are thus singled out, he looks for all the little signs of nervousness that might confirm his suspicions: the trembly, fidgeting fingers... the averted gaze... the pale, sweaty forehead... the squeaky, stammering voice.

He will ask for two things initially: proof of identification (i.e. a driver's license) and the airline ticket. Lack of suitable ID,[19] or a discrepancy between the name on the card and the one on the ticket,[11] suggests that the suspect is traveling under an alias in typical courier form. With the ticket in his hand, the agent can readily see two important sources of information: the passenger's itinerary and the baggage claims. He wants to see the itinerary because couriers often buy one-way tickets[11] for trips of short duration (usually with only a one-day layover),[3] and take peculiar routes. An itinerary going from Greensboro, N.C. to Los Angeles, then to Raleigh, N.C. the next day might be one such odyssey.[3] A flight from Los Angeles to New Orleans by the circuitous way of St. Louis might be another.[11] He's interested in the baggage claims (which are usually stapled to the ticker folder) because (1) the lack of baggage claims fits the profile,[11] (2) if the suspect has removed and concealed them he's probably fearful of being associated with that luggage, and (3) once the agent gets the claim numbers he can go look at the luggage.

Armed with the names from the ID and the ticket, Sherlock can now get a full read-out from the airline computer on recent flights made, telephone numbers given, and whether the customer did indeed check in luggage. The phone numbers can be verified to see if they are phony[11] or suggest an illegal enterprise,[1] and the names can be run through police computers to find out if the suspect is a known trafficker[20] or otherwise of interest to the authorities. Thanks to the wondrous silicon chip, this can all be done within minutes — indeed, it's often done prior to even approaching the suspect when an agent has learned his name from a helpful ticket clerk.

At this point the agent will either be satisfied that the passenger's "clean" and let him be on his way, or he'll be suspicious enough to press the investigation. The usefulness of the drug courier profile is essentially over once there's a serious intent to investigate. Its role is basically to steer the policeman in the direction of an investigation that will have more probability of paying off, and at the same time give him the legal excuse to pry into the affairs of a citizen who's minding his own business. The Supreme Court has declared that, before the police may stop and interrogate a person, they have to be able to say exactly what it is about him that suggests that he may be breaking the law. This requirement for the existence of reasonable articulable suspicion is one of our few protections against arbitrary police harassment.[21] The mere preference of a person to dress casually and carry a shoulder bag on a flight out of L.A. doesn't justify a grilling by the cops; having been alerted by these innocent hallmarks, however, they might acquire their justification after watching him act out some cloak-and-dagger routine.

Let's assume, for the sake of illustration, that our agent has singled out a Ms. Coca White, who's been glancing furtively from side to side since getting off her flight from Miami. Feeling meddlesome and having nothing better to do, he'll tell her that he's looking for drugs and has reason to believe that she's carrying them. If she wasn't unsettled by the initial approach of a narcotics agent, a guilty person would certainly start sweating at that statement. Self-conscious at being put on the spot, she's more likely to trip up as she attempts to dissemble, and her clumsy, evasive answers will achieve only more suspicion.[6/13/20] Then Sherlock makes his move for the jugular — he asks for her consent to a search. With the perspiration starting to run down her forehead, her panty hose suddenly feeling uncomfortably tight, and sensing that everyone in the airport must be watching, it's easy for poor Coca to overlook the import of that request. Any hesitation to agree is swiftly met with the warning that "a warrant can be gotten." If Ms. White is like most people, she'll reluctantly consent, even knowing that there are drugs in her luggage.[22] She's even likely to accept it as a kindness when the agent offers to escort her to a room where the bags may be searched in privacy. Coca's lack of knowledge about the process and about her constitutional rights has seen her voluntarily place herself into police custody while she proceeds to hand them the rope to hang her with.

In the event that a person (wisely) refuses to consent to the search, police have the authority to temporarily detain the luggage while they "investigate" further.[23] They might try passing it through the fluoroscope, or subjecting it to sniffing by trained dogs,[12] but nothing they can do to it will give them the right to open it up without a search warrant.[2/24] While there's no fixed time limit on how long they may hold a person's luggage during one of these "limited investigations," the United States Supreme Court has recently ruled that 90 minutes is definitely too long.[23] The likelihood of getting a warrant that quickly is often slim. The officer needs hard facts, such as a positive dog-sniff test, an inside tip from a reliable informant, or a whole panoply of very suspicious observations, in order to justify to a magistrate that he has probable cause to believe there are drugs in the baggage. Assuming that he can come up with his probable cause at all, he's then faced with the formidable challenge of finding out which country club His Honor is hiding at, and hoping that he'll be sober enough to come to the telephone once he's finally located. Moreover, some state laws don't even provide for search warrants over the telephone,[25] and the agent may well end up filling out affidavits and waiting for three or four days before he gets his warrant.[26]

Having failed to wheedle the suspect out of his consent to a search, the agent's hope of lawfully hanging onto him lies partly in the chance that he can be duped into waiting around for his luggage. The suspect will be coaxed into going along to an "office" somewhere,[18] or perhaps invited to join in on the chase as the police scurry around to establish their probable cause.[23] Even if he insists on completing his flight, however, a suspect is under full police control;[23] he won't be getting off until the plane lands, and by that time a warranted search of his luggage might be done and a reception party arranged for him.

What the police fear most in such a situation is that their suspect will promptly leave the airport and become unavailable for their prosecution efforts. Under the law, that's precisely what the citizen is entitled to do.[18] Unless the police have probable cause to believe he's in some stage of committing a crime, they're not allowed to arrest him. They can "detain" him temporarily while they ask their questions and punch their computer buttons to see if he's wanted for anything, but on the sole basis of a few suspicious observations, they're not justified in making an arrest. The matches with their profile only serve to give them a reasonable articulable suspicion that something fishy is going on. It gives them a legal justification to stop a person for questioning.[21]/[23] Without those suspicious little things that singled the person out for attention, they wouldn't have been justified in stopping him at all.[27] Once they do, however, there's a limit on just how far they can go.

Assuming that he has wisely behaved like a gentleman, the police are restricted to just asking questions. The theory is that anything suspicious-looking, short of an obvious red-handed crime, may well have a perfectly logical explanation. Once the citizen explains himself to their satisfaction, he's entitled to go on his way.

It's critical to realize that a person doesn't have to answer the questions at all.[29] If his answers are unconvincing, or if he says or does something that raises more suspicion, that just gives the police the right to pursue the matter a little further.[26] Indeed, if the man asking the questions happens to be a federal officer, any little white lies that are told to him in an attempt to dispel his suspicion can themselves be grounds for an arrest and conviction.[30] It's a felony to lie to a federal agent, and it's amazing how quickly they can catch a person in a lie and thereby escalate an "investigative detention" into an arrest.[31]

Unless the suspect gives them some solid facts to use against him, the police can't carry on a detention indefinitely; the American Law Institute (A.L.I.) has recommended a maximum duration of 20 minutes for these stops.[32] Most of the time they will be far shorter than that, but the important thing to realize is that the police must decide within this brief time period to either arrest the suspect or release him. If they don't have probable cause to make an arrest (which means actually demonstrating the presence of drugs), the courier must be free to leave.[18]

Naturally, the police will demand to see a reliable form of identification, such as a state driver's license, that will assure them of where they can nab the suspect later if they find drugs in his luggage. A person isn't required by federal law to produce an ID when they ask for it,[29/33] but failure to do so might result in his being followed and kept under surveillance when he leaves. Moreover, the act of giving police a convincing name and address makes it clear to them that the person expects his luggage to be returned after they are finished with it. It's critical to insist on a possessory right to the luggage because that's the only thing preventing the cops from opening it immediately; the moment they can show that it's been abandoned, they no longer need a search warrant.[34]

The smart courier faced with an "investigative stop" would be truthful[50] but taciturn, producing a valid ID (which would pass muster on a computer check), and politely refuse to consent to any form of search or detention. He would immediately seek to leave the airport instead of attempting to continue his flight. If the police insisted on detaining his luggage, he would forcefully assert his ownership rights but promptly get himself away, leaving them "holding the bag." Insisting on a search warrant would, in effect, buy him enough time to successfully do his disappearing act. A really shrewd fellow will have the goods safely stashed on his person instead of in his luggage anyway. Hopefully, after reading this chapter, the educated courier will probably never be confronted in the first place, since he will scrupulously avoid conforming with any of the indicia of the drug courier profile; after all, an ounce of prevention is worth a pound of cocaine...

This isn't the only such profile that's being used at the airport. During the sixties, when it was fashionable to hijack planes and take them to Cuba, the Federal Aviation Administration (F.A.A.) created a special "skyjacker profile" which was designed to identify potential saboteurs and air pirates. The government is far more fearful of terrorists than of drug traffickers, and has taken pains to avoid advertising what's on their skyjacker profile.[35] Nevertheless, common sense should suggest what its features would be, and its basic concept and the method of deployment, using airline personnel as auxiliaries, is the same as for the drug courier profile. A slight departure in philosophy of the skyjacker profile from the courier profile is that, once they identify somebody they suspect of being a terrorist, they're probably not going to let him walk back out the door the way they would a courier. They don't want to give him the opportunity to come back later and try again, possibly with better success the next time.[36]

Another list of characteristics which the police use at the airport, and one which has many features in common with the drug courier profile, is the "mule profile" used by Customs agents. A courier who smuggles drugs into the U.S. from another country is known as a "mule." Since a person's luggage is subjected to much more Customs scrutiny than his body, mules have learned to stash the stuff on their person in various ways. Packages can be taped to the body, but the bulky clothing that's needed to conceal them is in itself a tipoff to Customs agents, who can then expose it by conducting a strip search.[37] A safer way of carrying small quantities of valuable contraband, such as heroin or cocaine, is to seal it within balloons or condoms and "keyster-stash" it — slip it into the rectum and/or vagina. This would require the cops to conduct a body cavity search in order to find the drugs. Safer still, the drug balloons can be swallowed, and up to 700 grams of merchandise can be transported at one time without being exposed to view.[38]

The internal techniques of transportation would be very difficult for Customs agents to detect, were it not for a pattern that's been demonstrated recently by South American "importers." They hire local peasants as mules, buy them plane tickets, and send them off to the U.S. with their bellies full of balloons. A number of features that are characteristic of these mules have been formulated by Customs into a profile.

As with the drug courier profile, the source of a flight provides the first clue; one which is arriving from a drug source country, such as Colombia or Peru, is highly scrutinized.[39]

Features of the general appearance are primarily those of a peasant, particularly one who has made a clumsy attempt to represent himself as being of a higher social class. Inability to speak English[39] and evidence of low education, such as poor handwriting,[40] are typical. A woman who has rough "worker's hands" is considered to be suspect when she sports a fresh manicure.[41]/[42] Exhibiting an excessively passive bearing and carrying only one small suitcase[39] are further features of the peasant-mule.

Like the domestic drug courier, a mule usually travels solo. This is particularly noticeable when it's a woman, since Latin women don't usually travel alone.[40]/[42]

The mule's airline ticket has usually been purchased with cash, and since somebody else has gotten it for him, he doesn't know where or when it was bought, how much it cost, or what means of payment was used.[40]/[41] There's often a peculiar itinerary as well, such as short flights to and from drug distribution cities.[41] The passport often reflects other recent short trips to the U.S.[39]/[44]

Mules typically carry about $1500 in U.S. currency, probably because that's their standard fee for the job,[42] and they lack the checks and credit cards that most international travelers carry to cover their expenses.[42]

Predominant in the mule profile is a pathetic lack of plausibility concerning the visitor's plans.[45] Customs agents savor this part of their interview in the same way that the D.E.A. agent does the investigatory phase of the drug courier profile; it's a great opportunity for them to belittle these people and toy with them while playing Sherlock Holmes. The name of the game is to see how badly they can discredit the traveler's cover story.

Typically, the mules have no family or friends in the U.S., and have no idea of where they're going to be staying.[39] They often claim to be visiting the U.S. on business, and frequently hold themselves out to be proprietors who have come to purchase electronic equipment. Unfortunately, they usually know nothing about the business they're supposed to be in,[40]/[41] and carry no business cards or other professional paraphernalia.[40]/[46] They have little or no knowledge about the items they're supposed to be purchasing, where to shop for them, or how much it'll cost; they usually don't have enough money to cover such purchases anyway.[44] When asked how they plan to get around to do their buying, they generally say they plan to have taxis take them around.[47] One fellow, who was supposed to be a Sony dealer, told the Customs agents that Sony and Toshiba products were made in America.[47] Another poor soul said that he planned to buy three or four Xerox color-copying machines with his $971 and bring them back to Colombia in his luggage.[43]

- 269 -

When a traveler's conformity to this profile leads the Customs agents to suspect that they might have a "swallower," they can exercise a much higher level of discretion in detaining and searching him than the police would have under similar circumstances on a domestic flight. The airport is the functional equivalent of the border for flights arriving from outside the country, and once a person has landed on such a flight, he's irreversibly committed to the power of the Customs agents until they decide to release him. He can't simply walk away like a domestic drug courier can. How long they can detain him, and how aggressive they'll get in looking for contraband, depends on what part of the country he's in and what grounds they have to search him.

As was discussed in Chapter 8, the standards of reasonableness for body searches at the border (or its airport equivalents) are: (1) frisk — no grounds are necessary; (2) strip search — "reasonable articulable suspicion" is necessary (which is supplied when the suspect matches the mule profile); (3) X-ray of the abdomen — "clear indication" is necessary in the Ninth Circuit (which is not supplied by mere conformity to the mule profile), but only "reasonable articulable suspicion" is required in the Eleventh Circuit; and (4) body cavity search — "clear indication" is necessary. It's obvious that a person is at greater risk of being asked to submit to an X-ray when he enters the country by one of the Eleventh Circuit states (Alabama, Florida or Georgia). What's more significant, however, is that if he refuses to consent to an X-ray, he's likely to be chained up and watched for the next 16 hours until he has passed the contents of his bowels. It's a whole different ball game from the "brief detention" that the domestic traveler is subject to; the suspected mule is forced to deliver up the evidence one way or another. Detention for such long periods of time on the basis of a mere profile match is considered reasonable in the Eleventh Circuit,[48] but not in the Ninth Circuit (the West Coast).[39]

If it hasn't been made eminently clear from the foregoing, it's worth an encore to emphasize that the American airport is a high-surveillance place. From the moment you step out of your taxicab[12] there are critical eyes watching your every move. If they don't like what they see, you can be having your phone number checked out,[12] your photograph taken, and a secret file made up on you while you're waiting in the terminal.[19] They'll squeeze the air out of your suitcases in the back room to help the dogs get a good whiff of what's inside,[49] and sometimes they'll even creep up behind you to give the dogs a smell of your bag as you sit with it in the lobby. It all sounds like the imaginings of a paranoid, but unfortunately this is one dream that's too true to be good. Everything that's been said came from real-life dramas, where people who were only expecting to make a little trip ended up in prison. Think of these case citations as a reading list, and you'll see for yourself what can happen at an airport.

REFERENCES

1. *U.S. v Van Lewis*, 556 F2d 385 (6th Cir. 1977)

2. *U.S. v Chadwick*, 431 US 1, 97 SCt 2476 (1977)

3. *U.S. v Hill*, 626 F2d 429 (5th Cir. 1980)

4. *Florida v Royer*, 460 US __, 103 SCt 1319 (1983)

5. *U.S. v McClain*, 452 FSupp 195 (E.D. Mich. 1977)

6. *U.S. v Diaz*, 503 F2d 1025 (3d Cir. 1974)

7. *U.S. v Smith*, 574 F2d 882 (6th Cir. 1978)

8. *U.S. v Gooding*, 695 F2d 78 (4th Cir. 1982)

9. *U.S. v McCaleb*, 552 F2d 717 (6th Cir. 1977)

10. *U.S. v Forero-Rincon*, 626 F2d 218 (2d Cir. 1980)

11. *U.S. v Ballard*, 573 F2d 913 (5th Cir. 1978)

12. *U.S. v Sullivan*, 625 F2d 13 (4th Cir. 1980)

13. *U.S. v Vasquez,* 612 F2d 1338 (2d Cir. 1979)

14. *U.S. v Collis,* 699 F2d 832 (6th Cir. 1983)

15. *U.S. v Moya,* 704 F2d 337 (7th Cir. 1983)

16. *U.S. v Price,* 599 F2d 494 (2d Cir. 1979)

17. *People v Kiser,* Ill. App. Ct., 1st Dist., 3/21/83

18. *U.S. v Mendenhall,* 446 US 544, 100 SCt 1870 (1980)

19. *U.S. v Pope,* 561 F2d 663 (6th Cir. 1977)

20. *U.S. v Beck,* 598 F2d 497 (9th Cir. 1979)

21. *Terry v Ohio,* 392 US 1, 88 SCt 1868 (1968)

22. *U.S. v Canales,* 572 F2d 1182 (6th Cir. 1978)

23. *U.S. v Place,* 462 US __, 103 SCt 2637 (1983)

24. *Robbins v California,* 453 US 420, 101 SCt 2841 (1981)

25. *State v Valencia,* New Jersey Sup. Ct., 5/16/83

26. *U.S. v Jodoin,* 672 F2d 232 (1st Cir. 1982)

27. *Reid v Georgia,* 448 US 440, 100 SCt 2752 (1980)

28. *Coolidge v New Hampshire,* 403 US 443, 91 SCt 2022 (1971)

29. *Kolender v Lawson,* __ US, __, 103 SCt 1855 (1983)

30. Title 18 U.S.C. Section 1001

31. *U.S. v Parten,* 462 F2d 430 (5th Cir. 1972)

32. A.L.I., *A Model Code of Pre-Arraignment Procedure,* Section 110.2 (1), 1975

33. *Brown v Texas,* 443 US 47, 99 SCt 2637 (1979)

34. *U.S. v Tolbert,* 692 F2d 1041 (6th Cir. 1982)

35. *U.S. v Bell,* 464 F2d 667, 669-670 (2d Cir. 1972)

36. *U.S. v Skipwith,* 482 F2d 1272, 1281 (5th Cir. 1973)

37. *U.S. v Vega-Barvo,* 729 F2d 1341, 1345 (11th Cir. 1984)

38. *U.S. v Pino,* 729 F2d 1357, 1359 (11th Cir. 1984)

39. *U.S. v de Hernandez,* (9th Cir. 1984)

40. *U.S. v Vega-Barvo,* 729 F2d at 1343

41. *U.S. v Castaneda-Castaneda,* 729 F2d 1360, 1362 (11th Cir. 1984)

42. *U.S. v De Montoya,* 729 F2d 1369, 1370 (11th Cir. 1984)

43. *U.S. v Padilla,* 729 F2d 1367, 1368 (11th Cir. 1984)

44. *U.S. v Mosquera-Ramirez,* 729 F2d 1353, 1354 (11th Cir. 1984)

45. *U.S. v Vega-Barvo,* 729 F2d at 1350

46. *U.S. v Pino,* 729 F2d at 1358

47. *U.S. v Henao-Castano,* 729 F2d 1364, 1366 (11th Cir. 1984)

48. *U.S. v Mosquera-Ramirez,* 729 F2d at 1355

49. *Sprowls v State,* Florida Ct. App., 3d Dist., 6/28/83

50. There is one lie that a person can (and should) tell a questioning federal agent; when asked if he has committed a crime (e.g. having drugs) a person should always say "no." He cannot be convicted under 18 U.S.C. 1001 for telling an exculpatory lie to a police investigator. *U.S. v Hajecate,* 683 F2d 894, 899-900 (5th Cir. 1982).

Chapter 17

THE
TEN COMMANDMENTS

"The wind sits in the shoulder of your sail, And you are stayed for. There — my blessing with thee, And these few precepts in thy memory Look thou character..."

William Shakespeare, *Hamlet,* Act I, scene iii, lines 56-59 (1600)

We've seen how the police can carry out search and seizure in order to get evidence of a crime, and how both the search and the seizure can be applied to the four basic areas of an individual's privacy — the person, his property, his house, and his statements. A search of the person can be as minimal as a simple inquiry, and can progress to a "frisk," a "field search," or more intrusive physical measures such as body cavity searches, blood-drawing, and surgery. Similarly, the seizure can be a mere approach premised upon an "articulable basis," an intermediate *Terry* detention based on "reasonable articulable suspicion," an arrest based on "probable cause," or the seizure of some fluid or item that's been extracted from the body.

The scope of the search and seizure of personal property (generally speaking, an automobile) and of a house (or other building) depends primarily on the grounds for searching it — consent, warrant, or some exception to the warrant requirement.

As with the person, search and seizure of somebody's statements can be of varying degrees of intrusiveness. The "search" may be an electronic bugging or wiretap, the exploitation of an informer, the reading of one's papers, the offer of an opportunity to talk, interrogation, or a court's subpoena. The seizure can be the acquisition of consent (for some intrusion), leads to new evidence or witnesses, statements that can be used for the impeachment of testimony, evidentiary statements, and confessions.

The law has defined a regular crazy-quilt of limits and exceptions to these search-and-seizure intrusions, and it changes in little ways from one day to the next, much as a coastline does under the effects of wind and waves. Such changes don't prevent the mariner from navigating the coastline based upon a reasonable knowledge of where the shoals lie, and the same principle holds true for the citizen as he carries out his business over the treacherous reefs of the law.

Without getting bogged down in the vagaries of local laws, it's possible to lay down some general axioms that will provide guidance for a person on his voyage through the reefs — "rules of thumb," so to speak, to keep the old tub floating safely in deep water. Now, it's far from this author's intention to recommend that anyone should intentionally break the law — heaven forbid! That would probably subject the author to about twenty federal charges and several hundred state charges (they have so damned many statutes on the books that they can find three or four of them to use against you for doing practically anything you can name). Knowing human nature as he does, however, the author recognizes that most people will run afoul of the law sooner or later in one way or another, and for some of them it will be sooner and more often. People in this category — the "outlaws" of society — will be especially benefitted by a written "code of conduct" which can help them avoid the System. The presentation of such a code, which is a distillation of the major constitutional truths that have been discussed in the previous chapters, is the object of this final chapter. The author judges no one, and hopes that whatever kind of mischief you're into, this set of guidelines will help you avoid the full fury of The Beast.

It's well at this point to interject a note of sobriety, because when people get to talking about "beating the System" and using "loopholes" it's all too easy to jump to the conclusion that, with a little finesse, anybody can break the law and get away with it. Young and unsophisticated criminals are frequently caught because they place their reliance on the likelihood that police will observe their constitutional rights. Sometimes the cops will stop short of an impermissible intrusion, but other times they won't; and if their impermissible intrusion results in the discovery of criminal evidence, that suspect is in for a long struggle. The police realize that some of their busts will be thrown out of court, and that some of the ones that do get convicted will be overturned on appeal. That doesn't bother them, though, because they know that the court system operates so slowly that, even if a person has sure-fire grounds for reversal, it'll take a couple of years for the conviction to be overturned. Meanwhile, the guy who thought "they can't do this" will be sitting in prison twiddling his thumbs. They've gotten him off the street for a while, caused him to lose a lot of money, and broken up whatever game he had going — precisely what they wanted to do.

For those who make their living by breaking one law or another, it's safe to predict that inevitably they're going to get caught and punished. As TV detective Tony Baretta used to say, "if you can't do the time, don't do the crime." This isn't a reflection of the great efficiency of the police; to the contrary, they're an indolent and stupid lot for the most part. What it does reflect is (1) the consequence of Murphy's Law: if anything can possibly go wrong, it probably will; (2) the high chance of somebody becoming a snitch; and (3) the probability that the police will cross over the line of permissible conduct if they need to. As we've said earlier, they tend to stop playing by the rules when it looks as though they might lose the game.

The advice in this chapter, then, is calculated to provide you with the most accurate yet practical strategy for avoiding detection, frustrating apprehension, and minimizing penalties based on an understanding of your constitutional rights. If it helps you to escape detection altogether, "far out." If you're detected by the police but manage to slip through their fingers, "bravissimo!" But in the event that the unthinkable happens and you're caught, the attention that you've paid to the precepts in this chapter could pay off with the greatest dividends of all. It might mean the difference between your spending a few short weeks in jail and spending the rest of your life in prison. No set of rules can guarantee that you'll never get caught, but if you consistently follow these you'll shift the odds immensely in your favor, and avoid making the needless mistakes which have resulted in the destruction of so many lives.

Commandment I:
BE AWARE OF THE RULES

Nobody can know it all, but a general familiarity with basic practical considerations should precede the operation of any business or profession. A doctor or lawyer wouldn't hang out his shingle without first having prepared himself through the appropriate program of study. Neither should anyone presume to conduct an illegal enterprise without first educating himself in the technicalities of the field. Learning through error may be a fine method for the aspiring artist, but it's far too costly for the would-be outlaw.

    A. A *general knowledge of criminal procedure* is useful for anyone who may become a "guest" of the System. The material in this book is a good start, and if you can develop an occasional taste for text books about criminal law and evidence, you'll be far ahead of the pack.

An example of how this kind of knowledge can be practically applied is evident in the case of a warranted search. The magistrate who issues a warrant has no business participating in the search. Therefore, you should always *take down the names of everyone present during a police search.* Bystanders can be used later as witnesses to any constitutional violations, and if the magistrate's name shows up on the list, the warrant becomes invalid.

B. *Know the state and federal laws concerning your particular type of business.* In Michigan, for example, there's a mandatory life sentence for possession of Schedule 2 drugs in quantities exceeding 650 grams (22.88 oz.).[1] The sensible cocaine dealer there would avoid the risk of incurring this maximum penalty by simply making it a policy to never handle more than a pound at a time. At $300,000 a pound, nobody but a large-scale importer would ever need to have more than that on hand anyway.

Commandment II:
DON'T ATTRACT ATTENTION

Many people get into trouble with the law because they have an emotional hunger for self-esteem which they try to feed by showing the world what bad-asses they are. For them crime is a macho trip, and some of them aren't truly satisfied until they do get caught. Many others, whose sole motive for breaking the law is profit, make an attempt to be inconspicuous, but botch it through carelessness and lack of perception. What both these classes of people have in common is their tendency to attract the attention of the police, something which is avoidable if a person will just think ahead and use common sense.

A. *Avoid conforming to profiles.* Whatever you're up to, a police inquiry isn't likely to do you any good. Since they often use police profiles as a means of selecting likely candidates for inquiry, you should make a studied effort to avoid conforming to the indicia as much as possible.

1. *At airports, while making domestic flights,*

   a. Avoid flying

      i. from a "drug source city."

      ii. at off-peak hours.

      iii. on a round-trip ticket with a short layover.

      iv. on a ticket with a peculiar itinerary.

The inconvenience and delay of taking a car or a bus from a source city to the nearest non-source city before boarding a plane could save you much more time in the long run.

The ticket problem can be solved by always purchasing a round-trip ticket at the lowest rate possible (long layover). Cops are always suspicious of anyone who pays more for the short-layover tickets because a typical middle-class schmuck would rather stay a few days longer and save on the cost of his flight. You don't really need to stay, of course; you can get a refund on the unused portion of the round-trip ticket, and leave again whenever you want. If you do so, you should mail your ID ahead and register on your flight under a different name, because the airline computers are coordinated nation-wide, and such a change of itineraries would look suspicious if they should decide to check your recent flight record later. A bizarre itinerary should be broken up into a series of separate trips under separate names, while always exercising caution that no evidence of any other identity be on hand.

b. Avoid purchasing your ticket

    i. at the ticket desk.

    ii. on the same day as the flight.

    iii. with cash (particularly small bills).

    iv. changing flights enroute.

Call for reservations on the telephone as much in advance as possible, and pay with a check. If you're using an alternate name you'll probably have to pay in cash, but make sure that it's mostly in twenties rather than small denomination bills.

If you cash in the unused portion of a round-trip ticket, don't turn right around and buy another one then; come back later, after you've changed clothes and the airlines have changed shifts.

c. Avoid traveling

    i. alone.

    ii. without luggage.

    iii. with empty luggage.

    iv. with untagged or improperly tagged luggage.

    v. with padlocks on your luggage.

    vi. with a shoulder bag.

It's well to think about the type and amount of luggage that you'd be carrying if you really were going on the sort of trip you claim to be taking. The cops will be.

d. Avoid being attired

    i. differently from the other passengers.

    ii. inappropriately for the weather.

    iii. during your return flight with the same clothes you wore when you left town.

    iv. so as to reveal strange bulges.

e. Don't engage in suspicious behavior, such as

   i. scanning.

   ii. cloak-and-dagger stuff.

   iii. cautious, hesitant, nervous, or furtive behavior.

   iv. killing time inappropriately (e.g. making frequent trips to the water fountain or bathroom).

   v. inordinate haste.

   vi. going directly to the telephone.

   vii. not acting like friends with your traveling companion.

An ordinary traveler (whom you will presumably want to be taken for) generally has one of two objectives on his mind when he enters the airport: (1) to get his ticket and get to the proper boarding gate, or (2) to meet his greeting party and pick up his luggage. Either way, whether he's coming or going, he isn't interested in the other people who are there. He's thinking about golf games, steak dinners, corporate plans, and the like, and as he goes from one place to the next he moves naturally and confidently, totally oblivious to the security measures around him. If he has to wait for a flight, he might browse in the gift shop, have a snack in the coffee shop, or read a book in the lobby. If he's arriving off a flight, and nobody's there to meet him, he'll simply go to the baggage area and pick up his luggage. Once he has it, he'll go rent a car or grab a taxi and leave. He's likely to be cheerful, enthused about his trip, and generally cordial toward airline personnel and security police alike; after all, he has no reason to fear the police.

2. *At airports, when entering the U.S. from another country,*

a. Avoid coming directly from a "drug source country," if possible.
b. With regard to your airline ticket,
    i. Avoid purchasing it with cash.
    ii. Know
        A) When it was purchased
        B) Where it was purchased (which travel agency or airport)
        C) How much it cost
        D) How it was paid for (by cash, check, credit card, etc.)
    iii. Avoid booking an itinerary with short trips to drug distribution cities.
c. Avoid traveling
    i. alone, particularly if you're a Latin woman.
    ii. with only one small piece of luggage.
d. Avoid certain features of outward appearance:
    i. Shabby clothing
    ii. Bulky clothing
    iii. A fresh manicure of a woman's hands when their rough condition betrays her background of manual labor.
e. Avoid making repeated short trips to and from the U.S. on the same passport.
f. Don't exhibit:
    i. Extreme passivity
    ii. Excessively talkative or overly helpful behavior with the Customs agents
    iii. Nervousness
    iv. Indignation. It may help you escape police inquiries during a domestic flight, but it will

probably make things worse when dealing with Customs agents upon entering the U.S.[2]

g. Have at least the appearance of being dependent upon commercial paper and plastic for your financial needs.

   i. Carry a checkbook, traveler's checks, and/or credit cards while making international trips.

   ii. Avoid carrying large sums of cash.

h. When asked by Customs about your plans, have a *plausible* story ready which will withstand detailed inquiry.

   i. If you claim to be on a sight-seeing visit, have a tourist-type itinerary planned out, including hotels, activities, etc.

   ii. If you claim to be visiting friends or relatives,

      A) Be prepared to give their names, addresses, telephone numbers, and enough details about them to satisfy the Customs agents.

      B) Avoid disclosing any plans you may have to stay at hotels, since a visitor from abroad would ordinarily be expected to stay with the people he's visiting.

   iii. If you claim to be visiting on business,

      A) Make your representations for a business that you really *know* about and have the bearing for.

      B) Have business cards, manuals, forms, etc. to substantiate your claim that you're in that business.

      C) Have an itinerary planned out, including hotels you plan to stay at, the addresses of businesses you plan to visit, the precise description and cost of merchandise you plan to purchase, etc.

D) Have at least the appearance of ample credit and commercial paper with you to cover the travel expenses, purchases, etc. you claim you're going to be making.

If it seems as though all these details regarding your cover story are superfluous and unnecessary, read the cases cited in Chapter 16 under the discussion of the "mule profile." An implausible or inconsistent cover story was ultimately what got all those folks busted.

3. *In the vicinity of our national borders*, avoid driving

   a. an enclosed truck, van, or station wagon.

   b. with numerous passengers.

   c. on infrequently traveled roads.

The Border Patrol is constantly on the look-out for vehicles that might be carrying illegal aliens, so why invite trouble?

4. *When crossing our national borders*, avoid driving

   a. alone, especially if you're an elderly man.

   b. a rented car (which is usually evident from the decal in the window).

   c. with out-of-state license plates.

   d. an empty car.

The Bureau of Customs has recently become interested in a class of older retired men who have developed a pattern of making frequent solo trips south of the border in their automobiles. Some of them have discovered that they can supplement their social security checks by carrying back an occasional load of drugs for somebody, and Customs has therefore designated the elderly "gypsy-type" individual as a target of special attention.

Unusual features concerning the automobile tend to suggest various smuggling schemes, so Customs is less likely to be suspicious of a local, privately owned car packed with the usual fishing rods and vacation gear.

5. *When you're likely to be under surveillance,* avoid incongruous behavior such as

   a. using taxis for short distances.

   b. leaving your hotel to use a pay phone when there are phones in the rooms.

   c. Changing motels.

   d. making unlikely transactions (such as renting a safe deposit box on a short visit.)

   e. crossing back over the border at sites other than the Customs gate (when the feds put someone under surveillance, they keep track of his border crossings).

Any time you're involved in some major skul-duggery, there's a considerable chance that the police have noticed something going on, and are watching to see if it bears looking into. Under such circumstances, things which would ordinarily not raise any suspicion at all can begin to look very incriminating and prompt further unwanted attention.

6. *While boating on the Intracoastal Waterway:*[3]

   a. Avoid being loaded heavily enough to cause the boat to ride low in the water.

   b. Keep the boat wiped free of salt spray.

   c. Keep the cabin windows and doors open.

   d. Be prepared to give plausible answers con-cerning:

      i. where you're coming from.

ii. what you're doing (fishing, diving, etc.).

iii. who owns the boat.

iv. how many people are aboard.

v. whether there are any firearms aboard (avoid carrying them, and don't admit it if you do).

vi. whether you have the boat's documents with you.

e. Have the boat's documents all together and handy to reach in case they're requested.

f. Don't carry marijuana on board if it's packaged such that the odor is detectable.

B. *Avoid evoking attention or suspicion in general.* For example:

1. *Don't be a walking social statement.* If you're proud to be a member of some special interest or minority group, that's terrific, but leave the costume, song and dance at home. Bikers, cholos, players, gays, nazis, and other such groups all have outspoken enemies who occasionally want to start something. Ordinary, dull, everyday people have no such problems. Look ordinary, and do yourself a favor.

2. *Don't be abrasive, belligerant, or wierd.*

3. *Don't make wisecracks to the police.*[A]

4. *Don't do things in public that are dead giveaways* of criminal activity (e.g. sniffing the merchandise during a drug transaction).

5. *Don't place incriminating items where they can be seen.*

6. *Don't drive erratically.*

C. *Maintain an attitude of legitimacy.*

1. *Be sincerely convincing* in everything you say and do.

2. If you're singled out for inquiry by the police,
   a. *be confident.*
   b. *be politely indignant* — not because you "know your rights" (which suggests a criminal background), but because you've "done nothing wrong" (which suggests a legitimate citizen who's unaccustomed to being bothered by the police).
3. In the case of airport police,
   a. *show your ID only if it's solid enough to withstand a computer check.*
   b. *present your ticket with the baggage stubs attached* (don't remove them and attempt to hide them).

Commandment III:
KEEP QUIET

A. *Don't disclose information to anyone unless he has a specific "need to know."* This is standard policy for intelligence organizations, and while your secrets may not be as big as those of the CIA, they're every bit as important to you.
   1. *That includes the people closest to you* — your family and trusted friends (particularly in times of stress, e.g. when you're in jail).
   2. Be particularly cautious in so-called "privileged" relationships, such as:
      a. The doctor-patient relationship
         i. *Never give a physician or psychotherapist information or admissions pertaining to a crime.*
         ii. Be advised that doctors are generally required by state law to report all gunshot wounds to the police.

b. The attorney-client relationship

   i. *Never tell a lawyer anything that he doesn't need to know to defend your present case.*

   ii. *Never tell a lawyer about your plans* concerning a future illegal activity.

3. *Regard business associates and casual acquaintances presumptively as undercover police.*

   a. Take precautions to assure that they aren't "wired" during a transaction.

   b. Avoid conducting transactions in places that might be bugged (especially a hotel, jail, or the other person's place).

4. *Don't talk to police.* In the words of Justice Jackson, "any lawyer worth his salt will tell the suspect in no uncertain terms to make no statement to police under any circumstances."[6] Be rude, if necessary. Let them think whatever they want, but no matter what they do or say, don't provide them with your words; they'll find a way to use them against you. The kinds of volunteered statements which must especially be guarded against include:

a. pleasantries and chit-chat.

b. admissions of one's knowledge about facts in a crime.

c. admissions of one's awareness of his rights and responsibilities.

d. remarks which are prompted by ego or emotion.

5. When dialogue with police is unavoidable:

   a. *Always have a solid, irrefutable cover story prepared,* right down to the minutiae. For example, if you give the telephone number and address of a friend's house instead of your own when you call in your airline reservation, be prepared to give a plausible explanation of why, in case the cops check it out later. Surprises are only fun at Christmas and birthdays.

   b. *Don't tell a lie which can be refuted by checking.*

   c. Be especially wary of private-duty police, foreign police, probation and parole officers, and other "irregulars."

6. Avoid giving the police any information about your car or where you're staying.

   a. *Have your car key made so that it doesn't show what type of car it goes to.*

   b. *Don't carry your hotel key* around with you; leave it at the hotel desk.

   c. *Don't tell the police you have a car* if you're arrested. Don't tell them *what type* it is or *where it's located* if they ask.

   d. *Don't tell the police which hotel you're using.*

B. *Don't engage in conspiratorial dialogue over the telephone.* Unless you're using code words which are totally meaningless to the uninformed listener, it isn't safe to use the telephone for secret conversations. Merely couching your words so as to hint at what you're trying to say without coming right out and saying it doesn't fool anybody; if your partner can understand it, so can the cops who are listening in.

C. *Take a firm defensive stand as soon as you suspect that an adversary situation exists.*

1. *Once the police have decided to arrest you, don't go into explanations in an attempt to change their minds.* You won't prevent the arrest, and your statements could hurt you later.

2. Don't wait for them to read you your rights after they arrest you; *announce your own*

Miranda rights to the police. University of Michigan Law Professor Yale Kamisar recommends something like this:

> I believe I have a perfectly good defense, but I want to talk to my lawyer about it first. I understand that I have a right to remain silent, and a right to discuss my situation with a lawyer before saying anything to the authorities, and I intend to do just that. I intend to exercise my constitutional rights. Nothing personal, you understand.[7]

If you're slick enough to do this, the cops won't be able to impeach you later with your post-arrest silence.

3. *Invoke silence by demanding counsel,* and do so again *every time they give the Miranda warnings.*

4. *Never waive your silence thereafter.* Pay no attention to their innuendos and threats. Ignore their offers of leniency. Turn a deaf ear even to an emergency plea for your help. The devil can cite Scripture for his purpose, and if you let his entreaties loosen your tongue you'll be sorry.

D. *Avoid becoming a grand jury witness.*

1. If you anticipate that you may be useful as a witness, both you and your associates may be better off if *you can't be located when the subpoena comes out.*

2. If you are subpoenaed, seek to *have yourself declared incompetent to testify.*

3. If you're forced to testify, *invoke the Fifth Amendment right to silence to every question* beyond your name, no matter how harmless. *Don't answer even one question,* because doing so will be a waiver of your right to be silent. If you persist with your silence, they'll be forced

to grant you immunity from the use of your testimony.

4. If you're granted immunity, *find as soon as possible some clue which suggests that an illegal wiretap might have occurred, and make the allegation. Refuse to give further testimony* on that basis.

5. *Be taciturn* and as unhelpful as possible.

Commandment IV:
DON'T CONSENT

A. *Don't let people into your home* (or other parts of your property) *unless you summon them yourself* for a specific reason. When you do bring a stranger in, such as for repair work, be extremely cautious to *patrol the place ahead of time* in order to remove anything that may be incriminating or suspicious, and *accompany him at all times* while he's there.

A strict closed-door policy is only necessary if you're into some type of crime, but you must realize that any crime at all places you in this category. Smoking a little weed or having a few eagle feathers on your wall might seem inconsequential and harmless enough from your point of view, but they *are* crimes. Even if the fruits of your particular brand of mischief aren't the sorts of things that you display in plain view, it's still possible that some unforeseen item that's lying around can tie you in — something that an undercover cop would recognize immediately. People who dabble in crime simply can't afford to lead a happy-go-lucky lifestyle.

B. *Never consent to a search.* If the cops have a warrant, or if they have the legal justification based on one of the exceptions to the warrant requirement, they'll do their search without your consent. If they don't have such justification, don't give it to them — not for a search of your person, your baggage, your car, your house — not for anything.

C. *Never consent to being detained.*

1. *Do not accompany the police* if they ask you to go with them somewhere. *Insist on an arrest warrant* (which will be useful to you for evidentiary purposes later). Force them to resort to physical restraint (arrest) in order to move you anywhere.

2. As soon as you've met their initial inquiry with the barest minimum of information, *seek to leave.* If they won't let you leave at first, *keep trying to leave* until they are forced to either arrest you or let you go.

3. If police inquiry occurs as you're about to make a flight, and there's any possibility of incriminating evidence being discovered, *abort your trip and leave the airport immediately.*

4. *If the police are detaining anything that belongs to you, announce that you will return for it later, but don't wait for it.*

D. *Never consent to having your property detained.*

1. *Don't voluntarily give them anything;* force them to seize whatever they wish to detain.

2. *If your ID is shaky, if it doesn't match your ticket, or if* it's good but you know that *there is incriminating evidence in your luggage, do not show the ID or admit even having it with you.*

E. *Avoid conferring your automatic consent.*

1. Beware of the automatic consent which is *inherent in government contracts,* the opera-

tion of *governmentally regulated businesses,* and passage through *governmental reservations.*

2. *Don't share a place with another person* if you can't sustain a police search of it.

3. *Don't place your confidential property into the hands* (or car, or house) *of another person.*

F. *Instruct your family and friends not to grant consent* for intrusions of your property; but don't rely heavily upon their compliance.

Commandment V:
TRUST ONLY WHAT YOU CONTROL

A. For privacy from police intrusion, *rely upon your home more than your person: your person more than your luggage;* and *your luggage more than your car.*

B. For privacy in your buildings, *rely upon living areas* more than non-living areas; non-public or infrequently-visited areas more than public or heavily visited areas; and *interior* more than exterior areas.

C. For privacy concerning your identity:

1. *Never transport illegal items without using an alternate identity,* in case you're forced to leave the parcel behind.

2. *Avoid conducting illegal transactions under your real identity and address,* in case your partners prove to be untrustworthy.

3. For alternate identity, *use only solid (verifiable, state-issued) ID and plausible address and tele-*

phone references (ones which won't lead to a vacant lot or a bewildered occupant when checked out).

4. *Never have more than one set of ID in your possession* (including your car) at one time.

D. Always *carry ample cash on your person to cover emergency expenses for which a check isn't accepted* (car towing and impoundment fees, bail bondsman fee, etc.). Carry it on your person, not in your baggage or car, where it might become unavailable.

E. *To assure the maximum legal right of privacy in your car, maintain complete control of it, take precautions to prevent intrusions into it, and be present to object* if the police seek to search it.

Commandment VI:
DON'T TRUST THE PRIVACY OF ANYTHING WHICH IS ACCESSIBLE TO THE PUBLIC

A. Be aware that *cars, luggage and lockers which are in public locations are vulnerable to dog-sniffing inspection.*

B. Be aware that *cars on public highways are vulnerable to electronic monitoring.*

C. *Don't give your private papers even a limited showing.*

D. *Don't put anything private into the garbage.*

E. *Don't keep a stolen car if its VIN number (serial number) is visible from the outside* of the vehicle.[8]

F. *Never leave contraband in the same container in which it was delivered.* Customs, postal or delivery service employees may well have had a preview of it.

G. *Avoid engaging in illegal activities while under official scrutiny* (e.g. investigation, bail, probation, etc.).

Commandment VII:
BE WARY OF EVERYONE

A. Be alert to any possible indications of treachery in *lovers and friends.*

B. *Don't deal with anyone whom you haven't independently checked out.*

C. Be supremely cautious of a deal where a *third party* shows up on the scene — particularly one who presumes to be a big shot or high-roller type.

D. Be triply cautious *if you're new to the business or to the locality,* and therefore unfamiliar with the people.

E. *Don't accept favors from the police,* and *don't do them any.*

Commandment VIII:
DON'T GIVE THE POLICE AN OPENING

Unless they have independent reason to believe that you're guilty of some crime, the cops won't ordinarily have occasion to pry into your affairs. There are, however, a number of situations which give them such an opportunity; avoid them if at all possible.

A. *Avoid letting petty offenses go unresolved until they eventuate into outstanding warrants.* Nobody likes to pay parking tickets, but they can hurt you a lot more if you let them pile up until they mature into an arrest warrant that might come at a disastrous time. The same holds true for court orders.

B. *Avoid providing an exception to the warrant requirement.*

1. Try to *keep incriminating evidence where it won't be exposed because of a fire, medical emergency, burglary, etc.*

2. As much as possible, *avoid keeping incriminating evidence in a vehicle.*

3. *If you suspect that you're being watched, if you're about to be arrested, or if you've just been arrested don't go to a place where there might be incriminating evidence.* (e.g. your house or car).

4. *Don't keep incriminating evidence within the confines of a business which is heavily regulated* by the government (e.g. mines, gun dealerships, liquor establishments, pharmacies, etc.).

5. If an alternative exists, *avoid entering zones of government domination* where both discretion and frequency of search and seizure is heightened. Examples of places to avoid include:

   a. military reservations

   b. prison grounds

   c. busy border-crossing areas

   d. Customs checkpoints

   e. fixed Border Patrol checkpoints

   f. agricultural inspection checkpoints

   g. roadblocks for checking on licensing and registration, drunk drivers, and manhunts

Different types of governmental control areas pose varying levels of intrusion. The sort of reception that you can expect at a licensing and registration checkpoint, for example, should be minimal.[9] Uniformed cops are supposed to make the inquiries, and only if they have reasonable suspicion of a crime are they entitled to order people from their cars or ask for consent to search. The narks and the sniff dogs aren't even supposed to be brought out where the motorists are unless they have probable cause. On the other hand, the Bureau of Customs has a virtually unlimited level of discretion to search and detain people who enter their domain. If you can't withstand a search or inquiry, and you aren't sure exactly what kind of show they're running up ahead, your safest move is to discreetly pull off the road and find another direction to take.

C. *Don't give the police grounds to suspect that you might be in possession of either a weapon or contraband.* If you're accustomed to putting on the gangster act, swallow your pride for a little while and try to look harmless while there are police around. Unless you enjoy the frisk, you really don't want to convince them that you're a "bad dude."

D. *Don't violate vehicular laws.* Because of automobile administrative regulations, traffic laws, and parking ordinances, police are successful in bringing about the unexpected arrest of more outlaws than by any other mechanism in their repertoire. These laws form a net in which fugitives, illegal aliens, drug dealers, thieves, republicans — every imaginable type of crook — can be caught. Notwithstanding all the rhetoric about highway death tolls, the government would certainly want to keep these laws intact even if all vehicles were accident-proof; they're too good a pretext for catching people who are wanted for other reasons. Be sure, therefore, that you:

1. *carry a valid driver's license.*

2. *carry a valid automobile registration.*

3. *have no mechanical violations on your vehicle* (e.g. broken lights, bad muffler, excessive exhaust, etc.).

4. *obey the rules of safe driving.*

5. *don't have the smell of alcohol or marijuana in the car.*

6. *park only in legal places during allowable times.* Don't forget that parking meters expire, and certain legal parking spots on the street become tow-away zones during rush hours.

Commandment IX:
DON'T LEAVE THE POLICE A HANDLE

Once the cops do become interested in you, it's still possible to frustrate much of their endeavors if you've taken certain routine precautions in advance. Without that one good handle on you — something to open the door for them — they'll often have to let you slip through their fingers.

A. Watch out for your personal property.

1. *Don't leave your confidential property in the hands of* somebody whom you know to be *a likely candidate for search and seizure.*

2. *Don't abandon your confidential property when the police have custody of it. Demand a search warrant, and promise to return for it later.*

3. Always try to have a local friend to call upon for favors wherever you go.

a. If you're arrested away from your dwelling, *have a friend pick up your car* before it's impounded. Speed is vital in order to accomplish this before the cops can figure out where your car is, or before it's impounded for a parking violation.

b. If you're arrested in a town where you have a hotel room, *have a friend go over and pick up your belongings from the room* before the police get their hands on them.

4. *Register your car in the name of somebody else who will not be locatable by police.* This reduces your status to that of borrower rather than owner of the car, and thereby allows you to legitimately deny knowledge of anything which might turn up from a search of the trunk (provided that you haven't left your fingerprints or other trademarks in there). It also prevents the cops from locating your car after they've arrested you, since they'll be trying to look up the registration file on a car registered in your name.

5. *Don't carry weapons or contraband inside the passenger compartment* of a car *or the back of a camper.*

6. If somebody should carry a weapon or contraband into the passenger compartment, be sure that he *gets out of the car with it promptly in the event that the car is stopped* by police.

7. Always *keep weapons and contraband:*

a. *locked in the trunk.*

b. *additionally locked inside a container.* Keep the key to the container well hidden in the trunk rather than on your person, thus *forcing the police to damage the container in order to open it.*

8. *Keep drugs and explosives in hermetically sealed containers whenever transporting them* so that a dog sniff cannot identify them. The outside of the containers must be washed clean, too, since any trace will alert the dogs.

9. *Park away from your property whenever there's contraband in your car.* This prevents it from falling within the reach of a warranted search of the house, in case that should occur. Don't make a routine habit of parking at a distance, however, or the cops might think to specify your car in their warrant.

B. Don't give them an excuse to detain or arrest you.

1. *Don't go near your place if the cops are already there searching it,* since that would entitle them to detain you as the occupant.

2. *Don't resist an illegitimate arrest.* You'll beat it in court if the arrest is improper, but you'll *make* it legitimate if you resist.

3. *Avoid associating yourself with a person or thing for which you know that the police have probable cause* to make a seizure. Probable cause is highly contagious.

Commandment X:
GET A LAWYER

Even if you know a considerable amount of law yourself, and are unwilling to completely trust your fate to the care of a shyster, you should always have one representing you from the earliest stages of a criminal beef, because:

A. A lawyer can *check out and challenge a complaint, a warrant, and the affidavit supporting the warrant.* As a defendant representing himself, you can't effectively do any of this. This simple expedient shouldn't be overlooked, because it might get you released immediately and cause the entire case to be dismissed.

B. A lawyer can *investigate the facts of your case to develop grounds for a defense.* You can't investigate anything from a jail cell.

C. A lawyer knows what to watch out for to *protect your interests from prejudice during pretrial proceedings.*

D. A lawyer knows trial and appeal procedure; he *knows what to object to and when to do it* so that it will be timely and effective. Chief Justice Earl Warren once said in this regard that "the jury system... becomes a trap for the layman because he is utterly without the ability to make it serve the ends of justice."[10] This is the proper job for a lawyer.

E. A lawyer can *negotiate deals with the prosecution more safely and effectively* than you can. You risk making evidentiary admissions every time you open your mouth in front of a prosecutor, a risk which doesn't exist if your mouthpiece does the talking. As an objective, experienced professional, the lawyer is also more likely to get you a better deal on a plea bargain than anything you'd be likely to swing yourself. You can't make a deal with the devil, but a lawyer certainly can (probably because they're so closely related).

F. You should have legal counsel if you're subpoenaed *as a witness before a grand jury,* even though you aren't charged with anything. There's a good possibility that you soon might be.

G. Always *be aware of the details of your case and of everything your lawyer does* (and doesn't do) in representing you, particularly if he's a public defender. *Don't hesitate to speak up to the court* if you suspect that he's screwing up; it's *your* case, and if you lose, it'll be *you* who goes to prison, not the lawyer...

REFERENCES

1. *People v Harman,* Mich. Ct. App., 3/10/83
2. *U.S. v Mosquera-Ramirez,* 729 F2d 1352-1355 (11th Cir. 1984)
3. *U.S. v Gollwitzer,* 697 F2d 1357, 1362 (11th Cir. 1983)
4. *U.S. v Place,* 462 US __, 103 SCt 2637, 2640 (1983)
5. *People v Bittner,* N.Y. Sup. Ct. App. Div. 2d Dept., 11/14/83
6. *Watts v Indiana,* 338 US 49, 59, 69 SCt 1347, 1357 (1949), J. Jackson concurring in part
7. Kamisar, *Supreme Court Review and Constitutional Law Symposium,* Washington, D.C. (September 1982)
8. *State v Simpson,* 95 Wash.2d 170, 622 P2d 1199, 1210 (1980)
9. *Garrett v Goodwin,* 569 FSupp 106, 118-121 (E.D. Ark. 1983)
10. *Carnley v Cochran,* 369 US 506, 524, 82 SCt 884, 894 (1962), C.J. Warren concurring

AFTERWORD

The author would leave you with a parting thought. As repressive as the cops are now, it's clear from the trends of the law that we're in for still harsher times ahead. It happened in Germany, it happened in Russia, and it's happening now in the United States. The individual's rights are being steadily reduced by the government, and the prediction made by Judge Grosscup ninety years ago seems to have come of age:

> The battle for personal liberty seems to have been attained, but in the absence of the din and clash, we cannot comprehend the meaning of all the safeguards employed... The oppression of crowns and principalities is unquestionably over, and merciless majorities may yet constitute one of the chapters of future history.[1]

The pertinence of this warning to current developments under the Moral Majority is too coincidental to ignore.

---

1. *U.S. v James,* 60 F 264, 265 (1894)

INDEX

Electronic surveillance
(continued)
authorized (con-
tinued),291
prevalence of, 17-18
in public, 185-186
unauthorized in grand
jury, 227-228, 294
legal protection
against, 59, 123-124, 129,
181
Emetic, 114, 115
Enhancement of penalty,
25
"Entrapment" defined,
248-250
prevalence of, 18
right to be free of, 251
sting operations, 240
Evidence
competency of, 226-227
dissipation of taint, 62-63
falsification of, 18
hearsay, 78-79
independent source of,
63, 210, 221-222
inevitable discovery
of, 63
informant testimony as
probable cause, 79, 113
live witness testimony,
63, 79
materiality of, 226-227
testimonial confession,
178, 220, 304
defined, 195

Evidence (continued)
papers, 165-166, 180,
184-185, 220
Exclusionary Rule
criticism of, 60, 64-65
evidence affected by, 60-
61
exceptions to, 63-64,
74, 127-128
mechanism of action,
61, 180
origin of, 60, 62
purpose of, 61-62,
65-66
as a right, 62
standing for, 62
Ex-con, loss of rights
See Civil rights, loss of
following conviction
Exigency
automobile exception,
87, 160-161
destruction of evidence,
87-88, 126, 140, 144-145
hot pursuit, 87, 140
as justification for body
intrusions, 114
for warrantless entry,
140-141, 145, 242, 298
for warrantless search,
112, 141-142, 242
to protect life and
render aid, 89, 126, 144,
160, 211, 298
public health as, 141

Expectation of privacy.
See Privacy interest

Fingerprinting, as nontestimonial evidence, 114, 188
Forfeiture, 154
Forgetfulness, 226, 230
Fourth Amendment
meaning of, 74
parties protected by, 74
Frisk, 88, 106, 107, 270
"Fruit of the poisonous
tree" doctrine, 60, 80,
196, 208, 209
Full field search, 88, 91, 112
Functional border
equivalents, 93, 155-156,
269, 284-285

Garbage, 147, 295
General warrant, 80, 160
"Good cop-bad cop" ploy,
199
"Good faith," as an ex-
ception to Exclusionary
Rule, 64, 111
"Grabbable area," 90-91,
145, 161-162
Grand jury
defined, 37-38
length of term, 220
mechanism, 226, 31, 247
Miranda warnings and,
201

Grand jury (continued)
representation by
counsel at, 226, 304
witness exemption,
227-230, 294

Habeas corpus, the Exclu-
sionary Rule under, 63
Halfway house, 50
Hearsay. *See* Evidence,
hearsay
"Heinousness," 26
Holding, of court, 58
Home intermediate
intrusion of, 137
inventory search of,
145, 164
privacy interest in
defeat of, 137
defined, 123-25
extent of, 124, 126-127
relative to other
property, 161, 294
from surveillance, 129
Hotel, 125, 138, 164, 302
See also Home key, 292
Hung jury, 26

Identification
alternate, 294, 295
as credibility, 265
as an investigatory
tool, 261-262
ordinances, 109-110, 241
Immunity
inadequacy of, 222-224

Immunity (con-
tinued)
mechanism of, 221, 225,
294
Impeachment
as an exception to
inadmissible evidence,
64, 212, 243
silence as, 207, 209
volunteered statements
as, 208
"Imperative of judicial
integrity," 62
Incarceration, 45-47
"Independent source"
doctrine. See Evidence,
independent source of
Indictment, 19, 38, 196
"Inevitable discovery"
doctrine, 63
Informants, 14-15, 129,
201, 219-220, 223-224, 225
Information, 19
Initial appearance, 23
"Innocent until proven
guilty," 28
Inquiry, right of, 104
Inquisitorial system,
179, 224
Intermediate intrusion,
89, 106-107, 137
Interrogation
during a Terry stop,
109, 265
reinitiation of, 204, 243
tactics, 198-199, 201,
225, 242-243
Intrusion
extension of, 103, 109

Intrusion (continued)
reasonableness of
method, 114-115
Inventory search, 92,
145, 163-164
Itinerary, 262, 269,
282, 284

Jail, 44-45
Judge, 30

Keepers, 50-51
Knock-and-announce Rule,
142-43

Land
possessory interest in,
127
privacy interest in,
127-129
Laws, awareness of, 280
Lawyers, See Attorney-
client privilege;
defense counsel;
Judge; Prosecutor
attitudes toward, 31-32
Legislature, and prison
affairs, 52
Lineup
justification for, 113-114
as nontestimonial evi-
dence, 188, 198, 211, 304
as a ploy, 199

"Plain view" doctrine
(continued)
   incident to lawful arrest,
   145, 242
   during an inventory
   search, 164
   as probable cause, 239-
   240, 294-295
   during a warranted
   search, 160
Plant quarantine station,
   92
Plea, 24
Plea bargain, 24-25, 304
Possession. *See* Control
Possessory interest
   in articles, 157, 265,
   301
   in land, 127
Preliminary hearing, 19
Prepping baggage, 155
Pre-sentence report,
   27-28
Pretext, 138, 241-243
Pre-trial hearing, 25, 61
Pre-trial psychological
   proceedings, 200, 211-
   212, 304
Pre-trial release, 23
Priors, 25
Prison administrative
   searches at, 93, 298
   custody levels, 45-46
   deprivations at, 47
   as an economic
   venture, 48-49

Privacy interest
   control as, 125, 154,
   301
   defined, 123
   ownership as, 154
Privileged statements,
   181-184, 196, 226
"Probable cause"
   associations as, 113,
   303
   conduct as, 113
   defined, 19, 64, 78, 113
   informant's tip as,
   244-245, 263
   as justification for
   intrusive, 112
   reasonable govern-
   mental standards
   as, 128-129
   timeless of, 80, 112
Probation, 45, 104, 246
Profiles, police, 108, 264,
   281. *See also* Drug
   courier profile; Mule
   profile; Skyjacker
   profile
Prosecutor, 10, 30, 38
Protective search. *See*
   Terry stop, protective
   search
Psychotherapist. *See*
   Doctor-patient privilege
Public defender, 30, 304
Public esteem, right to,
   124
Public health,

Supermax, 45-46
Suppression hearing
    See Pre-trial hearing
Surgery, 115
Surveillance. *See* Electronic surveillance
Swallower, 268-269

Telephone conversation,
    181-182, 293
Telephone numbers,
    dialing of 146
Terry stop
    defined, 106-107
    detention. *See* Detention
    identification during.
    See Identification
    protective search, 88,
    106-107, 156-157, 160, 299
    right to not answer, 88,
    110, 265
    use of force during,
    108, 111
Third degree, 199, 208
Threshold, of house, 125
Throw-down gun, 18-19
"Totality of circumstances," 79
Traffic stops, 158, 299-300
Transactional immunity,
    221
Transmitter, locational,
    147, 160, 295
Trial

Trial (continued)
    defined, 26, 304
    setting of date for, 24
Trial court
    general jurisdiction,
    36-37
    limited jurisdiction,
    36
Trustys, 46

United States Supreme
    Court, 37
Use immunity. *See*
    Immunity, grant of

Vehicles, privacy interest
    in, 158-161
Vessels, search of,
    156, 288-289
Voice analysis, 114
Voluntariness.
    See Consent,
    validity of

Waiver, of *Miranda*
    rights, 206-207, 293
Warrant
    defined, 19, 78, 137
    grounds for, 78, 108,
    114, 244
    as justification for
    body intrusions,

YOU WILL ALSO WANT TO READ:

☐ **16037 Getaway: Driving Techniques for Escape and Evasion,** *by Ronald George Eriksen 2.* This little number covers everything you need to know to become an expert wheelman. High-speed cornering, bootlegger's turn, evading pursuit, ramming through a roadblock, running another car off the road, and much more. *1983, 5½ x 8½, 46 pp, illustrated, soft cover. $6.95.*

☐ **40066 Escape From Controlled Custody,** *by Tony Lesce.* Right now, there are people held captive all over the world. Some of them will try to escape. A few will succeed. This book takes you captive to show you what it's like. You'll learn to make knives from toothbrushes and printing presses from shoes. You'll follow prisoners through tunnels and over walls. Along the way, you'll hear about some of the great escapes: acts of bravery and cunning that stir the human spirit. *1990, 5½ x 8½, 144 pp, illustrated, indexed, soft cover. $10.95.*

☐ **40070 Surviving In Prison,** *by Harold S. Long.* A disturbing account of life behind bars. The author has spent the last ten years in prison. He describes how prisons are run: the penal code and the cell-block code. He takes you out to the yard and into the hole. He explains why rehabilitation programs fail. And he reveals what is required to survive the personal degradation, brutality and humiliation found in contemporary American Prisons. *1990, 8½ x 11, 128 pp, soft cover. $14.95.*

☐ **40050 Making Crime Pay,** *by Harold S. Long.* What does it take to make crime pay? Written by a professional criminal, this book is packed with information not available anywhere else (except, maybe, in jail). It explains what makes some criminals successful while others get caught. Also covered are how to deal with police, courts, and the criminal justice system to minimize apprehension and conviction. *1988, 5½ x 8½, 81 pp, soft cover. $9.95.*
